# CORETTA SCOTT KING

—African-American Biographies—

# CORETTA SCOTT KING

## Striving for Civil Rights

*Series Consultant:*
*Dr. Russell L. Adams, Chairman*
*Department of Afro-American Studies, Howard University*

**Anne Schraff**

**Enslow Publishers, Inc.**

| 44 Fadem Road | PO Box 38 |
| Box 699 | Aldershot |
| Springfield, NJ 07081 | Hants GU12 6BP |
| USA | UK |

**Library of Congress Cataloging-in-Publication Data**

Schraff, Anne E.
    Coretta Scott King: striving for civil rights / Anne Schraff.
        p. cm.—(African-American biographies)
    Includes bibliographical references (p. ) and index.
    Summary: Explores the life and career of Coretta Scott King, from her
childhood in Alabama, through her work with the civil rights movement,
to her continuing efforts on behalf of the underprivileged.
    ISBN 0-89490-811-1
    1. King, Coretta Scott, 1927–    —Juvenile literature. 2. Afro-American
women—Biography—Juvenile literature. 3. Afro-Americans—Biography—
Juvenile literature. 4. Civil rights workers—United States—Biography—
Juvenile literature. 5. Civil rights movements—United States—History—
20th century—Juvenile literature. 6. King, Martin Luther, Jr.,
1929–1968—Juvenile literature. [1. King, Coretta Scott, 1927–    . 2. Civil
rights workers. 3. Afro-Americans—Biography. 4. Women—Biography.
5. King, Martin Luther, Jr., 1929-1968.] I. Title. II. Series.
E185.97.K47S37    1997
323'.092—dc20
[B]                                                          96-43141
                                                               CIP
                                                                AC

Printed in the United States of America

10 9 8 7 6 5 4 3 2 1

**Illustration Credits:** Alabama Bureau of Tourism and Travel, p. 39;
Antiochiana Collection, Antioch College, pp. 6, 21, 76; Boston
University Photo Services, pp. 93, 95; Bush Presidential Materials
Project, p. 106; Kevin Smith, Lyndon Baines Johnson Library, p. 83;
Library of Congress, p. 31; National Archives, p. 96; New England
Conservatory, pp. 29, 34, 36, 91; Ronald Reagan Library, p. 104; United
Nations, p. 71.

**Cover Illustration:** Jimmy Carter Library

# CONTENTS

Coretta Scott King

# 1

## "THIS MOMENT IN HISTORY"

y mid-January 1956, thirty to forty threatening phone calls and letters reached Coretta Scott King's Montgomery, Alabama, home each day. The twenty-eight-year-old African-American mother of a newborn baby was married to Martin Luther King, Jr., a Baptist minister. Together they hoped to work for a dream of a better, fairer world for all races.

Now they were caught in a cyclone of hatred. Postcards signed by the Ku Klux Klan (KKK) promised violence. Foul-mouthed callers insulted them. Still, as

her husband recalled later, Coretta Scott King was neither "bitter nor panicky."[1]

One angry caller warned, "You'll be sorry you ever came to Montgomery!"[2] Coretta Scott King thought of taking the phone off the hook to get some peace. However, too many important calls were coming in and they had to be taken.

The incident that led to this hate campaign against the Kings began in December 1955. An African-American tailor's assistant and civil rights activist named Rosa Parks was riding home from work on the Montgomery City Bus Lines. Parks had already been working with the National Association for the Advancement of Colored People (NAACP) on civil rights issues.

At this time the buses were segregated. The white section of the bus was full when more whites got on the bus. The bus driver, J. P. Blake, left his seat and came down the aisle. He told four blacks, including Rosa Parks, to get up and give their seats to the white new-comers. Some of them did, but Parks refused. Blake said that he would have to arrest her if she did not give up her seat. Parks told Blake to do what he had to do. Blake called a police officer, and Parks was arrested.

There had been civil rights activity against segre-gation for some time in Montgomery. The incident leading to the arrest of Parks was the last straw. The African Americans of Montgomery, Alabama, were so

angry that they decided to boycott the City Bus Lines until they were treated fairly. No longer would segregated busing be tolerated.

In order to press its demands, the African-American community formed the Montgomery Improvement Association (MIA). Martin Luther King, Jr., at age twenty-six, was chosen as its leader. King's involvement explains why so much rage was aimed at the King family in its home at 309 South Jackson Street.

The boycotted buses were running nearly empty as thirty thousand African-American riders stayed away. Wrath grew in the white community as money was lost. The African Americans who usually rode the buses were no longer paying fares. They were not shopping downtown anymore either, causing a greater loss of money.

Many times Martin Luther King, Jr., had to spend his evenings at MIA meetings. When friends worried about Coretta being alone with the baby while Martin was away she insisted, "I'm happy staying by myself."[3] Just the same, a friend of the family, Mary Lucy Williams, came to stay at the house on nights Martin was away speaking.

The King house was in a built-up neighborhood. Previous racially motivated bombings in Alabama occurred in the countryside. Surely nobody would bomb a house close to town like this.

A few days earlier, with the boycott effective and spirits high in the African-American community, Coretta said, "Oh Martin, how happy I am to be living in Montgomery, with you, at this moment in history."[4] But possible violence was on Martin's mind. He looked at his wife and baby daughter and thought, "They can be taken away from me at any moment; I can be taken away from them at any moment."[5]

On Monday, January 30, Coretta Scott King and Mary Williams were sitting and talking in the living room of the parsonage. Baby Yolanda was asleep in her bassinet. Suddenly there was the sickening thud of an object landing on the concrete porch.

At first Coretta Scott King told herself it was probably a brick thrown in anger. "But somehow I felt we should go to the back," she later recalled.[6] The two women made a break for the back of the house, racing directly through a guest bedroom.

As they moved, there was a thunderous blast. The house rocked as if in the grip of an earthquake. Coretta Scott King felt that the whole front of the house had been blown away. Smoke poured through the house as the sound of splintering glass crashed in their ears.

Cold air surged around the women as Williams grabbed King and screamed. Frightened and shaken, King ran to the baby. Fortunately, Yolanda was safe in a back bedroom. "Well," Coretta King thought, "It

finally happened."[7] The threats had turned to deadly action. Had she gone to the front of the house to investigate the thud on the porch, the dynamite would have blown up in her face.

The front windows of the house had been blown into the living room, where they now lay in shards of glass. The concrete porch was split, leaving a large hole.

Immediately after the bombing the doorbell rang. Coretta Scott King thought briefly to herself, "They are coming in now!"[8] She thought that the people who had thrown the bomb were coming for her and the baby. As smoke billowed through the shattered house, Coretta Scott King worried about her baby. But then she heard the familiar voices of neighbors coming to make sure that she was all right. Soon a large concerned crowd gathered.

At the church where he was speaking, Martin Luther King, Jr., was taken aside by his friend Ralph Abernathy. "Your house has been bombed," Abernathy told him.[9] Martin Luther King, Jr., rushed home to his family.

When he got home, Coretta reassured Martin that she and the baby were unharmed. The mood of the milling crowd outside had turned angry. They were outraged at what had happened. At the edges of the crowd nervous police officers watched. Martin Luther King, Jr., stepped onto the shattered porch and spoke to the people. He told them that they must love their

white brothers no matter what. He calmly asked them to resist any thought of revenge. Deeply moved by his words, the crowd quietly went away.[10]

That night the Kings took refuge in a friend's home. Then, outside in the darkness, the figure of a man was seen approaching. After an uneasy moment, the Kings recognized Obadiah Scott, Coretta Scott King's father. He too had heard of the bombing and had come to take his daughter and granddaughter home until things settled.

Coretta Scott King listened to her father's offer, but she would stay with her husband. Her place was with him, in the struggle for justice. Not even the shock of a bombing in the night could frighten her away. Nor would any of the jailings, the threats, or the ever-present possibility of death by violence *ever* stop Coretta Scott King from fighting for the dream that she and her husband believed in.

# 2

# FROM COTTON FIELDS TO CONCERT STAGE

oretta Scott was born on April 27, 1927, in Marion, Alabama, in the heart of the Black Belt, a cotton-growing region noted for its dark-colored soils. She was the middle child between older sister Edythe and younger brother Obadiah, Jr.

Coretta and her brother and sister grew up in an unpainted frame house with two large rooms—a bedroom and a kitchen. It also had a large front porch, which was useful given Alabama's hot humid summers. A backyard well provided year-round water,

making the Scotts luckier than many neighbors who had to carry water from a spring.

Coretta was the child of strong, proud, and incredibly hard-working people who were determined to get a piece of the American dream. Coretta's mother Bernice McMurry Scott had only a fourth-grade education. She was sent to school just three months of the year and the rest of the time she spent "minding cows" and working in the fields.[1] Married at sixteen, Bernice Scott had her children early.

She told Coretta that she had never really been a child herself.[2] With her hair in braids, Bernice Scott looked like a Native American. In fact, her father Martin McMurry was part Native American. A reserved and careful woman with strangers, Coretta's mother had great practical wisdom.[3] Some of her children's memories included their mother reading stories to them, such as "Little Match Girl" and "Rumpelstiltskin."

Coretta's father Obadiah Scott built the family home right after he was married. Coretta remembered him as a born leader with a passion for keeping busy. Every morning the family ate breakfast by lamplight. Coretta's father wanted everyone to get busy after that. "I won't have lazy people in my house," he said.[4]

In addition to farming, Scott hauled lumber with his own truck. The fact that an African American owned a truck when many poor whites could not

afford one was a sore spot with some local whites. Coretta later remembered that white men would stop her father on a lonely road and "curse him and threaten to kill him."[5] Scott always carried a pistol when he went into the woods to cut timber, and there was always fear. Scott believed that if you looked a white man right in the eye, there was less chance that he would hurt you. But Scott warned his wife, "I may not get back."[6]

"We were quite young then," Coretta remembered of herself and her siblings, "and we were afraid something would happen to him. He would go out at night to work, and we never knew whether he would be coming back or not."[7]

Scott also learned the barber's trade to make more money. On evenings and weekends long lines of men waiting for haircuts would appear at the Scott house. When Scott could not handle them all, his wife would pitch in and cut hair too.

The family home had an unfinished pine kitchen, dominated by a big, wood-burning stove. Water for washing was heated outdoors in a big iron pot over a fire. Then the water was poured into two large tin tubs with washboards.

The Scott farm produced corn, peas, potatoes, and garden vegetables. The family also raised hogs, cows, and chickens. Coretta, her siblings, and their mother tended the crops. When she was six or seven, Coretta

began planting and weeding. She hoed the soil and fed the animals. At ten, she worked in the cotton fields to earn extra money. Coretta hoed and chopped cotton in the summer, and picked it in the fall. In a regular season—about five months—she earned $4 or $5, but one year she made $7. She was an expert picker.

Coretta was a spirited child who would often scrap with her brother and sister as well as other children. She said of herself, "Mother said I was the meanest girl. I used to fight all the time."[8]

Coretta attended elementary school at Heiberger, a crossroads village three miles from home. The Scott children walked to school in all kinds of weather. As they walked, they would see school buses full of white children going by. One hundred African-American children shared a one-room schoolhouse. They had to buy their own books and use outdoor plumbing.

At the local white school, textbooks were free, each grade had a separate room, and there was even a library full of books. The African-American children went to school seven months of the year, and the white children went for nine months. Two dedicated African-American women taught Coretta and the others, and Coretta was always at the top of her class. Still she knew that she was getting a second-rate education because of her race.

Racial discrimination reared its ugly head in many other small ways while Coretta was growing up. When

the children went to the drugstore for ice cream cones, it was understood that white children were served first. White children chose the flavor of their cones, but African-American children could only get whatever flavor the drugstore had too much of.

It was a small matter, but it impressed on a child that she was not first-class. Coretta's mother tried to build the self-esteem of her children. She told Coretta to get an education and work hard to become somebody in life. She also told Coretta that nobody could push her around then and she would not have to depend on anybody for a living, "not even a man."[9]

A prized possession in the Scott house was a victrola—a 78 rpm record player. Coretta had an early love for music. She listened to good gospel music, and jitterbugged to the songs of Clara and Bessie Smith, as well as other jazz singers.

Coretta's first social experiences took place at Mount Tabor AME (African Methodist Episcopal) Zion Church. Sunday churchgoing was the highlight of the week. People came from far and wide in their good Sunday clothes for services. The Scotts walked four miles to church on Sunday. For Coretta, church was a "warm and heartening" experience.[10] Coretta's grandfathers often led the services. The entire extended family of uncles, aunts, and cousins were there. Church was the largest and most important part of Coretta's world, and the life of the whole community.

Coretta had remarkable grandparents. Her father was the son of Jeff and Cora Scott. Cora Scott died early, but Jeff Scott owned three hundred acres and was an important man in the community. He was a church leader and he ran the Sunday School. Everyone looked to Jeff Scott for advice and he often traveled to distant church conventions. He was a friendly outgoing man who was highly respected.

Coretta's mother was the daughter of Mollie and Martin McMurry. Mollie McMurry was a warm, loving, indulgent grandmother. A skilled seamstress, she made most of the children's clothing and tended a bountiful garden. Martin McMurry was a stern man with straight black hair. He attended school only two days in his life, but he taught himself to read the Bible.[11] He studied the Bible and became such an expert that when people disagreed about a passage they would ask him to settle the dispute. He also owned a three hundred-acre farm, and even when he was seventy years old, he would walk the twelve miles into town.

So Coretta had the example of grandparents who had risen to prominent positions in their community by hard work and integrity. This instilled in the young girl a sense of racial pride, self-respect, and dignity.

Lincoln High School was a semi-private school established by the American Missionary Association after the Civil War (1861–1865). Although Lincoln was

located in the heart of the segregated South, its teachers were racially mixed; they lived together in dormitories. The students, however, were all African Americans. Tuition was $4.50 a year—quite a sum in those days of the Great Depression. All the Scott children attended this school. Since it was ten miles from home, they had to board with African-American families in town. But the sacrifice was worth it. Lincoln nurtured Coretta's love of music and opened up a new world for the young girl.

At Lincoln, Coretta learned to play the flutaphone—a mid-sized flute. She had her first formal singing lessons, too. Coretta began performing in school programs with vocal solos. She learned the beginning repertoire of all new pianists. Soon she could play hymns, popular songs, and spirituals. At fifteen years old, Coretta became choir director and pianist of her church.

On Thanksgiving night in 1942, misfortune struck the Scott family. Their house, including all the good furniture they owned, caught fire and burned. The origins of the fire were suspicious, but nobody was ever charged. Obadiah Scott bought a sawmill then, angering some local whites who were envious of his success. The sawmill burned too, but Scott wasted no time on self-pity or bitterness. He pressed on and eventually owned a general store.

Coretta's older sister Edythe graduated from Lincoln High School with honors in 1943. At that time Antioch College in Yellow Springs, Ohio, was offering scholarships to African-American students. Edythe received a one-year scholarship to Antioch and was soon sending back glowing reports of life there. "Oh, you'd just love it here, Coretta," she wrote.[12]

While in twelfth grade at Lincoln, Coretta received a partial scholarship to Antioch, too. She was now firmly set on a career in music. After graduating from Lincoln in 1945, she set out for Antioch and her first experience in integrated education. When Coretta first arrived, Edythe was still there. That made it more pleasant. However, when Edythe left for Ohio State in 1946, Coretta was on her own—one of only three African Americans in her class (another woman and one man).

Coretta quickly joined the NAACP and the Civil Liberties Committee. She already had strong feelings about the need for equality, and she took to heart the stirring words of the founder of Antioch, Horace Mann: "Be ashamed to die until you have won some victory for humanity."[13]

At Antioch, Coretta Scott learned to function in a white world. She was a waitress and camp counselor, and she worked at Friendly Inn, a settlement house in Cleveland, Ohio. The house was a center for poor women and children. She also seriously studied music.

Coretta Scott set out for Antioch College, and her first experience in integrated education, in 1945.

Coretta Scott's first public concert was held in 1948 in Springfield, Ohio. She appeared on a program with famed African-American baritone Paul Robeson, who praised the quality of her voice. Coretta admired Robeson not only for his own magnificent voice, but also because he was a political activist. She resolved to be politically active, too, and not "just an artist."[14]

Buoyed by Robeson's praise and the applause of the crowd, Coretta was more eager than ever to pursue her career. She majored in elementary education at Antioch—the first African American ever to do so.

After teaching for one year at Antioch's private school, she was required to spend a year teaching in the Ohio public schools. However, when she applied to student teach in the Yellow Springs district, she was turned down because of her race. The Yellow Springs schools were segregated. Her advisor told her that she had two choices—either spend another year teaching at Antioch's private school or teach for a year at the all-black schools in Xenia, Ohio. "They were so casual about it," Coretta recalled. "I was so hurt."[15]

Coretta Scott's inferior elementary school education and inadequate courses at Lincoln made college difficult. She did not graduate from Antioch, leaving in 1951. However, she credited her years at Antioch with helping to "broaden and enrich my whole life."[16]

# 3

# A BRAND-NEW DREAM

 oretta Scott entered the New England Conservatory of Music in Boston, Massachusetts, in 1951. She wanted a degree in music education. When she left the family home in Alabama after summer vacation, she had a grant of $600 and just $50 in her pocket for living expenses. By the time Scott reached Boston she was down to $15 for food. For the next few days she lived on peanut butter, graham crackers, and fruit.

When she first arrived in Boston, Scott did house-keeping chores in exchange for room and board in a house provided by an Antioch patron. Scott was

determined to make any sacrifice necessary to reach her goal of a musical career. Later she was able to move into the school dormitory on Hemenway Street. Scott studied voice with Madame Marie Sundelius. Scott also studied music education so that she could teach music at schools while her singing career developed. Scott's social life was placed very much in the background. She had no plans to marry for a long time.

In Boston at the same time, working on his doctorate in theology, was a young man named Martin Luther King, Jr. He was from Atlanta, Georgia, and unlike Scott, he was eager for romance. He confided to a friend, Mary Powell, "I wish I knew a few girls from down home to go out with."[1] Powell happened also to know Coretta Scott. She described her to King in very glowing terms. King was eager to meet Scott, but Powell had a harder time getting Scott interested in meeting King.

In January 1952, Powell asked Scott if she had ever heard of Martin Luther King, Jr. Scott said that she had not.[2] Powell then described King as a brilliant and promising young man whom Scott may well enjoy meeting.[3] Scott was mildly interested until Powell mentioned that King was a minister.

Though Scott was deeply religious, she had been turning away from fundamentalism—the very traditional and conservative Protestantism of her southern roots. While in Boston she usually prayed in her room,

going to no organized church services. Scott recalled later that she had stereotypes of ministers. They did not appeal to her because they seemed "narrow minded overly pious people."[4] She did not believe that such a person was right for her.

So when the call came from King, Scott did not expect much to come out of it. King introduced himself and seemed very enthusiastic. "I am like Napoleon at Waterloo before your charms," he said. Scott replied, "Why that's absurd. You haven't seen me yet."[5] They made a lunch date for the following day.

In a cold January drizzle, her coat collar up and a scarf over her head, Scott waited as King's green Chevrolet pulled up. At first glance Scott noticed how short King was. She recalled thinking "how unimpressive he looks."[6]

The young couple went to Sharaf's Restaurant on Massachusetts Avenue. King was totally charming. "The more I saw of him the more I liked him," Scott recalled.[7]

As a student, Scott had resolved never to marry a man unless he was highly intelligent and a civil rights activist.[8] On that first date the couple discussed politics and philosophy. King was pleased to discover that Scott could hold her own in the weighty conversation. "Oh, I see you know about some other things besides music," he said.[9]

In a book he later wrote, King recorded his own first impression of Coretta Scott. She was, he wrote,

"an attractive young singer whose gentle manner and air of repose did not disguise her lively spirit."[10]

The young couple got along very well on that first date, but nothing prepared Scott for what King would say when they finished lunch. He told her frankly that she had everything that he looked for in a wife. When Scott protested that she hardly knew her, King said that what he wanted in a wife was character, intelligence, personality, and beauty and "you have them all."[11]

Scott was troubled. She did not want her budding musical career derailed by a serious romance. Yet King seemed so sincere, and she did like him. When King phoned the next day for another date, she agreed to go with him to a party in Watertown.

Scott noticed that everyone at the party seemed to know and like King. She could see why—he was warm and compelling. Scott felt tenderness toward King, and at the party she thought, "He has taken me to the party. I was his girlfriend."[12] To be the girlfriend of a young man so obviously admired by all those people made an impression on Scott. From then on King pursued Scott. "Not that I ran very hard," Scott admitted later.[13]

During the time of their steady dating Scott and King went to movies and concerts. They went to hear Arthur Rubinstein play the piano in Symphony Hall, walked in Boston's parks, and ice skated.[14] King loved to dance, and they danced a lot. They bought clams

and they went to the Western Lunch Box for King's favorite dish—greens and ham hocks, cuts of pork.

Scott was growing very impressed with King's sense of mission. "He talked often about what he planned to do with his life," she recalled, "of what he hoped to contribute to the race and to humanity at large."[15] One Sunday, Scott heard King preach at the Twelfth Street Baptist Church in Roxbury. The pastor there allowed young preachers to try out their preaching styles at his church. Scott thought that King was wonderful in the pulpit that Sunday.

The young couple now began some serious planning. King frankly said that he wanted a wife who would be a homemaker and a full-time mother to his children. That was not Scott's dream. As a concert singer she certainly would not have time to be a full-time homemaker and mother. She was torn between her cherished dream of a musical career and her growing feeling for King.

Scott prayed for wisdom in making her choice. Soon she began to realize how much she wanted marriage and children. She was also falling in love with Martin Luther King, Jr. The young couple took the next important step. King planned to take Scott to meet his parents in Atlanta.

In his book, Reverend Martin Luther King, Sr., recounts his first impression of Scott. "Coretta was a beautiful young woman. She came from among

strong, solid, courageous black folks who'd worked the land and built up businesses for themselves."[16] Scott was struck by the elder King's large physical presence. He was gentle and courteous, but he did not seem to pay too much attention to Scott.

Coretta told Martin's father that she was planning a musical career and he thought that would not fit in with being a minister's wife. He thought that Scott would be happier with a man from the music business.[17]

After the meeting in Atlanta, King's parents came to Boston to visit their son and his girlfriend. King, Sr., mentioned to Scott that his son dated the daughters of fine Atlanta families, women "who have much to share and much to offer." Scott replied, "I have something to offer, Reverend King."[18] The senior King remained unenthusiastic about the match, but King said firmly, "I must marry Coretta. She's the most important person to come into my life Dad. I know you don't really approve, but this is what I have to do."[19]

King, Sr., resigned himself to the marriage. His son would marry Coretta Scott during the coming June 1953.

Coretta Scott had resigned herself too. She would be a minister's wife, not a major concert star. She did this because, as she later recalled, Martin Luther King, Jr., was "unlike anyone else I had ever met. And he was committed to making changes in society. We both were."[20]

Coretta Scott was a serious music student at the New England
Conservatory. She planned a musical career.

Scott would no longer be training for a musical career on the concert stage. She was finishing her junior year at New England Conservatory of Music. For her senior year she would focus entirely on music education. This way she could teach music wherever her husband's church was. She had made up her mind that her future was with Martin Luther King, Jr. "Whatever he does, I will be involved in it," she said.[21]

The wedding was held on June 18, 1953, on land owned by Scott's parents in Marion, Alabama. Obadiah Scott, Coretta's father, now had a nice home beside his general store, and there was a little arch in the garden. Coretta and Martin stood beneath that arch to exchange wedding vows. Reverend Martin Luther King, Sr., conducted the ceremony. The bride wore a pastel blue lace waltz-length gown with matching net gloves and shoes. Her veil had a crown made of flowers.

Although Martin came from middle-class Atlanta, and Coretta was a country girl, Martin fit in perfectly with her family. Martin rushed into the Scott home and greeted Coretta's mother as "Mom."

The newlyweds could not find a bridal suite for African Americans in any Alabama hotels, so they spent their wedding night at the home of a friend—a funeral director. Afterwards, King would often turn to his wife and joke, "Do you know we spent our honeymoon at a funeral parlor?"[22]

Coretta Scott married Martin Luther King, Jr., (shown here) on
June 18, 1953. Martin fit in perfectly with her family.

Now the young couple set out together to build a future. There was so much to do: finish their educations in Boston, find a church for King, and settle into their first home as a married couple. Within less than two years Coretta Scott King would be a mother in the center of a history-making civil rights struggle. But she did not know that yet. For what was left of the summer of 1953, Coretta and Martin would have the joy of being free of responsibilities with time to enjoy one another.

# 4

## BACK HOME TO ALABAMA

n the Sunday after her marriage, Coretta Scott King was baptized by immersion at Ebenezer Baptist Church in Atlanta, Georgia. The newlyweds lived with Martin's parents all summer, and in the fall they headed back to Boston and a hectic school schedule.

In September 1953, Martin began writing the thesis for his doctorate. Coretta was finishing her music education degree and singing several recitals. The Kings lived in a large old Boston home.

Coretta Scott King needed thirteen courses to complete her degree so that she could teach music.

Newlywed Coretta Scott King sang in several recitals. This photo is from the program of a 1954 recital.

Her education had to cover the theory of all instruments from piano to woodwinds and brass. She learned choir directing, orchestral arrangement, and percussion.

Martin tried to help Coretta with the housework. He did the heavy cleaning and washing. He put the dirty clothes in a kitchen tub to soak, washed them, and then hung them out to dry. Coretta appreciated his intentions, but she was not satisfied with how the wash looked. It was not clean and bright enough.[1]

The Kings did their grocery shopping together on Saturdays, and Thursday night was Martin's turn to cook. He was proud of his cooking skills, especially his specialties—smothered cabbage, pork chops, fried chicken, and the feet, snouts, and ears of pigs. Coretta did not care for pig's ears, but Martin insisted, "They're good and they're cheap."[2] Martin also liked to cook turnip greens, southern style, with ham hocks and bacon drippings. Both Coretta and Martin enjoyed soul food—seasoned, overcooked, and delicious southern cooking.

Martin Luther King, Jr., had strong ideas on the different roles of husbands and wives. The woman's place was definitely in the home and a woman's primary role was that of wife and mother. Martin considered himself the head of the family.[3] Coretta admitted that if she had not married a strong man she would have "worn the pants" in the family.[4]

Coretta Scott King performed here, in Jordan Hall, during her time at the New England Conservatory.

It is interesting that an independent, spirited young woman like Coretta Scott cheerfully accepted this strong young man's leadership in the family. It can only be explained by her love for him, and the fact that the goals they both passionately believed in dominated their lives. Coretta saw herself and Martin as a team destined to make the world a better place.

In January 1954, with both their educations completed, the Kings were ready for their first church. Martin Luther King, Jr., was invited to Dexter Avenue Baptist Church in Montgomery, Alabama, to preach a trial sermon. If the congregation liked him, he would be offered a pastorate.

When the Kings arrived in Montgomery, they drove around the neighborhood near the church. They saw African Americans riding in the backs of buses and signs indicating second-rate accommodations for non-whites. Everything was segregated, from drinking fountains to restrooms. The Kings knew that this is how they would have to live if they moved here. They had both enjoyed the much different atmosphere of New England, and it would require a painful adjustment to live here now. With all that, Coretta Scott King still told her husband, "If this is what you want, I'll make myself happy in Montgomery."[5]

Coretta Scott King was born only eighty miles from Montgomery and she knew well the reality of separate and unequal. Growing up in Alabama she had suffered

the many slights an African-American child had to endure. If she moved here her own children would have to face the same problems.

When Martin Luther King, Jr., preached his trial sermon, it was received with enthusiasm. The people loved him and he was offered the pastorate.

The Kings looked at the fine, solid, brick church on Dexter Avenue. Martin cried, "I like this church!"[6] Coretta knew from the light in his eyes that he would make a special contribution here.

The white frame parsonage was on Jackson Street, sixteen blocks from the church, in a segregated neighborhood. It was a nice seven-room house, though a little rundown. In September 1954, the Kings moved in. Coretta enthusiastically entered her new life. Martin would try out his sermons on Coretta before Sunday morning. She would offer suggestions on them. She worked as his secretary and joined several church committees. With her musical training she improved the Dexter choir and also sang in the choir herself—often performing solo parts of anthems.

The spring of 1955 was a joyful time for the Kings. Martin received his doctorate in theology, and Coretta had received a bachelor of music degree in music education in June 1954. Martin impressed his church with his strong authority. "Leadership never ascends from the pew to the pulpit but descends from the pulpit to the pew," he said.[7]

The Kings liked the Dexter Avenue Baptist Church in Montgomery, Alabama, right from the start.

On November 17, 1955, Yolanda Denise (nicknamed Yokie), the Kings' first child, was born at St. Jude's Catholic Hospital. Then, on December 1, 1955, Rosa Parks made her now-famous refusal to yield her bus seat to a white man. So the black community, under Martin Luther King, Jr., began to lead a boycott of the City Bus Lines.

Protests against the jailing of Parks were organized at Dexter Avenue Baptist Church. December 5, 1955, was chosen as the date for the boycott to begin. All African Americans were asked not to ride buses to work, to town, to school, or anywhere else. These buses were the only source of transportation for tens of thousands of African Americans. Leaflets were printed and distributed throughout the African-American communities.

At 5:30 A.M. on December 5, lights were already on at the King house. The first bus was due at the bus stop outside. Coretta watched from the window until the first bus appeared in the dim dawn light. Then she called Martin, who joined her at the window. They saw the success of the bus boycott in the making. There was not a single person on the usually crowded bus. It was only the beginning.

Bus after bus passed by with no black passengers. Yet though the buses were empty, the streets and side-walks were not. African Americans trudged long distances to work or they formed car pools. A few

banded together to hire taxis, and some rode mules, or came to work in horse-drawn buggies.

The MIA issued its demands for ending the bus boycott. They were:

1. Courteous treatment of African Americans by bus drivers.

2. Passengers should be seated on a first-come, first-serve basis. Blacks would be seated from the back going forward, and the whites from the front going back. If the bus was filled with black passengers, whites boarding the bus would have to stand.

3. Black bus drivers would be hired on predominately black routes.

The white establishment, not used to hearing demands from the black community, was angry. In fact, many were outraged. Rather than thinking about negotiating the MIA demands, they planned strategies to undermine the boycott. One scheme was to get an injunction against car pools. More and more African Americans were getting to work that way, so the whites tried to make it illegal.

Martin Luther King, Jr., feared that the injunction against car pools would undermine the boycott. Weary black workers could not be expected to walk long distances on a daily basis. The temptation to return to the buses would be strong.

Martin was at a low point when his wife tried to lift his spirits. Coretta said that she was somehow certain that the Supreme Court would save them. "I don't know whether I really believed that such perfect timing would ever come about," she said later, "but Martin and the movement needed desperately to believe in near miracles at this stage of the struggle."[8]

During the strife the police began to harass black drivers. They were stopped, questioned, and often arrested. On January 26, Martin Luther King, Jr., himself was arrested for a minor traffic violation. Two days later the parsonage was bombed with his family inside.

After the bombing, Coretta called the church where her husband was speaking. She told Reverend Ralph Abernathy that she and Yolanda were unhurt. A shaken Martin hurried home. After he had assured himself that his family was really safe, Martin went outside to calm the gathering crowd. Coretta held her baby in her arms and watched her husband through the broken window.

"We must not return violence under any condition," Martin Luther King, Jr., told the crowd. "I know this is difficult advice to follow, especially since we have been the victims of no less than ten bombings. But this is the way of Christ."[9]

On that shocking night, Coretta Scott King had seen the price that she and her family might have to

pay to achieve their dream of racial equality. The walls of discrimination were tough and strong, and dangerous passions defended them. But she had also seen the awesome power of love over vengeance as the enraged black crowd quietly fell back and went home. It was only the beginning of a dramatic and dangerous odyssey for Coretta Scott King and those she loved.

# 5

# "I WILL ALWAYS
# BE WITH YOU"

he damaged parsonage was repaired and the Kings moved back in. Floodlights were installed on the house, and an unarmed man guarded the premises. Martin Luther King, Jr., was indicted for his role in the bus boycott and he faced jail. The local grand jury indicted the entire MIA leadership, about a hundred people, for violating an old anti-boycott law intended to stop labor unions. Coretta Scott King told her husband, "I want you to know that whatever you decide to do, I will always be with you."[1]

Martin Luther King, Jr., surrendered at the courthouse and the trial was set for March 19, 1956. It took just one day to find him guilty. When bail was granted, Coretta and Martin walked hand-in-hand from court. A large crowd outside shouted good wishes and encouragement. The penalty for the conviction was a $500 fine or a year and a day in county jail, but pending appeal the penalty was stayed.

By mid-1956, Martin Luther King, Jr.'s, reputation had spread around the country. The media descended on the little parsonage on Jackson Avenue. The house was almost always crammed with friends and news people. Coretta Scott King learned to cook in large quantities, and hungry reporters sat at the family table with friends and parishioners.

December 5, 1956, was the first anniversary of the bus boycott. To mark the day Coretta Scott King was to appear at a major fund-raising concert at Manhattan Center in New York. Other performers included Harry Belafonte and Duke Ellington. Still, all eyes were focused on the featured performer, twenty-nine-year-old Coretta Scott King.

She sang a program of classical music and told the story of the Montgomery struggle in story and song. She used powerful black spirituals to illustrate the courage of the African Americans in Montgomery who rode mules or walked many miles rather than ride segregated buses. She sang "Walk Together, Chillun',

Don't You Get Weary," and "Keep Your Hand on the Plow." The concert was a great success. Coretta Scott King was able to use her considerable musical gifts in the service of the struggle.

Then the brave prediction Coretta Scott King had made just to cheer her husband in the early dark days of the Montgomery boycott came true. Just as she said it would, on November 20, 1956, the United States Supreme Court declared Montgomery's bus segregation system unconstitutional. The official word reached Montgomery on December 20. The MIA had won a major victory, but the Kings and their supporters spent little time celebrating.

Although the mayor of Montgomery said that he would obey the Supreme Court decision, nobody could predict how the newly desegregated buses would fare. Would long-denied African Americans shame the movement with rudeness? Would there be a backlash from bitter whites who swore they would never accept integration on any terms?

One night after the court decision, forty carloads of robed and hooded whites rode through the black communities of Montgomery. The Klan was making a clear message of intimidation. But the blacks were not frightened. They "acted as if they were watching a circus," Martin Luther King, Jr., said.[2] The black people opened their doors, came out on their porches, watched, and waved greetings to the angry white men.

The Klansmen were so shocked and disappointed that they were not scaring anyone that they went home after driving just a few blocks.

When the day came for the desegregated buses to roll, a few racists throwing stones hit some buses. Shots were fired, but nobody was hit. On January 15, 1957, Martin Luther King, Jr., had pleaded for a peaceful transition. He stood with a white minister at the bus stop in front of his parsonage. The bus driver smiled and said, "We are glad to have you this morning."[3] On January 28 a smoking pile of fourteen sticks of dynamite was found on the King porch. It was removed safely. For the most part, peace and even cordiality reigned on the buses. Not a single black or white citizen of Montgomery had died as a result of the bus boycott. A stunning victory had been won by the nonviolent tactics of Martin Luther King, Jr.

Coretta Scott King saw her husband become a hero to African Americans across the country. She had seen in him a burning desire to change the world when they courted, and that was one of the traits that endeared him to her. Coretta Scott King wanted to help change the world too. Now after only three years of marriage, the young couple, working together, had really begun to make dramatic changes. People were calling the Montgomery Freedom Movement the Second American Revolution.

On January 10, 1957, African-American religious leaders from all over the country met in Atlanta, Georgia, to form the group that later became the Southern Christian Leadership Conference (SCLC). The organization planned to fight all forms of segregation and to register African-American voters, especially in areas of the South where African-American voter registration had been discouraged. The tactics would be nonviolent disobedience to unjust laws.

So-called "Jim Crow" laws had been in effect throughout the South since the 1880s, after the Civil War. They were designed to keep blacks separate from whites and condemned to second-rate status. In most of the South, African Americans could not easily vote, were denied access to desirable jobs, and were forced to live behind a color line. The Kings and their supporters were attempting nothing less than dismantling a repressive system that had stood for almost eighty years.

Because of the fame generated by the Montgomery success, the Kings were invited to travel beyond the United States. Accounts of their experiences were appearing in many foreign newspapers. An invitation that was especially appealing came from Ghana. The Kings were asked to witness Ghana's move to independence in March 1957. It would be the first trip outside the United States for both of the Kings.

On March 3 the Kings boarded a plane for Africa. They landed in Accra, the capital of Ghana. They

looked forward to witnessing the birth of a new African nation.[4] Both Coretta and Martin, however, were offended by the servile demeanor of the black servants in Ghana. The Kings were guests at the home of a white English professor and the black servants' "cringing manner" towards the professor and his guests disturbed the Kings.[5]

The independence ceremonies were very stirring, especially to African Americans who could see the link in African nations becoming independent and their struggles to be equal in their own country. The Kings watched the last British parliament adjourn. Fifty thousand Ghanians, many in tribal dress, crowded into the square to watch the green flag of the new nation rise. "We were so proud of our African heritage," Coretta Scott King said.[6]

The Kings left Ghana and went to Lagos, Nigeria. Coretta Scott King was very distressed at the terrible poverty that they saw there.[7] After leaving Africa, the Kings visited Rome, Geneva, Paris, and London. At the Vatican the Kings were impressed by the great beauty of St. Peter's Basilica. Coretta recalled that Martin was so moved by the ancient church that he knelt "on the basilica floor and prayed."[8]

Back home after the trip, Coretta Scott King learned she was pregnant with their second child. On October 23, 1957, the Kings welcomed their first son, Martin Luther King, III. A time of relative peace and

quiet followed. The Kings were able to enjoy Yolanda and the new baby as well as Martin's ministry. During all the time that he struggled with the civil rights movement, Martin was also spiritual counselor to his parishioners. He was balancing his work with the MIA with trying to resolve marital splits and help parents with wayward children. As busy as Martin was with his leadership of the civil rights movement, he never stopped being an involved minister.

One Sunday, Martin Luther King, Jr., was invited to deliver a sermon at Holt Street Baptist Church. He gave a very eloquent talk, and afterwards Coretta Scott King was asked if he was always so electrifying. She smiled and said, "Sometimes he's even better."[9]

Although Coretta Scott King usually offered a pleasant smile to all who came her way, her heart was not at peace. There always lurked an ever-present danger of disaster. She confided in the wife of Harris Wofford (an early white admirer and advisor to Martin Luther King, Jr.) that she had a recurring nightmare of her husband being killed.[10]

In the summer of 1958, the Kings enjoyed their first real vacation since their marriage—a trip to Mexico. Martin spent some of the time working on a book, but for Coretta it was a time of pure rest from the struggles of the civil rights movement. The only sad aspect of the trip, according to Coretta, was that

Martin was in a state of "rage and despair" over the conditions of poverty he observed in Mexico.[11]

The issue of poverty and so many people apparently in a hopeless condition continued to haunt Martin Luther King, Jr., and he would address it a great deal in his last years. It would also be an ongoing cause for Coretta Scott King, continuing to this present day.

In September 1958, the Kings were back in Montgomery at a courthouse where their friend Reverend Ralph Abernathy was involved in a civil matter. A police officer spotted Martin Luther King, Jr., and ordered him to leave the courthouse. When he refused, two police officers appeared to grab him roughly and force his arms behind his back. Martin was obviously in pain as he was shoved down a flight of stairs in a hurried march. Coretta followed Martin, desperate for some way to help him. A police officer turned to her and snapped, "You want to go to jail too, gal?"[12] Coretta turned and rushed to get help for Martin, but when she returned her husband was nowhere in sight. After the roughing-up, he was released on bail.

At this point Martin Luther King, Jr., made a decision. The next time he was facing jail he would not post bail. He would serve the time. He believed that this was necessary to dramatize the cause. He felt his sacrifice would bear fruit.

On September 3, 1958, Martin Luther King, Jr., went to court on charges of disobeying an officer. He was found guilty and sentenced to pay a $10 fine or serve fourteen days in jail. The Montgomery authorities did not want Martin Luther King, Jr., in their jail system. He was too famous and they feared bad publicity. So when he lined up with the other prisoners to go to jail, someone paid his fine—over his objections. Martin was sent home.

During September 1958, Martin went on a book-signing tour with his first book, *Stride Toward Freedom: The Montgomery Story.* On September 19, he was at a Harlem, New York, department store autographing books when a demented African-American woman attacked him. Coretta had already made plans to pick up her husband at the airport the next day upon his return to Atlanta. Instead, the phone rang with frightening news. Coretta was told that Martin had been stabbed. He was alive, but the wound was very, very serious.

Fighting back tears, Coretta rushed to the hospital after arriving in New York. "If this is the way it's got to be, then this is the way it's got to be," she told herself, steeling herself against the possibility that the wound would prove fatal.[13]

The knife had entered Martin's chest and was touching the aorta (the heart's largest artery). Had he sneezed or moved suddenly, he would have died.

Doctors removed two ribs to free the blade. When Coretta saw her husband he was lying with a tube in his nose and throat, but he would survive. "I thanked God," she recalled later, "for what seemed almost a miracle."[14]

Thousands of cards and letters arrived at the hospital for Martin. Coretta spent most of her time at Martin's bedside or greeting the visitors who came to pay their respects. Martin asked about the woman who had attacked him and then said, "This person needs help. Don't do anything to her; don't prosecute her. Get her healed."[15] The woman was eventually sent to a mental hospital.

Pneumonia slowed Martin's recovery, but on October 3, 1958, Coretta took him to a friend's house where he recuperated for the next three weeks. The Kings had to stay in New York for medical follow-up.

Martin Luther King, Jr., had an invitation from the Gandhi Peace Foundation to make a speaking tour of India when he had some free time. He was a strong believer in the tactic of nonviolence practiced by the great Indian leader Mohandas Gandhi, and he carried Gandhi's principles into his own crusade. This seemed an ideal time to go. So, after the Christmas holidays of 1958, the Kings went to India.

Coretta Scott King and her husband were again heartsick to see the terrible poverty in Bombay, India. When they asked about all the people sleeping in the streets, they were told that they had no other place to

go. They were homeless.[16] Coretta said, "We loved the Indian people for the warmth and spiritual quality they possessed."[17]

The Kings enjoyed a special moment together when they sat on a rock right at the point in southernmost India where the Indian Ocean, the Arabian Sea, and the Bay of Bengal meet at Cape Comorin. Coretta watched the sun become a sliver of orange as the moon came up on the other side of the ocean. She touched Martin's shoulder and said, "Look Martin, isn't that beautiful."[18] It was a rare interlude for the Kings, whose lives had become usually too busy for such moments of quiet joy.

Coretta Scott King was greeted with great enthusiasm in India. Her dark beautiful features were much like the faces of many Indian women, and her sari garb touched the hearts of the people. Martin recalled after the trip, "Coretta ended up singing as much as I lectured."[19]

At this point in their lives, the Kings had a serious decision to make. Martin's vast national obligations were taking him more and more away from his work at Dexter Avenue Baptist Church. He was loved by the congregation and they were not complaining that he was neglecting them, but he felt that he was. He believed that he was cheating them of what they deserved—a full-time pastor. The Kings felt that they could no longer do justice to the Alabama congregation

while being of service to the national civil rights struggle.

Martin Luther King, Sr., offered his son the co-pastorate at Ebenezer Baptist Church in Atlanta. Martin could devote himself to his national work then with a clear conscience because he would not be the only pastor at the church. With this in mind, he offered his resignation at Dexter Avenue Baptist Church on November 29, 1959, taking effect the last Sunday in January 1960.

An emotional farewell was given the Kings at their beloved little church. "For almost four years now," Martin Luther King, Jr., told his weeping congregation, "I have been trying to do as one man, what five or six people ought to be doing."[20] He apologized for neglecting the people at Dexter, and the Kings wept along with the congregation during the hymn "Blest Be the Tie That Binds."

Coretta Scott King had grown to love Dexter Avenue Baptist Church. She would name her second son after it. Now she was leaving Alabama where she had been born, raised, and married, and she was going to her husband's Georgian roots—Atlanta. However, Martin and Coretta were leaving Alabama a better place than they had found it.

# 6

## WE SHALL OVERCOME

As soon as they arrived in Atlanta, the Kings learned that a Montgomery, Alabama, grand jury had indicted Martin Luther King, Jr., on charges that his 1956-1958 state tax returns were dishonest. He was accused of personally using money intended for the MIA and SCLC. Martin was crushed as he talked over the charges with Coretta. He feared that many of his supporters would believe that he was guilty. He grieved that such a charge was leveled against him when he prided himself on "my honesty where money is concerned."[1] Martin never mixed his own meager resources with

donations intended for the civil rights cause that he received. Coretta recalled, "I tried desperately to assure him that the vast majority of people believed in him and understood the motivation of the State of Alabama."[2] Powerful political interests in Alabama still resented the dramatic success of the MIA. The discrediting of Martin Luther King, Jr., would have been a welcome development for them.

Coretta Scott King was scheduled to speak in Cleveland, Ohio, for the Antioch Baptist Church Women's Day, but she was so upset that she was not sure she could go through with it. Then, before her appearance, the verdict came in on the income tax charges against her husband. A jury of twelve white southern men took less than four hours before finding him not guilty. Coretta Scott King called it a "triumph of justice," adding that it was a miracle "that restored your faith in human good."[3] She went to Cleveland, and without using notes, she spoke from her heart about what her family had just been through. She spoke passionately, describing her anxiety over the false charges. Afterwards, a friend, Mrs. Leola Whitted, said, "Girl, you held that audience spellbound. I am so proud of you."[4]

As the Kings settled into their new Atlanta home, Coretta Scott King fully realized that, in spite of its cosmopolitan qualities, Atlanta was still the segregated South. All across the city, restaurants, theaters, lunch

counters, and most parks were closed to African Americans. Coretta Scott King noted sadly that an African American wanting a soda at a downtown restaurant still had to order it from a side door.[5]

After they had lived in Atlanta for a while, Coretta Scott King talked to an interviewer about her life there. She discussed the stress the family often had to endure. "It takes a toll on the family," she said. "We like to read and listen to music, but we don't have time for it. We can't sit down to supper without somebody coming to the door."[6] She talked about the constant pressure of expecting something bad to happen. She described one night when men came and burned a cross on the lawn. "Martin was away, and the children were asleep. But when I went outside and looked, I wasn't afraid. It just seemed like a piece of wood burning to me."[7]

In 1960 the thrust of the civil rights movement had turned to the desegregation of lunch counters and restaurants in the South. The song "We Shall Overcome," based on a black spiritual, had been played and sung at so many marches and demonstrations, that it became the official anthem of the movement. African Americans on their way to lunch-counter sit-ins would sing it as they went.

Whenever Martin Luther King, Jr., sat-in at Rich's Department Store lunch counter in Atlanta, he was routinely arrested. The King children were now old

enough to realize what was going on. Five-year-old Yolanda had heard on the radio that her father was jailed. She came home crying to her mother and demanded to know why her father had gone to jail.

Coretta Scott King tried to explain in a way that a five-year-old could grasp. Yolanda could not have understood the details of segregation, but she could understand how life in the South made it hard on African Americans as they tried to live.

Coretta explained to Yolanda that her father had gone to jail to help people. He wanted to make life better for people and to do that he had to sacrifice his own freedom for a while.[8]

Three-year-old Marty, who was in love with airplanes, only wanted to know if Daddy had gone to jail on a plane. Later the boy would be thrilled when his father came home from jail in an airplane.

Yolanda attended an integrated Quaker school in Atlanta. When a classmate taunted her about her father being in jail, she remembered what her mother said and told the other girl how her father was helping people.[9]

Martin Luther King, Jr., and the others who sat-in at Rich's went on trial in October 1960. All but Martin were released. While he was in jail, the authorities uncovered an old suspended sentence on a traffic violation. They used this as a pretense to sentence him to six months of hard labor in the tough state prison at

Reidsville. Coretta described Martin's sentence as "viciously unjust."[10]

Coretta Scott King was five months pregnant and extremely upset. For the first time since the movement began, she cried in public. The long sentence given Martin meant that he would not be there when Coretta gave birth to their third child.

When Coretta visited Martin in jail, along with Martin Luther King, Sr., tears flowed again. "Corrie, dear," Martin said, "you have to be strong. I've never seen you like this before. You have to be strong for me."[11] Martin's father said, "You don't see Daddy King crying, Coretta. I am ready to fight. When you see Daddy King crying, then you can start crying."[12]

Men came in the pre-dawn darkness to take Martin Luther King, Jr., from the county jail. He was handcuffed, put in leg irons, and driven some three hundred miles to Reidsville. He was placed in a narrow cell with hardened criminals and forced to wear a prison uniform. "Dad," Coretta cried to Martin's father when she heard that he had been taken to Reidsville in the dark of night, "what's going to happen to him down there?"[13] Martin Luther King, Sr., admitted to great fear on his own. "I knew the jeopardy my son was in," he said.[14]

As Coretta and Martin's father agonized over Martin's fate, a telephone call came from Senator John F. Kennedy of Massachusetts. At the time,

Kennedy was locked in a close election battle with Vice President Richard Nixon for the presidency of the United States. When Coretta Scott King took the phone she said that she would be grateful for anything Kennedy might be able to do.

Kennedy's brother Robert placed a call to a Georgia judge and Martin Luther King, Jr., was quickly granted bail. There was little doubt that pressure from the Kennedys made the difference.[15] Martin was freed and he boarded a plane chartered by the SCLC to return to Atlanta, where Coretta waited with the children.

Martin Luther King, Sr., was supporting Nixon for president up to this point, but he soon switched to Kennedy. Many others might have done the same thing. Nobody knows for sure how many votes went to Kennedy that November because of his compassionate call to Coretta Scott King and his persuasive efforts to free her husband. A few days later John F. Kennedy was elected president by a very slim margin. It is possible that those calls tipped the scales in his favor.

On January 30, 1961, Dexter Scott, the family's second son, was born. He was named for the beloved church where the Kings had first served.

In February 1962, Martin Luther King, Jr., was convicted of leading a civil rights march in Albany, Georgia. In July he was sent to jail. For the first time in their lives, the King children would actually see

their father in jail. Martin was allowed to meet with his family in the corridor, so that the children did not see him behind bars. Coretta was concerned that Martin was missing so much time with his family. "If you stay away much longer," she told him, "the baby won't know you."[16] Still, the visit buoyed Martin's spirits. Coming out of jail with the children Coretta said, "I think he feels much better after seeing the children. It gave him a lift."[17]

In March 1962, Coretta Scott King was invited by the Women's Strike for Peace to go to Geneva, Switzerland, as a delegate. Martin was out of jail and free to take care of the children, so she went.

Ever since her college days, Coretta had been vitally interested in the cause of peace. She joined Quaker peace groups at Antioch, and in Atlanta, she joined the Women's International League for Peace. Now she joined fifty other American women in Geneva to plead for a ban on atomic testing. Coretta Scott King met with the American representative to the atomic test ban talks, but he treated her and the others like "hysterical females."[18]

During these years of civil rights struggle, the Kings were the parents of young children with all the responsibilities that carried. Sometimes the children felt the pressure of being well known. Yolanda told her mother that she was tired of being the daughter of a famous person and longed to be treated like an ordinary

child.[19] Marty was afraid to tell two white playmates who his father was for fear they might beat him up.[20]

A new amusement park called Funtown opened in Atlanta, and the King children watched the extensive publicity campaign on television. They wanted to go to Funtown, but their parents kept putting it off. Finally Coretta and Martin had to tell the children the truth—African-American children were not welcome at Funtown. Like her mother had done with her, Coretta told her children that they were just as good as any other children in spite of this discrimination. And she promised them that it would not be long before they could go to Funtown.[21] In the spring of 1963 Funtown was quietly desegregated. The King family was among the first African Americans through the turnstiles.

When Martin was with the children, Coretta recalled, he always had a wonderful time. Martin had a game he would play with each of his children. He put them on top of the refrigerator, and they would then leap into his arms. Later, older King children leaped from the stairs into their father's arms. Coretta worried that he would miss catching the leaping children, but he never did.[22]

In 1963 the Kings were disappointed that President Kennedy was planning no civil rights legislation. They had expected more action from this

🔲🔲🔲🔲🔲🔲🔲🔲🔲🔲🔲🔲🔲🔲🔲🔲🔲🔲🔲🔲🔲🔲🔲🔲🔲🔲🔲🔲🔲🔲🔲🔲🔲

president, but he had other items on his agenda that he wanted to pass first.

On March 28, 1963, the Kings' fourth child, Bernice Albertine (nicknamed Bunny) was born. At the time, Martin Luther King, Jr., was involved in a struggle to desegregate Birmingham, Alabama, lunch counters. The police chief there, Eugene "Bull" Connor, was known for harshly repressing demonstrations—sometimes with fire hoses and police dogs. Once again, on April 12, Martin was put in jail. This time he was not even allowed to communicate with the outside world. Attorney General Robert Kennedy, the president's brother, called Coretta Scott King offering help. Then the president himself called her to reassure her that the Federal Bureau of Investigation (FBI) would check on Martin's condition to make sure he was all right.

Martin Luther King, Jr., spent eight days in jail and wrote his now-famous "Letter from a Birmingham Jail," explaining why African Americans could wait no longer for equality. On Saturday, April 20, 1963, he was freed from jail. Coretta flew to meet Martin. Then, finally, black and white businesspeople in Birmingham hammered out a settlement of the public accommodations issue. Lunch counters, drinking fountains, and rest rooms would be desegregated, and bus companies agreed to hire more African Americans.

Because of the events in Birmingham, and the desegregation of the University of Alabama on June 11, 1963, President Kennedy took another look at his civil rights agenda. He moved it to the front burner. On the evening of June 11, Kennedy made a nationally televised address to the nation. He called civil rights a moral issue and he urged all Americans to support it. The Civil Rights Bill of 1964 was designed to open all public accommodations to African Americans. The battle for desegregation would not then have to be waged on a city-by-city basis. If passed, the Civil Rights Bill would effectively end segregation in the South.

Coretta Scott King and her husband had good reason to be optimistic. Martin's suffering in jail after numerous arrests, and Coretta's fortitude during the anxiety and loneliness of those times seemed to be bearing fruit.

So many blacks and their white friends had marched and struggled and endured punishment for the cause. Now they had a real friend in the White House, and he was moving forward with a bold civil rights law. It was the spring of 1963 and spirits in the civil rights movement were soaring with fresh hope. But in the months ahead the Kings and their supporters would experience triumph in Washington, D.C., and profound tragedy in Dallas, Texas.

# 7

## IN SEARCH OF PEACE

fter the success of the Birmingham struggle, Coretta Scott King suggested to her husband that so many Americans were so inspired by the civil rights movement that now was the time to call for a "massive march on Washington." This would encourage the passage of legislation to completely end the exclusion of African Americans from American society.[1] Martin Luther King, Jr., began discussing the idea with other African-American leaders, and they quickly agreed that it was a good idea. The date for a march on Washington, D.C., was set—August 28, 1963.

The Kings, along with thousands of other Americans, arrived in Washington, D.C., on that day. Coretta and Martin watched from their hotel window and wondered how many people would show up. Those opposed to the march and civil rights goals were hoping for a small unimpressive turnout.

When the Kings reached the mall, their spirits soared. A quarter of a million people milled in the bright sunshine. They had come by plane, train, bus, car, and some even walked. About one-fourth of the crowd was white.

Coretta was seated right behind Martin when he made his memorable "I Have a Dream" address. His stirring words rang through the crowd with enormous power. He said, in part:

> I have a dream that my four little children will one day live in a nation where they will not be judged by the color of their skin, but by the content of their character. I have a dream today! I have a dream that one day down in Alabama . . . little black boys and black girls will be able to join hands with little white boys and white girls as sisters and brothers. I have a dream today![2]

Martin Luther King, Jr., concluded with these words:

> We will be able to speed up that day when all God's children, black men and white men, Jews and gentiles, Protestants and Catholics, will be able to join hands and sing in the words of the old Negro spiritual: "Free at last. Free at last. Thank God almighty, we are free at last."[3]

Coretta Scott King recalled that when her husband finished his speech the applause was thunderous.[4] One writer described the crowd's reaction this way: "It was a stunning, heart-wrenching tour de force. Thousands were shouting King's name, shouting for joy, weeping for happiness."[5]

As the Kings left the platform, they held on to one another. Martin went into the White House with the other African-American leaders of the march, and Coretta remained outside with the other wives. Martin Luther King, Jr., met with President Kennedy. Later, Martin and Coretta had their private celebration of the remarkable day in their hotel suite.

Everyone was in high spirits after the successful Washington march, but only three weeks later a terrible crime took place in Birmingham, Alabama. A bomb was planted at the Sixteenth Street Baptist Church. It exploded during Sunday School, killing four little African-American girls. Martin Luther King, Jr., went to Birmingham to console the grieving parents. He then spoke the eulogy at a joint funeral for three of the victims.

On November 22, 1963, the Kings were at home in Atlanta when news from Dallas, Texas, flashed across the television screen. Martin called to Coretta with the news that President Kennedy had been shot, perhaps fatally. Coretta joined Martin to watch the dreadful

announcement that the President had, indeed, been shot to death in a motorcade.

As Martin and Coretta viewed the unfolding events in Dallas, Martin said he feared that he would meet the same fate as President Kennedy had. He said he did not expect to reach the age of forty.[6] Coretta could not console him by saying that she was sure such a thing would not happen. In her heart she believed that Martin was probably right.[7] The older King children came running to their parents in tears. Coretta and Martin comforted them and tried to assure them that however awful the death of President Kennedy was, the cause that they all fought for would continue.

Soon after he took his oath of office, President Lyndon B. Johnson announced that he would consider Kennedy's civil rights agenda his first priority. And he signed the Civil Rights Bill in July 1964, keeping his pledge.

In October 1964, Martin Luther King, Jr., was in the hospital for a checkup when the phone rang back home. Coretta Scott King was soon speaking to someone from the Associated Press, who told her that her husband had been given the 1964 Nobel Peace Prize. Coretta called Martin at the hospital and told him the good news. Then Coretta thanked God for the blessing of the Nobel Peace Prize and what it meant to Martin, herself, and the children.[8]

🞑🞑🞑🞑🞑🞑🞑🞑🞑🞑🞑🞑🞑🞑🞑🞑🞑🞑🞑🞑🞑🞑🞑🞑🞑🞑🞑🞑🞑🞑🞑🞑🞑🞑🞑🞑🞑🞑

The Kings meet with Ralph Bunche, undersecretary of political affairs for the United Nations, in 1964. It was the same year Martin Luther King, Jr., was awarded the Nobel Peace Prize.

The Kings wanted to take their two older children—almost nine-year-old Yolanda and seven-year-old Marty—to the Nobel Prize award ceremonies, but they were advised against taking children under the age of twelve. So the Kings left the children at home and went to Norway in December 1964. On their arrival in Norway, the Kings were given bouquets of flowers. They were received by the king of Norway. On December 10, 1964, Martin Luther King, Jr., received the Nobel Peace Prize in Aula Hall in Oslo with Coretta Scott King watching. After the ceremonies ended, the Kings went to Paris for a wonderful holiday.

Homecoming to New York for the Kings was a festive affair. They received a hero's welcome with fireboats on the Hudson River jetting streams of water and Mayor Robert Wagner giving them the keys to the city.

Hometown Atlanta wanted to add to their welcome as well, but in this city it was not a unanimous sentiment. A reception was arranged for the Kings at the Dinkler Hotel in January 1965. Black and white businesspeople as well as celebrities were among the fifteen hundred guests who came to honor the Kings. Three of the King children were also on hand to see their father being honored. The police were also out in force because of bomb threats, and Ku Klux Klansmen in full regalia marched on the sidewalk outside the

hotel. Inside there was a warm interracial banquet. Nothing but kind wishes were offered for the first native son of Atlanta who had won the world's most prestigious prize.

Also in January 1965, a troubling incident occurred that revealed a high-level FBI campaign to discredit Martin Luther King, Jr. Coretta Scott King was at SCLC headquarters when a large anonymous package arrived. It turned out to be a tape supposedly containing evidence that Martin had been involved in extramarital affairs at a hotel.

Only then did the Kings discover that the FBI was planting listening devices at hotels where Martin stayed. It was a strategy by J. Edgar Hoover, then head of the FBI, to undermine the character of Martin Luther King, Jr., and erode his support. Hoover believed that Martin Luther King, Jr., was a bad influence on African Americans, that he was stirring up discontent, and that he was perhaps a communist. "They are out to break me. They are out to get me, harass me, break my spirit," Martin Luther King, Jr., said of the FBI campaign.[9]

Coretta and Martin listened to the tape together and later Coretta concluded, "We found much of it unintelligible. We concluded that there was nothing on the tape to discredit Martin."[10]

A march from Selma to Montgomery, Alabama, was planned for Sunday, March 7, 1965. Martin Luther

King, Jr., had planned to lead it, but he had to preach at Ebenezer Baptist Church that Sunday. He intended to join the march on Monday. The marchers planned to present Governor George Wallace with demands for an end to police brutality in Alabama and for voting rights for African Americans.

On March 7, on schedule, the marchers left Brown Chapel and moved down Highway 80, known as Jefferson Davis Highway. They crossed the Edmund Pettis Bridge and left Selma, where they met state troopers standing three deep. The troopers ordered the marchers to return to their church. When they did not immediately obey, "Bloody Sunday" occurred.

Alabama troopers waded into the crowd swinging billy clubs. Heads were cracked open, and people were knocked down and bloodied. Tear gas was lobbed into the crowd, and a mounted posse bullwhipped the marchers. Marchers fell back choking and crying in pain from the brutal onslaught.[11]

In Atlanta a grief-stricken and shocked Martin Luther King, Jr., said, "I shall never forget my agony of conscience for not being there when I heard of the dastardly acts perpetrated against nonviolent demonstrators."[12]

The Kings immediately rushed to Selma. After a minister's march of four hundred ministers, rabbis, priests, and nuns was also turned back by the troopers, another march was planned. On March 21, 1965, Martin

and Coretta were joined by over three thousand others—including college students, celebrities, nuns, clergymen, and mothers pushing baby carriages. They headed for Montgomery with courageous determination.

The marchers spent the nights of the three-day journey camping in tents by the roadside. There was entertainment by the likes of Harry Belafonte and Sammy Davis, Jr. It was all very moving to Coretta Scott King, who grew up in this region. She addressed the marchers one night and told them how much this march personally meant to her. She recited poetry about the racial struggle and buoyed the spirits of the people.

During the day the Kings led the marchers through thick mangroves and beside swamps in Lowndes County. In a driving rain they finally reached Montgomery, giving the civil rights movement a triumph. It was the largest civil rights demonstration in southern history.

Later in August 1965, President Johnson followed through on his promise to pursue vigorously a civil rights agenda. He signed the Voting Rights Bill. This law swept away all the discriminatory tests that whites had used to keep blacks from voting. Now in the South, blacks would be able to vote and be elected to office along with whites. This law was described as the "crowning achievement of the civil rights movement."[13]

Martin Luther King, Jr., was the commencement speaker at Antioch College on June 19, 1965. Here Martin and Coretta Scott King are shown with Antioch College administrators.

In 1965 Atlanta desegregated the public school system. The King children had been attending integrated private schools, but now the Kings felt they should take advantage of this change.

Spring Street Elementary School was considered a very good school in Atlanta, and the Kings wanted Yolanda and Marty to go there. However, they would have been the only two black children in an all-white school. So the Kings talked it over with their friends the Abernathys, who had three school-aged children. When the King and Abernathy children all enrolled at Spring Street it made the transition easier. The experience turned out well for all the children.

During 1965, Coretta Scott King was singing regularly in the Ebenezer Church choir. She often sang her husband's favorite hymn, "Sweet Little Jesus Boy," and the whole King family enjoyed singing right along. She also gave many freedom concerts to raise money for the SCLC.

Although incidents of racial violence continued to occur, the Kings were heartened to see momentum going in the right direction in the South. Walls of discrimination were crumbling. A visitor to the American South in the mid-1950s would have been astonished by the changes by the mid-1960s. The dream that the Kings had devoted their lives to appeared to be taking shape. But if there was increased optimism over successes in the South, Martin Luther King, Jr., saw a

much different situation in the North, where half of the entire African-American population lived.

In the North, blacks had for years enjoyed the same civil rights as whites. They could vote and attend integrated schools. There were no racist signs directing them to inferior accommodations. But there was subtle discrimination. Most African Americans in the North lived in all-black neighborhoods and attended all-black schools. Most lived in crowded cities, often in slums where poverty, crime, drugs, and despair took a heavy toll.

It was now time for the Kings to turn their attention toward the problems of the urban poor in the North. Martin Luther King, Jr., developed the Campaign to End Slums and headed north. The Kings also turned their energies to the increasingly divisive war in Vietnam. The two issues—poverty and Vietnam—were linked in their minds. They believed that money wasted on the futile war could be better spent improving the lives of the poor.

# 8

# THE DREAMER
# DIES

hicago, Illinois, was chosen for the SCLC's drive to dramatize the poverty and hopelessness of the ghetto. The Chicago movement was a pilot project to call attention to run-down tenements throughout the North, most often occupied by African-American families.

The Kings rented a slum apartment in Chicago so that they could, for a short time, share the living conditions of the people who had to live there all the time. Coretta and Martin and their children would spend part of the summer of 1966 in this apartment.

When Coretta Scott King first arrived at the third floor apartment in the run-down building, she walked carefully up the rickety stairs. There were no lights in the hall, and just one dim bulb at the head of the stairs. There was no lock on the front door of the building, so vagrants could come and go at will, often urinating on the plain dirt floor of the first story. The apartment was built railroad-style, with one room behind the next one. One entered the sitting room in front, but to reach the kitchen and bath, one had to go through the bedrooms.

Coretta Scott King found a dilapidated gas stove and a refrigerator that scarcely worked. She was told that the heating system was so poor in winter that the temperature inside and outside was about the same. Also, although the stench was sickening and the surroundings demoralizing, the rent was $90 per month—about the same as good housing in other neighborhoods. As if the miserable apartment was not bad enough, at the corner was a grocery store with bad meat and high prices, and a poorly stocked drugstore.

On July 10, 1996, Freedom Sunday, the whole King family, including their four children, were living in the slum apartment. In the stifling summer heat it was necessary to keep the windows open, but the noise level from the street was maddening. Coretta Scott King hung curtains, but there was little that she could do to relieve the grimness of the place.

The experience in the Chicago slum was an eye-opener for the King children. They had never seen such poverty. They grew up with grassy yards and trees, and plenty of nice places for play. Here, the only place to play was in bare dirt, and there was nothing green in sight. Nearby a family of ten lived in one small apartment with no running water and no heat in winter. The King children saw a world they never imagined before.

Some of the black teenagers in the neighborhood resented the Kings because white civil rights workers were part of Martin Luther King, Jr.'s, team. The teenagers did not want to see white faces in their part of town. Martin Luther King, Jr., spent time talking to the gang members and he won some of the boys over to non-violence. He convinced the rest to at least tolerate his white colleagues.

At a large civil rights march in Chicago, all the King children—even little Bernice—took part. Also during that difficult summer Martin and Coretta took time out to travel to Jackson, Mississippi, to help in that city's struggle for equality. In blistering heat, the marchers—including the Kings and their two oldest children, Yolanda and Marty—walked to the state house as a band played "When the Saints Go Marching In." Fifteen thousand people applauded as the Kings walked onto the capital grounds.

Then, early in 1967, the Kings began strong opposition to the war then being waged in Vietnam. Following a 1954 peace agreement, Vietnam was divided into North Vietnam under a communist government, and South Vietnam under a non-communist government. The United States supported the government of South Vietnam.

South Vietnamese who went north after the 1954 peace agreement started to return around 1957. By 1959 these people—known in the United States as Viet Cong—began a full-scale civil war against South Vietnam. The United States sent military advisors to help South Vietnam. Little by little the United States forces grew in South Vietnam until, by 1967, about half a million American military were fighting in a major war against the Viet Cong and North Vietnamese forces.

As early as 1965 Martin Luther King, Jr., pleaded for an end to American involvement in the Vietnam War. In 1966 he said that the war was wrong and we were wasting precious American lives and resources on it. On April 4, 1967, he went farther than he had gone before in a dramatic public statement against the war.

Speaking at Riverside Church in New York, Martin Luther King, Jr., said that he knew the problems of the poor in America would never be solved "so long as adventures like Vietnam continued to draw men and

The Kings were strongly opposed to the Vietnam War. Here, Coretta Scott King is seen at an anti-Vietnam War protest rally in 1967.

skills and money like some demoniacal destructive suction tube."[1]

Criticism rained on Martin Luther King, Jr.'s, head from President Johnson, who called the comments "right down the Commie line," to African-American columnist Carl Rowan, who called Martin's anti-war address "communist-influenced."[2]

Martin was hurt by the attacks, but he said to Coretta, "I know I'm right, I know this is an unjust and evil war."[3] For her part, Coretta addressed fify thousand at an anti-war rally in San Francisco.[4]

In 1968 the Kings became involved in the Poor People's Campaign to lift the poorest out of their predicament and guarantee an annual wage sufficient to survive for all workers.

Coretta and Martin decided that Marty and Dexter were now old enough to accompany their father on one of his trips. The Kings felt that the boys should see firsthand what their father was involved in.

So in March 1968, the boys accompanied their father through rural Georgia. Dexter especially was amazed at how much work his father did and how many people he talked to during a day.[5] Coretta would later be very thankful for the decision to send the boys on this trip with their father, because it would turn out to be the last chance for such an experience between father and sons.

In Memphis, Tennessee, there was a longstanding and bitter strike by the underpaid sanitation workers who were mostly African American. Martin Luther King, Jr., planned to march for the sanitation workers on Monday, April 8. As he left for the trip, Coretta kissed Martin goodbye and wished him well as she always did. He promised to call that evening and he did.

Martin Luther King, Jr., took rooms in the African-American owned and operated Lorraine Motel on Mulberry Street in Memphis. On Thursday, April 4, Coretta Scott King was shopping for Easter clothes for Yolanda. She had already bought new suits for the boys.

Soon after she got home, the telephone rang. It was Jesse Jackson, who was with Martin in Memphis. He said, "Doc just got shot. You better catch the first thing smoking."[6] Jackson did not tell Coretta how seriously wounded Martin was. She recalled that the children were in the room and they saw the television commentator talking about the shooting. "Yolanda looked at it and screamed and ran out."[7]

Coretta Scott King was getting the 8:25 P.M. flight to Memphis when she was paged at the Atlanta airport. Dora McDonald, Martin's longtime secretary, had gone with Coretta. Mayor Ivan Allen of Atlanta took both women into a lounge at the airport and said, "Your husband is dead."[8] "I knew that," Coretta

recalled later, "but hearing the words had a sad finality."[9]

Martin Luther King, Jr., was standing on the balcony of the Lorraine Motel talking to friends at 6 P.M., April 4, 1968, when he was shot. He fell back, mortally wounded. A white ex-convict, James Earl Ray, was later convicted of the crime and sentenced to ninety-nine years in prison. He never gave a motive for his act, but author William Bradford Huie, a friend of the King family, offered a theory. "He wanted the FBI and all of us to know that James Earl Ray, that poor, contemptible little man with a price of $50 on his head, had killed one of the great Americans of this century."[10]

Martin did not need her anymore, but the children did. So Coretta left the airport and returned home. When she arrived, Dexter and Bernice were in bed, but Yolanda was still up. Yolanda told her mother that she was not going to cry because her father was not really dead. She said that she was going to "see him again in heaven."[11]

Seven-year-old Dexter awoke suddenly to ask when his father was getting home. Coretta Scott King told him that his father was hurt and she would explain it more fully in the morning. Mercifully, Dexter went back to sleep.

President Lyndon Johnson called with condolences, and flags around America were lowered to half-mast.

The following Sunday was designated a day of national mourning. Coretta Scott King graciously accepted the words of sympathy, but she had children to comfort and that was her first priority. Five-year-old Bernice watched the plane land that carried her father's body. Bernice wanted to know where her daddy was. "Daddy has gone to live with God," Coretta Scott King told her daughter.[12]

Martin Luther King, Jr., lay in state at the Georgia State Capital in Atlanta from Saturday afternoon to Monday afternoon, when he was taken to Ebenezer Baptist Church for the funeral on April 9, 1968. The church held only 750 people, so thousands more stood outside to listen to the ceremony. They heard the voice of Martin Luther King, Jr., from an earlier sermon describing his own wishes for the day of his burial. He said that he would like somebody to mention that day that he was a man who "tried to give his life serving others."[13]

Martin Luther King, Jr.'s, casket was brought out, placed on a flatbed farm wagon, and drawn by a pair of mules through the streets of Atlanta to his burial plot in South View Cemetery. There, he was laid to rest.

Martin Luther King, Sr., said of Coretta Scott King's conduct at that time, "Coretta surrounded her children with love and guidance during a time when a lesser person's feelings might have torn her apart and

plunged her into the depths of despair she couldn't escape."[14]

Coretta Scott King expressed her own feelings four days after her husband's assassination. She said that there were moments in life when everything seemed dark, but the coming of Easter is a "time of resurrection."[15] She said she would carry on—that her husband would have wanted that.

# 9

## CARRYING ON THE DREAM

After Martin Luther King, Jr.'s, death, gifts and contributions poured into the King house. Coretta Scott King received useful items for her four children, and some financial help that she sorely needed. Although Martin was very famous, he was never wealthy. His salary as co-pastor of Ebenezer Baptist Church was only $6,000 a year. Upon his death he had about $5,000 in the bank, and an insurance policy worth $50,000. Coretta Scott King had four young children to raise and educate.

Immediately after Martin's death, Coretta began thinking about creating a living memorial to her

husband. But first she had to deal with a mountain of correspondence. One hundred and fifty thousand letters, telegrams, and bouquets had arrived, and Coretta was deeply touched by this outpouring of love.[1] Many were from famous people, but most were from humble men and women whose lives had been touched by the Kings.

Coretta Scott King turned a bedroom into an office so that she could be close to the children as she worked. It was, of course, impossible for one person to handle all the mail, so Coretta's sister Edythe, an English and dramatic arts teacher at Cheyney State Teachers College, came to help. Staff was set up, including young people from Senator Robert F. Kennedy's office. Eventually every piece of mail was answered.

King took virtually no time out for mourning. She just kept working on ways to carry on the dream. In May 1968, only a month after Martin's death, Coretta joined the Poor People's Campaign in Washington, D.C. About three thousand African Americans, Hispanic Americans, and Appalachian southerners set up a tent city called Resurrection City on sixteen acres beside the Lincoln Memorial. They pressed demands for what they called 29 million poor forgotten Americans.[2] On the last day of the encampment, King addressed the crowd and pleaded for an end to violence and for efforts to improve the welfare of the poor.

Coretta Scott King spoke at the New England Conservatory after
the death of her husband. Shown with her are the King children
(from left to right): Dexter; Yolanda; Martin Luther King, III;
and Bernice.

Also in 1968, King was invited to write a book. She was eager to share her own unique memories of her husband, and the advance of $500,000 would go far to guarantee financial stability for the family. The book, entitled *My Life with Martin Luther King, Jr.,* was published in 1969 and it reflected Coretta Scott King's calm undramatic persona, her sense of control and composure, and her deep love for her husband.[3]

Early in 1969 King announced her plan to build a center in Atlanta to promote Martin Luther King, Jr.'s, ideals. She insisted that the name be the Martin Luther King, Jr. Center for Non-Violent Social Change.[4] Getting the Center built would occupy much of her time over the next thirteen years. She bought property on Auburn Avenue and set out on the formidable task of raising millions of dollars for the project.

There were many small donations, but large gifts came from the Alpha Kappa Sorority and Henry Ford, Jr. President Jimmy Carter helped raise millions as well. Planning the Center was a foundation made up of many prominent people, including former Vice President Hubert Humphrey and Senators Hugh Scott and Edward Kennedy.

Coretta Scott King also devoted some of her time and considerable energy to a campaign to establish a national holiday honoring the memory of Martin Luther King, Jr. There was initially some opposition to the holiday because many simply opposed another

Coretta Scott King received an honorary doctorate from Boston University in 1969. Here she is shown with Boston University President Christ-Janer.

holiday because of a loss of productivity, while others were unsympathetic to Martin Luther King, Jr.'s, ideals.

Also in 1969, Coretta Scott King received an honorary doctorate degree from her husband's alma mater, Boston University. She delivered the Centennial Founder's Day address as well.

In the years following Martin's death, Coretta's time was occupied mostly in raising her four young children. The oldest, Yolanda, was twelve and the youngest, Bernice, just five when their father died. An excellent household staff cared for the children when it was necessary for King to travel to fulfill obligations.

In 1974 Coretta Scott King received the United Nations Ceres Medal for her work on behalf of underprivileged people. In 1977 she was chosen to be a member of President Carter's Commission for the First National Women's Conference in Houston, Texas. She also became a public delegate to the General Assembly of the United Nations.

In 1978, Yolanda King graduated from New York University with a master's degree in fine arts. She had already played Rosa Parks in a television movie titled *King*. Marty was graduated from Morehouse College. Dexter graduated from high school, and only Bernice remained in high school. King was nearing the end of her child-raising duties.

In October 1979, many celebrities and politicians joined Coretta Scott King for groundbreaking

Coretta Scott King delivered the Boston University Centennial
Founder's Day address in 1969.

Coretta Scott King speaks to the crowd attending Solidarity Day,
at the Lincoln Memorial in Washington, D.C. King had a very
full schedule during the 1970s.

ceremonies at the Center in Atlanta. She had carefully assembled a mountain of memorabilia that would occupy the exhibition hall. She had saved everything she could of her husband's life—his speeches, notes, and also his suits that were neatly hung in a closet. Coretta even saved Martin's shoes—the battered muddy reminders of all those civil rights marches.

Coretta Scott King felt that her husband was a great man, and people needed to see his things to help them understand what his life was all about. She had now helped turn over a spadeful of dirt, and the impressive living memorial to Martin Luther King, Jr., was underway.

# 10

# "A COMPASSIONATE WORLD COMMUNITY"

n January 15, 1982, the Martin Luther King, Jr. Center for Non-Violent Social Change officially opened. Situated on a three-block area around historic Auburn Avenue, it existed solely because of the determination of Coretta Scott King. The founding president and chief executive of the impressive complex, she nurtured the concept in her heart and mind, and brought it to reality by her struggles.

The Freedom Hall Complex forms a rectangle around Martin Luther King, Jr.'s, elevated marble crypt. His body was taken from South View Cemetery and placed there. There is a large reflecting pool and

an eternal flame. Within the complex is an all-faiths chapel, exhibition hall, gift shop, auditorium, and administration building with meeting rooms. The architectural design of the Center complex itself is intended to promote a sense of calm reflection. Visitors to the exhibition hall find many mementoes of the key stages of Martin Luther King, Jr.'s, life, including the Nobel Peace Prize medal.

At the opening ceremonies, congratulations came from around the world, including from President Ronald Reagan, though during his administration a congressional bill offering millions for the complex was buried.

Coretta Scott King frankly admitted financial problems at the start. "The day-to-day survival of the Center plagues us," she said, adding, "realistically speaking, the survival of the Center is in jeopardy."[1] But optimistically she insisted:

> I believe we will come up with the necessary support to sustain us. There were many times when Martin never knew how he was going to get a campaign funded, but it always seemed to come from somewhere. Through the grace of God we will survive.[2]

Thousands of visitors immediately began coming to the Center, including youth who were trained in the six principles of non-violence that Martin Luther King, Jr., believed. They are:

1. Accepting non-violence as a way of life.

2. Trying to gain understanding through non-violence.

3. Working against injustice.

4. Believing that suffering educates and transforms.

5. Choosing love over hate.

6. Believing that the Universe is on the side of justice.

In 1983 about three hundred thousand visitors came to the Center, but by the mid-1990s about 1.5 million came annually. As visitors near the crypt, they approach it in respectful silence. The gift shop provides the only steady income, as visitors spend thousands of dollars on items related to Martin Luther King, Jr., and the civil rights movement. In January 1990, Coretta Scott King expressed the hope that by the year 2000, one hundred thousand people will have been trained in non-violent methods of social change.

In 1983 Coretta Scott King helped assemble some of her husband's most memorable speeches in a book, *The Words of Martin Luther King, Jr.* In the foreword to the book she described the triple evils of poverty, racism, and war that she tried to battle. "By reaching into and beyond ourselves," she wrote, "and tapping

the transcendent ethic of love, we shall overcome these evils."[3]

In 1984 a conference in Washington marked the twentieth anniversary of the 1964 Civil Rights Act. Coretta Scott King addressed the conference, saying that although segregationists no longer stood in schoolhouse doors, "segregated housing patterns and more subtle forms of racism prevent equal access to a quality public education."[4]

In 1985 Coretta Scott King and twenty-five hundred other civil rights activists commemorated the 1965 Selma to Montgomery march by crossing Edmund Pettis Bridge, where civil rights marchers had been brutally attacked twenty years earlier. The following year, 1986, Coretta Scott King demonstrated her longstanding concern for ending the system of apartheid in South Africa by journeying to that country to attend the installation of Desmond Tutu as Anglican Archbishop of Cape Town. It was a controversial trip. She originally planned to meet with Winnie Mandela, wife of the then imprisoned South African black leader Nelson Mandela (who, in 1994, was elected president of South Africa). She also planned meetings with white South African President P. W. Botha and Zulu leader Mangosuthu Buthelezi. However, Winnie Mandela made it clear that she would not see King if she also met with the others. So Coretta

Scott King cancelled the meetings with Botha and Buthelezi and met only with Mandela.

Coretta Scott King described the meeting with Winnie Mandela as "one of the greatest and most meaningful moments in my life," though later she admitted that the political situation in South Africa was "more complex than I initially thought," and she would need to gather more information about it.[5]

Having achieved the creation of the Center in Atlanta, Coretta Scott King now turned her attention more fully to promoting the Martin Luther King, Jr., national holiday. She lobbied politicians, entertainers, and ordinary Americans for years. She made speeches on the merits of the holiday, pointing out how much it would mean to so many people. Then finally, in 1986, Martin Luther King, Jr.'s, birthday, January 15, was declared a national holiday. He became the first African American and the first clergyman honored with a federal holiday. On January 16, 1986, a bronze bust of him was placed in the Capitol rotunda.

The Martin Luther King, Jr., national holiday meant a great deal to millions of Americans, and it had profound meaning for Coretta Scott King. It consoled her at those times when her husband's reputation was called into question. Responding to a recently published book that accused Martin of marital infidelity, Coretta said of him, "He doesn't need any defense. His life and his work speak for themselves. The fact that we

President Ronald Reagan signed the bill establishing Martin Luther King, Jr.'s, birthday as a national holiday in 1983. Here, Coretta Scott King is shown with President Reagan in the White House Rose Garden.

have a national holiday, the fact that people are celebrating around the world, the fact that every place you go in the world people honor and revere him."[6]

Every year at the annual commemorative service at Ebenezer Baptist Church during the Martin Luther King, Jr., holiday, Coretta Scott King has delivered her State of the Dream address, noting progress or lack of it in America's march toward justice and equality.

In January 1987, Coretta Scott King led fifteen thousand to twenty thousand marchers through all-white Forsyth County, Georgia. In 1912 a black man accused of rape was lynched in Forsyth County. Two other black men were hanged after a very brief trial, and all black people were then driven from the county. As over two thousand law officers watched, Coretta Scott King led a peaceful march to prove that Americans of color could walk anywhere they wanted.

On August 27, 1988, to commemorate the twenty-fifth anniversary of Martin Luther King, Jr.'s, "I Have a Dream" speech, Coretta Scott King walked with other activists to the Lincoln Memorial. She called for a national rededication to such social goals as adequate housing for all and an end to poverty.

Coretta Scott King's life has revolved around the Center in Atlanta since its opening. From here she meets with her staff, plans the learning center activities, answers mail, and receives visitors. In 1990 she walked to the Center's theater to watch "Stepping into

Coretta Scott King and Vice President Dan Quayle watch as President George Bush signs a proclamation extending the Martin Luther King, Jr., holiday in 1989.

Tomorrow," a production of the Nucleus Theatre Company, one of Yolanda King's projects.

In November 1990, Coretta Scott King spoke at length about her hopes for the future. "When we achieve equality here in America, we will set an irresistible example of hope for the entire world," she said. "We must envision a world free from the ravages of poverty, racism, war and militarism."[7] She went on to say:

> I know that some would say that this is an impractical utopian vision of a compassionate world community, but the God who sent us Frederick Douglass, Rosa Parks, Martin Luther King, Jr., and so many other great visionaries did not put us here to dream small dreams.[8]

Coretta Scott King favors more women being elected to public office so that they can help "shape the priorities" and strengthen families. She insists, "Every person needs at least a job, an income, and that is not asking for too much."[9]

Those who see Coretta Scott King on a daily basis say she seems to be working all the time. She wakes at 7 A.M. and watches the television news, has a cup of tea, and then meditates and prays about world problems and the specific difficulties ahead for her.[10] She has an office at the Center, and as she works through the day she often has lunch and dinner sent to her so that she does not have to stop. "I think I am a pretty easy person

to get along with," she said, but she also admitted to being a perfectionist with an always orderly desk.[11]

Coretta Scott King's motherly instincts are evident in the warm way she relates to the children at the Martin Luther King, Jr., day-care center across the street, and in her regular visits with her own four grown children, most of whom have worked at the Center. Coretta Scott King obviously enjoys people and graciously welcomes many of the visitors to the Center. She is in constant demand as a speaker and she travels throughout the country. A widow for almost thirty years, she says that she is never lonely, nor at a loss to entertain herself.[12]

When asked in 1990 if she might ever remarry, Coretta Scott King said:

> I don't know. That is one of those things that is left in the hands of God. I had such a fulfilling marriage. I don't ever expect to have anything like that again. Marriage really means making a lot of adjustments at this stage in my life, and I'm not sure I can make those adjustments, or that I want to make them.[13]

The youngest of the King children, Bernice, was seen by the nation in an award-winning photograph. It shows her at five years old laying asleep in her mother's lap at her father's funeral. Now Bernice King serves as assistant pastor at Greater Rising Star Baptist Church in Atlanta, Georgia. She credits her mother for holding the family together in spite of the violence and struggles of the times. "She's always been able to

stay committed and focused on God, family and humanity," Bernice King said. "I admire the passion and compassion that she has in her."[14] Bernice King added, "I heard about my father and saw him on film, but I witnessed it up close with my mother."[15]

Coretta Scott King's hope is that her life will have made a difference. "That means helping people and improving conditions in the lives of people."[16]

As a young woman, Coretta Scott worked in a Cleveland settlement house, and all through her life she has not spared herself in fighting for the betterment of human lives. She continues to do so and her millions of admirers believe that she has fulfilled her hope of making a difference many times over. However, she is not finished yet. In her life, and in the lives she has changed for the better, the dream is alive and well.

# CHRONOLOGY

1927—Born in Marion, Alabama, on April 27.

1937—Started Lincoln School.

1945—Graduated Lincoln School.

1951—Left Antioch College; started New England Conservatory of Music in Boston, Massachusetts.

1953—Married Martin Luther King, Jr., on June 18.

1954—Graduated from New England Conservatory of Music; moved to Montgomery, Alabama.

1955—First child, Yolanda, was born in November.

1956—Escaped injury in parsonage bombing in Montgomery, Alabama.

1957—Visited Ghana with husband (first trip outside the United States); Martin Luther, III, was born in October.

1958—Visited India with husband.

1960—Moved to Atlanta, Georgia, with family.

1961—Dexter, third child, was born in January.

1963—Bernice Albertine, fourth child, was born in March.

1964—Accompanied husband to Oslo, Norway, when Martin Luther King, Jr., received the Nobel Peace Prize.

1968—Widowed upon the assassination of Martin Luther King, Jr., on April 4.

1969—Published first book, *My Life with Martin Luther King, Jr.*; made plans for establishment of Martin Luther King, Jr. Center for Non-Violent Social Change in Atlanta.

1974—Awarded United Nations Ceres Medal.

1977—Chosen delegate to first National Women's Conference in Houston, Texas; chosen public delegate to the General Assembly of the United Nations.

1982—Martin Luther King, Jr. Center for Non-Violent Social Change officially opened on January 15.

1983—Edited book *The Words of Martin Luther King, Jr.*

1986—Saw years of efforts realized when Martin Luther King, Jr.'s birthday was declared a national holiday.

# Chapter Notes

## Chapter 1

1. Martin Luther King, Jr., *Stride Toward Freedom: The Montgomery Story* (New York: Harper and Row, 1958), p. 136.

2. Coretta Scott King, *My Life with Martin Luther King, Jr.* (New York: Holt, Rinehart and Winston, 1969), p. 126.

3. Ibid.

4. Ibid., p. 123

5. William Roger Witherspoon, *Martin Luther King: To the Mountaintop* (New York: Doubleday, 1985), p. 36.

6. Lerone Bennett, Jr., *What Manner of Man: A Biography of Martin Luther King, Jr.* (Chicago: Johnson Pub. Co., 1976), p. 69.

7. Ibid.

8. Ibid.

9. Ibid.

10. Witherspoon, p. 37.

## Chapter 2

1. Coretta Scott King, *My Life with Martin Luther King, Jr.* (New York: Holt, Rinehart and Winston, 1969), p. 32.

2. Ibid.

3. Ibid.

4. Ibid., p. 26.

5. William Roger Witherspoon, *Martin Luther King: To the Mountaintop* (New York: Doubleday, 1985), p. 11.

6. Ibid.

7. Lerone Bennett, Jr., *What Manner of Man: A Biography of Martin Luther King, Jr.* (Chicago: Johnson Pub. Co., 1976), p. 41.

8. Ibid.

9. King, p. 34.

10. Ibid., p. 32.

11. Ibid., p. 22.

12. Ibid., p. 40.

13. Ibid., p. 44.

14. Witherspoon, p. 13.

15. Bennett, p. 45.

16. King, p. 46.

## Chapter 3

1. William Roger Witherspoon, *Martin Luther King: To the Mountaintop* (New York: Doubleday, 1985), p. 11.

2 Coretta Scott King, *My Life with Martin Luther King, Jr.* (New York: Holt, Rinehart and Winston, 1969), p. 52.

3. Witherspoon, p. 13.

4. King, p. 54.

5. David L. Lewis, *King: A Biography* (Urbana, Ill.: University of Illinois Press, 1978), p. 41.

6. King, p. 54.

7. Lewis, p. 42.

8. Ibid.

9. Ibid.

10. Martin Luther King, Jr., *Stride Toward Freedom: The Montgomery Story* (New York: Harper and Row, 1958), p. 23.

11. Coretta Scott King, p. 55.

12. Stephen B. Oates, *Let the Trumpet Sound: The Life of Martin Luther King, Jr.* (New York: Harper and Row, 1982), p. 44.

13. Coretta Scott King, p. 57.

14. Oates, p. 44.

15. Lerone Bennett, Jr., *What Manner of Man: A Biography of Martin Luther King, Jr.* (Chicago: Johnson Pub. Co., 1976), p. 47.

16. Rev. Martin Luther King, Sr., *Daddy King: An Autobiography* (New York: William Morrow and Co., Inc., 1980), p. 149.

17. Ibid.

18. Ibid., p. 150.

19. Ibid., p. 151.

20. Witherspoon, p. 13.

21. Coretta Scott King, p. 70.

22. Ibid., p. 74.

## Chapter 4

1. Coretta Scott King, *My Life with Martin Luther King, Jr.* (New York: Holt, Rinehart and Winston, 1969), p. 90.

2. Ibid.

3. Ibid., p. 91.

4. Ibid., p. 90.

5. Stephen B. Oates, *Let the Trumpet Sound: The Life of Martin Luther King, Jr.* (New York: Harper and Row, 1982), p. 51.

6. William Roger Witherspoon, *Martin Luther King: To the Mountaintop* (New York: Doubleday, 1985), p. 21.

7. Adam Fairclough, *Martin Luther King, Jr.* (Athens, Ga.: The University of Georgia Press, 1990), p. 19.

8. David L. Lewis, *King: A Biography* (Urbana, Ill.: University of Illinois Press, 1978), pp. 78-79.

9. Witherspoon, p. 51.

## Chapter 5

1. Coretta Scott King, *My Life with Martin Luther King, Jr.* (New York: Holt, Rinehart and Winston, 1969), p. 135.

2. William Roger Witherspoon, *Martin Luther King: To the Mountaintop* (New York: Doubleday, 1985), p. 43.

3. Ibid., p. 45.

4. Ibid., p. 52.

5. Ibid.

6. King, p. 156.

7. Ibid., p. 157.

8. Ibid.

9. Stephen B. Oates, *Let the Trumpet Sound: The Life of Martin Luther King, Jr.* (New York: Harper and Row, 1982), p. 128.

10. Ibid.

11. Ibid., p. 134.

12. King, p. 163.
13. Oates, p. 138.
14. King, p. 178.
15. Witherspoon, p. 61.
16. King, p. 173.
17. Ibid., p. 177.
18. Oates, p. 143.
19. David L. Lewis, *King: A Biography* (Urbana, Ill.: University of Illinois Press, 1978), p. 99.
20. Oates, p. 146.

## Chapter 6

1. William Roger Witherspoon, *Martin Luther King: To the Mountaintop* (New York: Doubleday, 1985), p. 70.
2. David L. Lewis, *King: A Biography* (Urbana, Ill.: University of Illinois Press, 1978), p. 122.
3. Coretta Scott King, *My Life with Martin Luther King, Jr.* (New York: Holt, Rinehart and Winston, 1969), p. 187.
4. Ibid., p. 188.
5. Stephen B. Oates, *Let the Trumpet Sound: The Life of Martin Luther King, Jr.* (New York: Harper and Row, 1982), p. 150.
6. Ibid., p. 161.
7. Ibid.
8. King, p. 191.
9. Ibid.
10. Ibid., p. 192.
11. Oates, p. 163.
12. Ibid.

13. Rev. Martin Luther King, Sr., *Daddy King: An Autobiography* (New York: William Morrow and Co., Inc., 1980), p. 174.

14. Ibid., p. 175.

15. Lewis, p. 128.

16. Ibid., p. 166.

17. Oates, p. 198.

18. Coretta Scott King, p. 209.

19. Ibid., p. 210.

20. Ibid., p. 211.

21. Ibid., p. 213.

22. Witherspoon, p. 107.

## Chapter 7

1. Coretta Scott King, *My Life with Martin Luther King, Jr.* (New York: Holt, Rinehart and Winston, 1969), p. 235.

2. Adam Fairclough, *Martin Luther King, Jr.* (Athens, Ga.: The University of Georgia Press, 1990), p. 90.

3. Ibid., p. 91.

4. King, p. 244.

5. William Roger Witherspoon, *Martin Luther King: To the Mountaintop* (New York: Doubleday, 1985), p. 143.

6. Ibid., p. 150.

7. Ibid.

8. King, p. 3.

9. Witherspoon, p. 168.

10. Stephen B. Oates, *Let the Trumpet Sound: The Life of Martin Luther King, Jr.* (New York: Harper and Row, 1982), p. 332.

11. Ibid., p. 348.

12. Ibid.

13. Fairclough, p. 103.

## Chapter 8

1. William Roger Witherspoon, *Martin Luther King: To the Mountaintop* (New York: Doubleday, 1985), p. 210.

2. Ibid.

3. Ibid.

4. Stephen B. Oates, *Let the Trumpet Sound: The Life of Martin Luther King, Jr.* (New York: Harper and Row, 1982), p. 440.

5. Coretta Scott King, *My Life with Martin Luther King, Jr.* (New York: Holt, Rinehart and Winston, 1969), p. 307.

6. Witherspoon, p. 222.

7. Ibid.

8. Ibid., p. 223.

9. Ibid.

10. W. B. Huie, "The Story of James Earl Ray and the Plot to Assassinate Martin Luther King," *Look,* November 1968, p. 86.

11. King, p. 321.

12. Ibid.

13. Ibid., p. 330.

14. Rev. Martin Luther King, Sr., *Daddy King: An Autobiography* (New York: William Morrow and Co., Inc., 1980), p. 193.

15. Coretta Scott King, p. 345.

## Chapter 9

1. Coretta Scott King, *My Life with Martin Luther King, Jr.* (New York: Holt, Rinehart and Winston, 1969), p. vii.

2. Rayford W. Logan and Irving S. Cohen, *The American Negro* (Boston: Houghton Mifflin, 1970), p. 286.

3. Lynn Norment, "Coretta Scott King: The Woman Behind the King Anniversary," *Ebony,* January 1990, p. 117.

4. Ibid.

## Chapter 10

1. Walter Leavy, "A Living Memorial to the Drum Major for Justice," *Ebony,* February 1983, p. 124.

2. Ibid., p. 125.

3. Coretta Scott King, ed., *The Words of Martin Luther King, Jr.* (New York: Newmarket Press, 1983), p. 13.

4. Muriel Grindrod and Donald Young, "Black in the United States," *1985 Yearbook* (New York: Funk and Wagnalls, Inc., 1985), p. 92.

5. John Greenwald, "Into the Racial Maelstrom," *Time*, September 22, 1986, p. 45.

6. Lynn Normant, "Coretta Scott King: The Woman Behind the King Anniversary," *Ebony,* January 1990, p. 117.

7. Coretta Scott King, "45 from Today," *Ebony,* November, 1990, p. 60.

8. Ibid.

9. Normant, p. 118.

10. Ibid., p. 116.

11. Ibid.

12. Cheryl Heckler-Feltz, "Time Will Tell of This King's Mark," *The San Diego Union Tribune,* February 24, 1996, p. E4.

13. Ibid.

14. Normant, p. 122.

15. Heckler-Feltz, p. E4.

16. Ibid.

# FURTHER READING

Bennett, Lerone, Jr. *What Manner of Man: A Biography of Martin Luther King, Jr.* Chicago: Johnson Pub. Co., 1976.

Fairclough, Adam. *Martin Luther King, Jr.* Athens, Ga.: The University of Georgia Press, 1990.

King, Coretta Scott. *My Life with Martin Luther King, Jr.* New York: Holt, Rinehart and Winston, 1969.

King, Martin Luther, Jr. *Stride Toward Freedom: The Montgomery Story.* New York: Harper and Row, 1958.

King, Martin Luther, Sr., with Clayton Riley. *Daddy King: An Autobiography.* New York: William Morrow and Co., Inc., 1980.

Lewis, David L. *King: A Biography.* Urbana, Ill.: University of Illinois Press, 1978.

Lucas, Eileen. *Civil Rights: The Long Struggle.* Springfield, N.J.: Enslow Publishers, 1996.

Medearis, Angela S. *Dare to Dream: Coretta Scott King and the Civil Rights Movement.* New York: Dutton Children's Books, 1994.

Oates, Stephen B. *Let the Trumpet Sound: The Life of Martin Luther King, Jr.* New York: Harper and Row, 1982.

Robinson, Joann Gibson. *The Montgomery Bus Boycott and the Women Who Started It.* Knoxville, Tenn.: University of Tennessee Press, 1987.

Schuman, Michael A. *Martin Luther King, Jr.: Leader for Civil Rights.* Springfield, N.J.: Enslow Publishers, 1996.

Witherspoon, William Roger. *Martin Luther King.: To the Mountaintop.* New York: Doubleday, 1985.

# INDEX

# About the Author

Anne Schraff is the author of numerous works of fiction and nonfiction for young people, including *Colin Powell: Soldier and Patriot* for Enslow Publishers, Inc. A graduate of California State University Northridge with a master's degree, Ms. Schraff maintains a keen interest in United States and world history. When not writing she enjoys horseback riding, and hiking with her two nephews.

# AWAKEN THE ADVENTURE!

The Death Walkers are rising and
bringing plagues of evil to the world.
It's up to YOU to stop them!

1. Go to Scholastic.com/TombQuest

2. Log in to create your character
   and enter the tombs.

3. Have your book ready and enter
   the code below to play:

## R372N9JPWC

## Scholastic.com/TombQuest

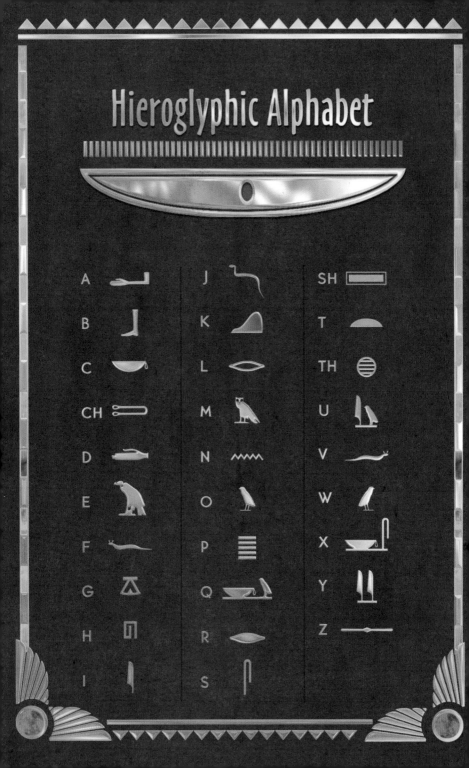

SEP 0 9 2022

# THE FINAL KINGDOM

X

# MICHAEL NORTHROP

SCHOLASTIC INC.

# For the readers:
## To all the awesome TombQuesters who've followed me through every twist and turn (and chase and trap and spell) of this epic adventure, this one is definitely for you.

Library of Congress Control Number Available

ISBN 978-0-545-72342-8

10 9 8 7 6 5 4 3 2 1          16 17 18 19 20

Printed in the U.S.A.   23
First edition, April 2016
Book design by Keirsten Geise

Scholastic US: 557 Broadway · New York, NY 10012
Scholastic Canada: 604 King Street West · Toronto, ON M5V 1E1
Scholastic New Zealand Limited: Private Bag 94407 · Greenmount, Manukau 2141
Scholastic UK Ltd.: Euston House · 24 Eversholt Street · London NW1 1DB

# Prologue

Making mummies is an ancient and grisly business, but business was good once again. The bodies lay on low stone tables beneath the timeless sands of Egypt, lit only by flickering torchlight.

Half a dozen acolytes in ancient dress gathered their implements nervously, the jewels and glass beads of their thick collar necklaces glinting, and the light linen of their shendyt kilts shining a pure, audacious white. They began with the body on the highest platform. For while all men may be created equal, all mummies are not. This body was taller than the others, and broader in the shoulders, with skin the color of wet sand, a hawklike nose, and sharp features that seemed determined even in death.

The acolytes dipped their cloths in a bucket of cool well water, wrung them out, and got to work washing the corpse.

Their hands trembled slightly as they put down their rags and picked up their blades. They were nervous as they made the first cuts: Everything had to go perfectly. The blood was

drained from the man's body and taken out in buckets. Once that was done, the internal organs were removed, one by one. Only the steadiest hands made these cuts. The others busied themselves packing the carefully culled pieces into sacred canopic jars for the trip to the afterlife. Only the man's heart was left in his body: the most vital organ, the home of the soul.

The clay lid clinked into place on the last of the jars.

The workers washed their hands in the water buckets and then rubbed the body with natron salt to preserve and dry it. They packed the hollowed-out frame with still more natron and plugged the skull with linen.

By now, the acolytes' foreheads and bare chests glowed with sweat. They anointed and sealed the body with a thick, sticky resin. They lifted its shoulders from the stone — the broad torso not nearly so heavy now, filled only with salt — and wrapped it in strips of fresh linen.

Finally, they placed a heavy mask on the man's head, transforming his own sharp features into those of an Egyptian vulture. Solid gold, except for the sharp, iron point of the cunning predator's beak.

The acolytes repeated their grim work with methodical care, and one by one, the bodies were transformed. As they neared completion on the fifth, blood-spattered and exhausted, a chorus of voices rose in the chamber behind them. Beneath the largest of the torches, a group of three men, priests of The Order, chanted words not heard for

millennia. They were reading from the Lost Spells of the ancient Egyptian Book of the Dead, legendary incantations of unimaginable power.

The priests released their final lines with full-throated fervor, then stood winded and wide-eyed in the sudden silence, in thrall to the unearthly power they'd felt surging through them.

The priests watched intently. The acolytes barely dared to blink.

*Had it worked?*

*Had the ancient Spells accomplished their dark task?*

These were no idle questions. Far more than a day's work was at stake here. The figures on these slabs had bet their lives on it. They had died for this.

But they had no intention of staying dead for long. Nor did they intend to remain in these frail human forms. There were other forms waiting for them in the afterlife — if they could get there.

# A World Walled and Dark

"Ren!" called Alex, and then, softer, "Ren?"

Nothing. No response, just like the last time — and the hundred times before that. It was clear that no one could hear him down here. At least no one who felt like responding. He took one last look out the small, square opening in the door and then took his hands off the grimy bars and retreated back into the darkness of his cramped cell.

He sat on his cot, the only furniture in the room, unless you counted the bucket that served as a bathroom and the small electric lamp that cast a weak yellow glow on the hard sandstone floor. A beam of stronger light from the hall was cut into three even slices by the bars on the door, and Alex watched a bug the size of a D battery skitter diagonally across them, like a winning move in tic-tac-toe.

*Not totally alone after all*, he thought as the insect disappeared into the darkness.

Alex got up and went to the door again. This time he called out for the person he'd traveled halfway across the world to find, whom he'd lost again in the blink of an eye.

"Mom!" he called. "Mom!"

He remembered how she had looked, her face over-whelmed with emotion, when his hunt for her and the Spells had finally come to an end in that desert village. He remembered the despair on her face when they were captured by The Order, the Spells stolen from their grasp. Even though he feared the answer, he wondered again: *What would the ancient cult do with such awesome power?*

Suddenly, a sound broke through his muddled thoughts: footsteps. It was the guard again. Alex walked over and flicked off his lamp, then returned to the door.

"Stand back from the door, stupid boy," called the guard in heavily accented English, "or you get no food."

Alex crouched down beside the door. He was hoping that the guard would open it this time and he could catch him by surprise. He flexed his hands, ready for a fight.

But once again, he was disappointed.

*Flink* went the slot in the bottom of the door as it opened. *Shhish* went the empty tray from the day before as it was pulled out into the corridor. *SHHUNNKK* went the new tray as it slid across the floor. In the little slice of light, he saw a single piece of the Egyptian pita bread known as *aish baladi*, a cup, and a handful of dull, shriveled dates.

The little slot slapped closed again, leaving the tray in darkness. Leaving Alex alone.

"Wait!" called Alex. "Come back! My bucket needs to be emptied!"

Which was true — every inch of the small cell stank with

its contents. But it was also an excuse, one more attempt to get the door to open, to give himself a fighting chance.

The guard seemed to understand that, too. A laugh, joyless and cruel, rose in the hallway only to fade along with the slap of the guard's sandals.

Silence.

Darkness.

Alex flicked the lamp switch again, but it wouldn't turn back on. With a sigh, he reached down and felt around for the tray. He grabbed the cup and lifted it to his dry, cracked lips. Two big swigs later, it was empty.

He squatted down in the darkness and reached around for the bread. It moved under his hand and he let out a screech that would have been embarrassing if there was anyone to hear him. The bug had gotten there first. But he needed his strength: He knew he should eat the bread, anyway — the bread and probably the bug.

He split the difference, shaking the bug loose. It landed with a clack on the floor behind him. It skittered off, but the silence didn't return.

Footsteps.

Alex held his breath and froze in the darkness by the door.

Because these footsteps were different.

They were coming from *inside* the cell.

6

"Alex?" said Ren, and then, louder, "Anyone?"

Nothing, but she wasn't surprised. Renata Duran was the kind of girl who always considered the odds. If no one had answered the first ten times she'd called out, what were the odds someone would this time? She decided not to waste any more breath.

She went back and sat on the edge of her cot, in the soft light of her lamp.

Before long, a sound echoed through the corridor. She hurried over to the door. Like Alex, Ren was twelve years old. Unlike her best friend, the noise didn't catch her off guard. In fact, she'd been waiting for it.

"Did you bring me soup, like I asked?" she said once the guard sounded close enough. "I have a gluten allergy," she reminded him, even though it wasn't remotely true. "And problems with fruit, too!"

She heard a loud sigh from out in the corridor. "Step back, stupid girl," said the guard as he knelt down to open the slot at the bottom of the door. "I brought your soup."

Ren stepped back as the guard retrieved the previous tray and slid the new one into the cell. It held a bowl of dark, lumpy gruel.

It did *not* look appetizing, but that wasn't why she'd asked for it.

Partly, it was a test. She wanted to see if her captors cared at all about keeping her alive, thus the "dangerous" food allergies she'd concocted. And they did. Not in luxury,

clearly, but alive. That had to mean something, though she had no delusions that it would be good. The last time The Order had captured her and her friends, they'd tried to sacrifice them to a Death Walker.

Ren shuddered, thinking about what she'd learned of the Walkers. They were powerful, evil beings who had clung to the edge of the afterlife for centuries, desperately trying to avoid the weighing of the heart ceremony, where the old gods judged the spirits of the ancient Egyptian dead. Knowing they would fail and be destroyed forever, their souls devoured by Ammit, the Walkers had waited for an opportunity to escape. And Alex's mom had given them that chance when she'd used the Lost Spells to save his life back in New York — opening a rift between the worlds in the process.

Which made Ren think of New York, and her own parents there. She missed them desperately — and she definitely missed their clean, bright apartment.

Which reminded her of the main reason she'd asked for the soup in the first place.

She knelt down and found the bowl, then held it up to the light from the little window. She slowly shoveled a spoonful of the lumpy gunk into her mouth.

Dis.

Gus.

Ting.

"Bleck!" she said. Still, she licked the spoon clean and held it up to the light. Metal, just like she'd hoped.

She dumped the soup into her bathroom bucket. Then she picked up the bucket's handle, which she'd managed to remove with slow, repeated bending.

She returned to the door and ran her hand along the side. She felt the heavy plate that guarded the lock and desperately wished she still had her ibis. She'd been the last of the group to get an amulet of her own — and definitely the last to get a handle on its power. If she had the ancient artifact now, she could fill the cell with brilliant light and open the lock with a simple telekinetic click. It might even give her a clue what was waiting for her outside.

But The Order had taken her amulet, along with her phone and her friends.

So these were her tools: a metal spoon and bucket handle, a wooden soup bowl, a plastic tray, and a ceramic cup.

Once more, she thought of home.

It wasn't for sentimental reasons this time. Her dad had worked alongside Alex's mom at The Metropolitan Museum of Art, but he wasn't an Egyptologist like her. He was a senior engineer: a mechanical wizard and the museum's go-to Mr. Fix-It. And he'd taught his daughter a lot.

Ren went to work.

## II

# Visitors

Even in the dark, with his heart beating like a drum set, Alex knew who'd come for him. He could sense the powerful presence.

Alex felt the strong urge to say something and confirm his suspicions. But what should he call this man? He'd never really known him, and to the extent that he did, it was as his mortal enemy. And yet when Alex opened his mouth, all he could think to say was: "Hi, Dad."

The word felt explosive and unreal. He had found out just days before that the leader of The Order was his father, and there had been no time for explanations after their capture, so he knew no more than the bare, brutal fact of it.

"Hello, Alex," said the man.

It was the same voice he'd heard in the desert, but it was louder, bigger.

"What do you want?" Alex said. He meant it defiantly, but he ended up sounding like a servant addressing his master. Though he couldn't see it, he assumed the leader was

wearing the golden vulture mask that allowed him to bend people to his will.

"I want to talk to you," said the leader. "Now that you understand who I am. We never got to know each other, and that is . . . a shame."

Alex felt the powerful urge to agree with everything the leader said — *yes, such a shame* — but he knew that was the mask's magic. He fought it. He fought him. "You already talked to me," he said, each word a struggle. "When you tried to sacrifice me in that pit."

Alex braced for an angry response, but the leader remained calm. "You are your mother's son," he said. "I have no doubt about that. And your actions leave no question whose side you're on. I lost you both, years ago."

Alex desperately wished he could fill in the blanks on this strange story. *His father had lost them? Or abandoned them? And for what?* His head swirled with hurt pride and unasked questions. "You didn't have to sacrifice me to a —"

"I don't *have* to do anything," said his father, cutting him off. "I am the leader of this organization, and soon of this world and the next. I chose to sacrifice you, and the others. You are my son, but you have cast yourself as my enemy — and what is one boy's life, in the face of the glory to come?"

*The glory to come* . . . Alex knew he meant the Final Kingdom. Now that the doors between worlds were open, The Order planned to use the power of the world of the dead to rule the world of the living.

Still, it wasn't just *one boy's life*.

"But I'm your son . . ." he said. Was it possible he wanted this madman to care about him?

"And you have chosen to be my enemy."

Alex knew he was right. He didn't know why his mom had married a power-hungry madman — or a man who became one, anyway — but he knew she hadn't raised one. "So why am I still alive?"

"Victory is close," said the leader. "But until then, you might be useful to me. You and the scarab."

"I would never help you," Alex managed, though challenging the leader's will felt like swimming against a riptide. He desperately wished he had that scarab now, the ancient amulet his mom had left for him when she'd first disappeared with the Spells. After a lifetime of being too sick and weak to do much of anything, it had given him power. The ability to move objects, to summon powerful winds, and activate the spells in the Book of the Dead. It also gave him a radar-like sense for the undead and the dark magic that made them.

And then the thought occurred to him — if the leader wanted to use Alex's powers with the scarab, maybe he had the amulet on him right now. Maybe . . .

The leader let out a little huff of laughter. "It doesn't matter if you want to help me. You don't have a choice."

Alex knew he was right again. The leader had made him tackle his own mom in the last battle. But if he could get his scarab back, maybe then he'd have a chance. He stalled for

**12**

time as he tried to peer through the darkness. "So you came to gloat?"

"I came to express my regrets," he said. "A useless emotion, really. It changes nothing. And yet —"

But as he spoke, the floor began to shake. A low, ominous rumble emerged from the stone all around. Soon, the whole room was shaking. Alex heard a few little chunks of the ceiling clink as they fell to the floor. It was another one of the tremors that had rocked the cell over the last few days, but this one was stronger. Alex imagined the whole place coming down around him, crushing him like a bug. But just as abruptly as it had started, it stopped.

"Another earthquake," he gasped.

"They are coming," said the leader.

"Wait, who is coming?" said Alex, but he could already feel that the powerful presence that had filled the cell was gone. His father had vanished without a sound — or at least without one his mind-bending mask had allowed Alex to hear.

But a moment later, Alex did hear something. Soft footsteps, coming from the hallway — had the leader returned? A hushed voice just outside the door answered his question. "Who's in there? Alex? Todtman? Dr. Bauer?"

"Ren!" he blurted. "How —"

"SHHHHHHH!" she hissed. "Hold on a second. I have to try something."

He heard a series of metallic clunks and scrapes, followed by a click.

Light fell across Alex as the big door swung open.

# Tunnel Vision

Alex blinked in the sudden light and saw Ren holding a bizarre device. A pointy, bent piece of metal stuck out of one side of a wooden bowl, while a strip of plastic stuck out of the other, its end shredded into a sort of fork.

"I am *so* glad to see you!" he said. He considered hugging her out of sheer gratitude, but it wasn't really something they did. Plus, she had that pointy thing in her hand.

"I'm glad I found you," she said, and then stepped forward and, awkwardly, hugged him. He hugged her back.

When they pulled apart, Alex pointed to the device. "Did you open the door with that thing?"

"Yeah!" she said. "It's a lot easier from the outside. It took me forever to get under the plate thingy from inside my cell. But I finally got the spoon underneath to pry it open a little."

"Where'd you get a spoon?"

Ren produced a slightly mangled spoon from her pocket. She was in the same outfit as the last time he'd seen her and looked pretty grubby. "It was for my soup."

Alex allowed himself a moment of amazement at his resourceful friend, then blurted, "Wait, where was your cell? Is my mom there, too? Is Todtman?"

Ren shook her head. "I haven't seen them since they brought us here. This is the first cell I found." She made a big circle with the spoon and added, "This place is big."

Alex stepped out of the cell and looked down the tunnel. It curved gradually and had a slight slope to it. The ceilings were at least twelve feet high, as if made for some other species entirely.

"Let's get out of here," he said. "We need to find my mom and Todtman."

"Okay, we should go this way," said Ren, pointing farther down the hallway, converting his vague wishes into an actual plan. "Because I came from the other direction, and I think mine was the first cell in this section."

They walked cautiously, sticking close to the walls and heading farther down the slope. Here and there, flickering lights buzzed above them. Alex peered through the uneven glow until he spotted something up ahead. Two doors, one on each side of the tunnel. One was solid and painted black, but the other had a barred window at face height — *another cell!*

Forgetting his caution, Alex rushed toward it. *My mom could be in there!*

The faintest hint of light escaped from the small window. Alex knew immediately that it came from another small electric lamp. Someone was inside.

"It could be anyone," whispered Ren. "Be careful."

Alex put his ear up to the barred window and heard a faint sound, like a cornered animal breathing. He peered inside.

"Who is it?" said Ren. "Do we know them?"

"Oh yeah," Alex managed despite his surprise. "Definitely."

On the floor of the cell, in between the cot and the lamp, a teenage boy was doing sit-ups. His arms were crossed over his chest and his head was just now rising above his raised knees. His eyes met Alex's and froze somewhere between the sit and the up. "Hey, cuz!" he said.

"Hey, Luke," said Alex. It was his cousin from home, Luke Bauer, the jock who had been spying on them for The Order. The one whose betrayal in the Valley of the Kings had nearly cost them their lives.

"Luke?" said Ren. She shoulder-checked Alex aside and, small for her age, hopped up to get a quick glimpse in the window.

"Hey, Ren," he said. "We have seriously got to stop meeting like this."

Despite the tension of the situation, Alex couldn't help but smile. The last time they'd seen Luke was in a different Order cell, in the lair of a Death Walker. But that Walker had been destroyed, and that location was no longer secret. Clearly, the cult was consolidating its holdings here.

"What do we do?" whispered Ren, keeping her voice low enough so that only Alex could hear.

Alex knew his answer immediately. The last time, they'd had to leave Luke in his cell, his pale, dirty face pressed up

to the bars, as they fled from The Order. Alex had regretted it ever since.

Luke had betrayed them, but he'd also been betrayed by the treacherous cult. His captivity seemed proof enough of that, but it was his words last time that had clinched it for Alex. Alex remembered his cousin's desperate cry: *They were going to kill my parents*. Alex didn't doubt that The Order would make such a threat — or that they'd follow through. In his mind, it was clear: Luke had been lured into spying on them by the promise of easy money. Once he realized what bad news The Order really was, it was too late. He'd been kept in line by the worst threat imaginable.

No, Alex would not leave his cousin to rot in a cell a second time.

"Can you open this lock, too?" he said to Ren.

"Yeah," she said, then softer: "But are you sure?"

He nodded. "I think we can trust him now."

Ren shrugged. "Keep an eye on him," she said. As she knelt down and got to work on the lock, she called up: "This doesn't mean I'm not mad at you!"

It was way too loud. Almost immediately, there was a muffled exclamation from inside the door across the tunnel.

"Dudes," hissed Luke, "that's the guardroom!"

Alex glared at his cousin's face. *Now you tell us?*

His heart began to hammer in his chest as something toppled over in the room across the way, the sound of a man standing up too quickly. "Hurry!" he hissed to Ren. "We need him."

Ren seemed to understand. Without their amulets, their only weapon was the two-time New York State Junior Olympic gold medalist behind the still-locked door. "Right," she said. She gave the curled piece of metal one final wiggle in the keyhole and then stuck the small piece of flayed plastic in beneath it.

The door flew open across the hall as Ren fished around in the lock.

The guard rushed straight toward them. Alex threw himself at his legs, but the man easily brushed aside the awkward tackle attempt. "Stupid boy," he said as Alex hit the ground.

Suddenly, there was a crisp, metallic click.

Ren dove to the side, and Luke's door flew open — smacking the lunging guard in the forehead just as he was straightening up.

Luke burst forth, crazy-eyed and ready for a fight.

But there was no need. The guard stumbled backward, holding his head in both hands, and crumpled gracelessly to the floor.

"Thanks for the spoon and stuff," Ren said as they locked the unconscious guard in the cell with his own keys. They left the lamp on for him, a small kindness in return for some bad soup.

They crept across the tunnel toward the open door of the guardroom. Ren kept a close eye on Luke as he padded

silently beside them in high-tech running sneakers, a dirt-streaked Under Armour top, and basketball shorts. In her mind, it was clear: He'd betrayed them again and again, and only stopped when he got caught. She kept Alex between her and Luke. If her friend trusted him so much, he could be the one to deal with the next betrayal.

As they approached the door, Alex whispered: "Hopefully there's a map of the other cells in here, or a list of prisoners, or . . . something."

*Hopefully there's not another guard*, thought Ren. "Shhh!" she hissed.

But the guardroom was unguarded now, just a small, simply furnished square. The soup can was still open on the counter of the tiny kitchenette, next to a bag of Egyptian bread and a stack of trays like the one she'd peeled her lockpick off of. The only thing out of the ordinary was a heavy-looking steel door built into the wall.

The three examined it closely. "I would love to see what's inside there," said Alex longingly. "Maybe weapons." Remembering his father's words, he thought of another possibility. *The scarab* . . .

Ren eyed the safe. The door was almost as tall as she was, and the lock was as big as her head. She tossed the remains of her lockpick kit on the table. "There's no way we can crack that thing."

"Oh, there's a way," said Luke, hooking a thumb over his shoulder. "The guard's still in my cell. Probably awake by now."

"Why would he help us?" said Ren.

Luke smiled — a devilish smile that Ren couldn't help but be a *little* charmed by. "Because if his bosses find him in there, after he let us escape, he is toast. *So* toast. Like the super burned kind you just have to throw away because —"

"I got it," she said. "Toast."

"Wait," said Alex. "You want us to, what, let him go in exchange for the combination?"

Luke shrugged. "How bad do you want to get in there?"

"Pretty bad," Alex admitted.

He looked over at Ren, and they both nodded.

"Okay," she said to Luke.

He was standing there watching them with that same look on his face. *The problem with devilish grins*, thought Ren, *is you can never tell if you're making a deal with the devil.*

**20**

# Treasure Beyond Measure

Alex looked through the bars to find the guard sitting on the cot with his head in his hands. "He's totally awake," he whispered back to the others.

But like many guards, this one had excellent hearing. "Because if they find me in here, I am done for," he said into his hands. After a brief pause he added, "Stupid boy."

The false bravado didn't fool any of them. This was a desperate man, and a deal was struck quickly. He seemed to like the idea of giving them the combination. "Yes," he said. "You free me, you open it and find what is inside. Then you cause the troubles, and I slip away. Am gone."

"Okay, but first you give us the combination, then we let you go," said Alex.

The man was silent, considering it. Finally, he looked up at Alex. "Bring to me pen and paper, from table," he said, his face pushed out through the bars.

"Why the paper?" asked Ren.

"Because the combination is in hieroglyphs, of course."

They grabbed the pen and paper from the guard-room, and a few minutes later he had scrawled a string of hieroglyphs — the small symbols the ancient Egyptians used to communicate information. The guard's last words as he scrawled the symbols: "You will want what is inside, yes, but wait a little. Then come back with the keys! You are the good ones, yes? The Amulet Keepers?"

Alex heard the fear in the man's voice. He wondered what horrible punishment he'd get if he was caught. "Sure," Alex called, as he rushed across the hall. *Did he mean it?* They were Amulet Keepers, not Boy Scouts.

Back in the guardroom, his hands shook as he began turning the large dial. The others crowded around, looking over his shoulders. Two turns to the falcon symbol, one back to the snake, three forward to a set of scales, back to a stack of lines.

*KLICK!*

"Sweet!" said Luke. "Open it!"

Alex began to pull, but Ren stopped him. "Wait a little," she said, quoting the guard.

Alex paused a few long seconds. Then he pulled the heavy steel door open. He peered into the dim shadowy interior and saw two vaporous, glowing orbs staring back at him. His breath caught as he realized they were *eyes*.

"What the —" blurted Luke, jumping back.

"Oh, shoot," said Ren. "It's a sheut!"

Alex gave the slightest of nods. It was a sheut, or shadow, a sort of ancient Egyptian ghost, a supernatural shell that

had lost its self and soul. One of these had nearly drained him of his own life one very dark night in Vienna. But this one wasn't attacking. It was just . . .

"It's *watching* you," whispered Ren, her voice horrified, her small body leaning back and away.

Not wanting to provoke it, Alex forced himself to stay very still. It seemed to work. The murky eyes narrowed.

"Is it falling asleep?" whispered Ren.

Alex nodded slowly. Opening the safe had woken the sleepy spirit, but now its eyes were little more than two narrow white lines hanging in the shadows. Alex exhaled and scanned the dim interior behind the drowsy apparition.

He saw something so familiar on a small shelf that the shadows did nothing to obscure it. "The scarab!" he blurted.

Forgetting himself, he lunged for it.

"No, wait!" said Ren, but Alex had already pushed his hand through the veil of shadows inside the safe.

The spirit eyes popped open.

Alex's fingers brushed the scarab, but before his hand could close on it, the shadow rushed forth. It hit Alex like an ice-cold wave, and a feeling of profound emptiness made him gasp and fall back to the floor.

Luke backpedaled expertly, like a cornerback dropping into coverage. Alex crab-walked awkwardly back, hands and feet underneath him, as Ren tugged unhelpfully on his shoulders. "That's what we were supposed to wait for," she moaned. "Till it went back to sleep!"

The sheut rose to its full height in front of the safe,

looming above them. A mouth formed underneath its milky eyes — a trembling circle of deeper darkness. There was a hissing gasp — a quick, deep inhalation — and then:

*ssskkrreeEEEEEEEEEEEEEEEEEEEEEEEEEEEEE EEE!*

Alex had never heard a scream more piercing or terrible. Still on the floor, he clamped his hands over his ears.

Luke had one index finger jammed into each ear and was shouting, "We have to get out of here!"

The desolate scream filled Alex with an unspeakable sorrow and he felt tears filling his eyes. The sadness was supernatural, he knew, but his fear was very real. The piercing scream would carry forever in the echoing stone tunnels.

They had to get out now, get as far away as possible. Luke already had one foot out the door, and Ren wasn't far behind. But Alex couldn't bring himself to go — and not just because he was still on his butt. His eyes were focused not on the wailing apparition, but on the open safe behind it.

He took one last deep breath and darted forward.

"Nooooo!" screamed Ren.

Alex tried to duck around the sheut, but the ringing in his ears made him disoriented and clumsy. Instead, he went right through. He felt as if he'd been painted with ice as he reluctantly removed his right hand from his ear. The scream pierced him down to his very soul, but he groped

around inside the safe, grabbing the first shiny object he saw.

He stumbled back and looked down. An amulet — Ren's ibis!

He held it up and saw her eyes gleam with recognition. He delivered the delicate carving of an Egyptian wading bird in an underhand arc. As it descended toward her, she lowered her left hand from her ear and plucked the amulet from the air.

As soon as she had a hold of it, she dropped her right hand and thrust it forward, shouting into the horrible noise all around: "Go!"

A loud *FWOOOP* cut through the horrid scream as a flash of brilliant white moonlight filled the room.

The ibis was a symbol of Thoth, the Egyptian god of moonlight, writing, and wisdom. He was also the one who kept track of where each spirit belonged — so when the light faded, the deathly shadow was gone from this world. Alex was pretty sure the screaming had stopped, too, but it was hard to tell with his ears ringing like fire alarms.

He wasted no more time, rushing forward and ransacking the safe.

He grabbed the scarab, instantly feeling the current of ancient energy flow through him as he threw the chain over his head.

Next to it was a third amulet: Todtman's falcon, the powerful mind-bending artifact known as the Watcher. He

grabbed that, as well as a fistful of money from a tall stack of bills and stuffed it all in his pocket.

"Why would they keep the amulets right here, so close to us?" shouted Ren as they rushed out of the room and into the hallway.

"Because they planned to make us use the amulets — for them!" called Alex.

"Who cares why?" called Luke. "You got your bug back, dude," he said to Alex. He turned to Ren: "And you got your, like, seagull!"

They all grinned crazily. None of them realized they were shouting. Alex even took a moment to step across the hall and unlock the cell door. The guard had done his part, he figured, and posed no real danger to them now that they had their amulets. Alex knew time was tight, so he hurried.

But he didn't know how tight.

With his ears ringing, he couldn't hear the stampede of approaching footsteps. He did wonder, briefly, why the guard suddenly refused to leave his cell.

## Deep Trouble

The friends hustled down the dim corridor, deeper into the earth. Ren shot another look over her shoulder, knowing the gentle curve of the tunnel would hide any pursuers until they were right on top of them — and nearly ran into a heavy door. The tunnel in front of her had ended.

"Think we reached the end of the cellblock," said Luke.

Ren looked over at him and something occurred to her. He could have taken off running toward daylight at any time — definitely when that sheut appeared — but he was still here. She grudgingly gave him one point and turned back toward the door. It was bigger than the others and with no barred window. If this length of tunnel really was just a cellblock, was another one next? Would they find Alex's mom and Todtman on the other side — or something much worse?

But Alex was already gripping his scarab. He reached out with the amulet's energy, probing the inside of the lock, pushing against it. The heavy lock turned.

"Ready?" said Alex.

Luke nodded and lowered himself into a wide athletic stance, as if there might be a charging running back on the other side of the door.

Ren considered the question. *Was she ready? Were they?* She took one more quick look back over her shoulder — and *now* she was ready. "Yeek!" she squeaked. Because barreling down the sloped tunnel was a menacing menagerie of enemies.

There were half a dozen of them, some living, some living dead.

The first thing Alex noticed was the mummy. Its ragged wrapping betrayed its formidable age, and though it dragged one leg slightly, it was still moving at a full run.

Three guards were on either side of the sprinting corpse, two of them already reaching for the pistols at their waists. *Uh-oh*, thought Alex as he tugged the heavy door open and Ren and Luke ducked under his arm and through.

Alex took one last glimpse and saw two more figures behind the others. The first was a man clad all in crimson: bloodred robes and a ruby red headdress. *Was he a wizard? A priest? A raspberry?* Gliding silently beside him was a creature of inky blackness. This one was more than a mere shadow. Alex could already feel its deathly chill.

He quickly ducked inside the door and pulled it closed as the first bullets thunked and pinged into the other side.

He reached for his amulet. The ancient energy surged through him, mixing potently with his fear and adrenaline. He found a weak point in the lock — a small gear deep inside — and snapped it off. "That ought to hold 'em!" he crowed.

"I doubt it," muttered Ren.

But with his hearing clearing and a thick door blocking their pursuers, Alex was more optimistic.

Ahead of them was another cellblock, and a familiar face pushed outward between the bars of the nearest cell. He recognized the froggy features immediately — the sloping chin, the bulging eyes.

"TODTMAN!" screamed Ren.

"Hallo, Ren!" he called in his crisp German accent. But even as he said it, the smile fell from his bar-pinched face. "Look out behind you!"

The friends turned too late. The gliding apparition had come straight through the thick door and was swarming over Luke.

"Aah, get it off!" he shouted.

Ren grabbed her amulet and felt the ibis's edges press sharply into her palm. She felt its power surge through her,

a prickling, electric rush. Then she raised her right hand in a fist and opened it suddenly. "Go!" she shouted.

Once again, a blast of concentrated moonlight brightened the dim tunnel. But this spirit was different: bigger and darker and more dangerous. It didn't vanish. It steamed. Gray vapor hissed upward from the inky edges of its frame. Its head spun around, and two glowing eyes focused on Ren.

"Uh-oh," she mumbled.

The ghostly presence released Luke, who fell to the floor clutching his arms to his chest and shivering visibly. Then it rushed toward Ren. She heard the click behind her, the creaking arc of a door unaccustomed to opening, but she didn't dare look back.

Instead, she took a deep breath and opened her fist once more. "Go!"

*FWOOP!*

The thing shimmered and steamed in the second blast of light, and for just a moment it seemed to stumble in its stepless movement. But the moment passed and it resumed its swift attack. As Ren bumbled backward, the toe of her left boot caught the heel of the right.

"Guh," she said as she went down in a heap.

The spirit shot forward and loomed over her. She felt its lifeless chill.

And then — *Oh no!* — a second dark silhouette appeared in front of her, slicing in from the side. *I'm done for!* she

thought. Her last thought was of her family, who she missed more than anything. But that's when she realized what she was seeing.

It wasn't the front of another spirit. It was the back of Dr. Ernst Todtman in his trademark black suit. In his first act as a free man, he had stepped in front of the onrushing menace. The evil presence enveloped him, as it had Luke, and for a moment he seemed to be completely eclipsed by it.

Then it broke apart like a wave hitting a rock. For a moment, it hung shredded in the air around him, like a flock of scattered crows. Then it pulled back and began to re-form, the dark patches reconnecting like liquid pooling in the air.

Pushing it all back was the silver chain and falcon amulet hanging loosely from Todtman's left hand.

"Ready, Ren!" he called.

She gathered herself and took hold of her own amulet. The spirit had almost entirely re-formed now. But as the last few wisps rejoined its hanging frame, Todtman swung his left hand, and the falcon amulet sliced the apparition's head clean off. "Now!" called Todtman.

The spirit's head hung in the air like a black balloon; its glowing eyes blinked twice in seeming disbelief. Ren aimed her blast right between them.

*FWOOP!*

The floating orb hissed and steamed and then Ren heard the faintest *pop!* and it was gone. The rest of its body fell to the floor and faded into nothingness.

For a few long seconds, everyone was silent. All Ren could hear was her own labored breathing and her own pounding heart. As she began to calm down, she managed a few words: "What was that? Another sheut?"

"No," said Todtman. "The taxonomy of the Egyptian afterlife is long and complex . . ." Ren smiled despite her frayed nerves: *Such a Todtman thing to say.* "But that was older, more dangerous. A dark khu, perhaps."

"Felt like a walk-in freezer," said Luke, rising to his feet, still hugging himself and shivering slightly. "But it's good to see you again, Dr. T."

Todtman did a quick double take. Ren wasn't sure if it was because no one had ever called him that before, or because last he'd heard, Luke was a traitor and a spy.

"He's okay, I think," said Ren, offering the firmest endorsement she felt ready for. "Anyway, we let him out. And he's right: It is nice to see you."

"Yeah," agreed Alex. "I wasn't sure I'd ever see you again." He looked around the little group. "Any of you."

Todtman was not an overly emotional man, but he flashed a big, froggy smile now. "Well, then," he said, glancing back toward his cell. "There is someone else here I am *sure* you will be glad to see."

"Mom?" Alex called, rushing past Todtman into the cell.

Todtman grabbed his shoulder. "Be careful. She is badly hurt."

*Badly hurt?* Alex shook Todtman off and darted inside.

"Alex, honey, is that you?" he heard.

And there she was, holding her side and just now rising from a cot. "Hi, hun," she said, her voice soft and hesitant.

*Holding her side . . . Oh no.*

"Are you okay, Mom?" said Alex. "Are you hurt?"

The dim light from the hallway filtered in through the door, and the little lamp shone weakly from the floor, but her face remained in shadow. Alex stepped forward, his arms already open to hug her. Over the last few weeks, he'd lost her and found her and lost her again, and he wouldn't let it happen anymore.

She put her arm out to block him. "*Careful*," she warned.

Alex stopped short. "You're hurt."

"It's my ribs," she said. "Mostly."

Alex took the news like a kick to his own ribs.

"What happened?" asked Ren from the door.

Dr. Bauer managed a quick, mischievous grin. "What, you think you're the only ones who can try to escape? After they caught me, they threw me back into Todtman's cell — so that he could take care of me."

"I tried to tell them, I am a doctor of *Egyptology*," said the German ruefully. "I begged them to get her a real doctor."

Not knowing what else to do, Alex reached out and gently

took his mom's hand. She leaned down to wrap him in an awkward one-armed hug.

Ever the pragmatist, Todtman cut the emotional reunion short. "We have to go now," he said sharply.

Alex's mom straightened up and wiped a tear from her eye. "I can walk, but I'll just slow you down."

Todtman gestured down at his own bad leg, crippled by a scorpion sting in their battle with the first Death Walker in New York: "That is my job."

For a moment, the two old friends shared the smallest of smiles. Alex was watching them intently and smiled when his mom did, a sort of sympathetic reflex. He'd grown up sharing the same small apartment with her, their schedules wrapping around each other like vines. Early morning drop-offs on the way to work, doctor's visits scheduled for half-days. They knew each other's moods and expressions the way ship captains know the tides.

The moment was broken by another sound echoing down the tunnel. It was the cry of a mummy, the ragged, rattling product of a time-shriveled tongue. A second hoarse cry rose up to answer the first. Their pursuers had broken through and were on the way.

The hobbled crew hurried down the hallway as best they could. Dr. Bauer had one arm pressed against her injured left side, and Alex, doing his best to support her, pressed against

her right. Their pursuers were so close that they could see their dim shadows playing at the edge of the curved tunnel, a nightmarish mix of stretched and distorted shapes, arms and heads and gun barrels.

"The tunnel branches off up here!" called Ren, who'd rushed ahead of the others.

Alex rounded the corner and saw the two passages, like gaping mouths in the earth. Ren was standing with her eyes closed, focused on the ibis amulet clutched in her hand, but her feet were tapping nervously. The amulet's main power was information. It gave her images to interpret: scenes from the past, present, or future, and she was trying to find out which way led to freedom.

As Alex watched, her eyes flew open.

"I can't get anything clear — it takes time to interpret —"

But their time was up. Behind them, the twisty shadows and angry shouts were drawing closer.

"If we're going to guess, I'd go left," said his mom. "To the sun."

It was a cryptic comment, but her son understood immediately. In ancient Egypt, everything had been oriented around the north-flowing Nile. The maps were drawn with south at the top instead of the bottom, making the eastern bank on the left and the western bank on the right. For the Egyptians, the eastern bank represented the sunlit land of the living. The Order still followed the old ways, which meant the friends needed to go left to leave these tombs and find the sun.

Todtman seemed to understand, too. "Good thinking. Alex, buy us some time," he called. "They must not see which tunnel we take."

Alex nodded. As the others hurried to the left, he grasped the scarab. His pulse pounded; his eyes focused. The scarab was a symbol of rebirth, but rebirth took many forms in Egypt. Alex extended his right hand and whispered: "The wind that comes before the rain." Instantly, a whipping column of wind shot back up the tunnel. Confused shouts rose up, only to be drowned out by the hurricane howl. The shadows were beaten back, disappearing from view.

Alex gave it everything he had. When it was over, he stood gulping down air, the bright, hot cinder of a headache just beginning to burn in his skull. He turned to see the others disappearing into the shadows fifteen yards down the tunnel.

Except for one. As Alex turned to hustle after them, he was surprised to find Luke waiting beside him. "Let's go, cuz," he said. "That won't hold 'em for long."

The boys rushed up the tunnel. The sounds of argument and confusion grew behind them as the hunting party debated directions. Soon, the voices faded.

Silent and fast, the boys raced toward the others. The way was harder here, but they didn't mind at all.

It was harder because this tunnel had begun sloping ever so slightly upward.

# A Whiff of War

Alex and Luke quickly caught up with the others, who were waiting at the next fork in the tunnel. It split again after that, and the friends relaxed ever so slightly, confident they had lost their pursuers. The tunnels continued to slope upward and a hundred yards farther along the group paused to examine a tall archway built into the wall. As Todtman ran his fingers across the hieroglyphic symbols cut deep into the framing stone, Alex knew exactly what he was looking for. They needed to figure out what The Order was doing with the Lost Spells, and ultimately, they needed those Spells back. Their power was the only thing that could set things right again.

Alex turned his eyes to the hieroglyphs and saw one symbol more than any other: the lioness. Again and again, the elegant predator was carved into the stone entrance. Sometimes crouched on its own and sometimes in the midst of a swirl of other symbols.

"It's a tomb," he said. "And I think I know whose." He remembered all too well the vicious Order operative who

wore the skull of a lioness as her mask. "See that symbol, the lioness?"

"Peshwar," said Luke, spitting the word out bitterly. "I hate that cat lady."

"But if this is a tomb," said Ren, "does that mean she's dead now?"

"Perhaps," said Todtman. "We need to know what The Order is up to now. And there is one way to find out . . . I'll be right back."

He took a step toward the tomb mouth and winced as his weight landed on his injured left leg. Alex could tell that all this hobbled running was catching up to Todtman. His limp was worse than ever. A few feet away, Alex's mom was leaning against the wall and holding her side. Alex's concern mixed with guilt. In his tireless quest to find her, he'd led The Order straight to her — and to the Spells she'd tried so hard to hide.

"No, wait," he said. "I'll go."

"We'll go," chirped Ren, stepping forward.

"Me too," said Luke, but Ren shook her head.

"No," she said firmly. "You should stay here and look out for Todtman and Dr. Bauer." Alex could tell she was cutting him out because she still didn't trust him. But it seemed to work.

Luke nodded. "Can do," he said. He didn't seem particularly disappointed not to be sneaking inside yet another dark, creepy tomb.

⟨——|——|——|——⟩

Alex and Ren crept forward.

A dim passageway gave way to a huge room lit by two iron cauldrons with flames floating on the surface of the liquid within. Alex had been in enough tomb chapels to know that this was the outer chamber. Through an archway at the far end of the room he could see flickering firelight and shifting shadows in the inner chamber. Muffled voices came from within.

Alex and Ren slunk silently forward. They were in the middle of the floor now: If one of those shadows emerged, they would be caught in the open like deer in the headlights. Alex took the lead, as they passed between the two flaming cauldrons. He eyed the eerie flames — barely daring to breathe — and that's when it happened. The floor started to move.

The floor. The walls. The world around them.

It was another tremor. The room jolted and jerked like a carnival ride, and Alex toppled to the side. Ren reached for him but she was too late.

Desperate to avoid the burning liquid, he put his hand out toward the iron side of the cauldron. He winced, anticipating the searing metal burning into his hand. But the iron was cool to the touch. These flames burned cold. He pushed himself up. "I'm okay," he whispered, reminding himself to forget everything he knew about the laws of science. It was the laws of magic that ruled down here.

They moved past the cauldrons, arms out for balance as if they were on a tightrope. A few steps later, the room fell still.

The talking started up again in the next room. The words were in an ancient dialect, and Alex closed his hand around his amulet so that he could understand them. He was close enough now to recognize the first voice — and the powerful presence behind it.

He sucked a short, sharp breath into a chest gone tight with fear. Even at this distance, his father's words had the solemn weight of a judge pronouncing a death sentence. And there was something else about them, something outsized and otherworldly.

He turned back to Ren. Her eyes were round with fear, the whites gone pink in the flickering glow. They reached the tall archway and slowly, carefully peered inside.

Alex's heart raced. The tomb chapel's inner chamber was bright with the light of four flaming iron pots. Carved lionesses lounged on stone platforms, eyes of bloodred rubies all staring at the ornate gold-painted sarcophagus in the room's center. Intricate paintings and deep-cut hieroglyphs covered the walls. The ceiling was high, as the archways and indeed the tunnels themselves had been. And now Alex knew why. For inside walls stood two massive figures.

He'd expected his father to be one of them, and he was half right. The larger of the two had once been his dad. The mask, the voice, the *presence* were all unmistakable. But the figure standing before him was more than ten feet tall — higher than a basketball hoop.

*He'd done it.* The cult's plan had worked. His father, whom he had never really known in life, was standing before him now in death. Warm bile rose in Alex's throat, seeking an exit. He swallowed hard.

Ren squeezed his shoulder in support. Alex felt a sudden emptiness inside, as if something big had been taken from him. And it had been. Whatever his father had once been, that man was gone now. He had left the living world and used the power of the Lost Spells to inhabit a new form: the massive statue he'd had made in his own image. Then he'd used that power to escape the afterlife. He had become a Death Walker.

And he wasn't alone.

Peshwar, the woman for whom this tomb was built, now stood nearly as tall as the leader and had the outsized skull of a lioness perched atop her shoulders. Beneath her crimson robes, her frame was almost as skeletal.

Both Walkers were facing away from the entrance, allowing Alex to peer into the room unnoticed. He followed their gaze: They were staring at a large false door. He knew from experience that Egyptian tombs contained at least one of these symbolic gateways to the afterlife, just a recessed indentation in the stone to serve as the door, and a raised border to form the frame. But he had never seen one so large.

"And what if I cannot find my way?" rasped the creature who had once been Peshwar.

"You will know," said the leader. "A path has been cleared and you are our finest tracker. We have constructed these portals especially for our purposes. Keep to the borderlands and travel as if to Aswan."

As Alex watched in breathless horror, he couldn't help but remember the last time he'd seen these two together, during that fateful battle in Minyahur. They'd been humans in masks then; now they were monsters.

He glanced once more at Peshwar's sarcophagus. *Just a relic now*, he knew. The body beneath that golden lid had been needed only for the trip into the afterlife. It had been abandoned there, like a discarded rocket booster falling back to earth. Thanks to the power of the Lost Spells, her spirit, too, now resided in one of the massive stone statues he had seen in the desert.

He looked back at the leader and watched the firelight wash across his avian features. *There used to be a human face under there*, he thought. *Maybe it even looked like mine.* No more. Now it had been transformed by the magic of the Spells into pockmarked bird flesh and a cruelly curved beak. All in the name of power.

"And once I arrive?" asked Peshwar.

"Prepare the way," said the leader. "The tremors grow more frequent. The undying army's arrival draws near. I will go to the seat of power and consult the Spells."

The stunning words went off like cherry bombs in Alex's head: *the undying army, the seat of power, the Spells . . .*

"And then our conquest begins in the west," added Peshwar.

*Conquest.*

The leader nodded. "Yes, where this all started."

"Then let it begin." Peshwar's tall wraithlike figure stepped toward the false door. As the sun-bleached snout of the lioness skull touched the recessed doorway, the painted stone shimmered like the surface of a lake. Peshwar stepped forward into the rippling gateway — and disappeared.

The orange ripples faded and the stone regained its solidity.

Then the leader turned his huge body and cruel bird eyes toward the doorway.

But there was no longer anyone to see there.

*Where this all started* . . . The words echoed in Ren's head. That's where The Order's conquest of the world of the living would start, and she didn't like the sound of that one bit. Because she'd been there when it had all started.

She'd been home, in New York City. Her parents were still there.

*Was Peshwar headed for New York?* She needed to know for sure. As she and Alex slipped back through the outer chamber, she reached up for her amulet once again.

This was the trickiest of the ibis's tricks, and she'd struggled with it in the past. Now she reminded herself that

it didn't provide answers, just information. *It's like extra credit. A bonus: Anything it gives you is more than you have now.* And the girl known as Plus Ten Ren back at school had plenty of experience with extra credit.

Her pulse racing with the power of the amulet, she began to form the first question in her mind: *Where* — But before she got any further, she was rocked by a wave of images.

A panicked crowd on the run, with tall buildings burning behind them.

A horde of ragged figures advancing down a broad street at night.

Flashing police lights seen through wafting smoke.

The intensity of it buckled Ren's knees, and she released the amulet with a gasp as she wobbled forward.

Alex reached out to catch her. "What is it?" he whispered.

Ren blinked twice, refocusing her vision on the world around her. She noticed that he had plucked a jewel-topped staff from the wall of the heavily decorated chamber. She ignored the treasure and looked him straight in the eyes. This involved him, too. Because the buildings, the streets, and even the police cars: She'd recognized them all. She took another deep breath and tried to calm herself for what she had to tell him.

"It was New York," she said. "And it was burning."

## The Road Ahead

Alex and Ren told the group what they'd seen and heard as they continued up the tunnel.

Alex heard his mom's labored breath catch as he told them about the leader.

"So he's dead, then," she said. Even through the pain, her voice sounded far off. He could tell that she was asking about the present but remembering the past.

"Yes and no," said Todtman, using the jeweled staff Alex had given him like a five-dollar walking stick. "He is a Death Walker. The same Spells that allowed the first Walkers to escape have now created new ones."

But Maggie Bauer had a more human take. "Amir is gone."

*Amir* . . . The word ricocheted through Alex's mind. He had learned his father's name only in death, as if reading it from a tombstone.

It was too much to process, and there was still so much Alex didn't know. He wanted answers, but he knew this was

not the time. His mom needed to save her breath — and he needed to save his mom.

"And Peshwar is going to New York?" Luke asked Ren. "I mean, good riddance, but that *cannot* be good."

As Ren eyed the former spy suspiciously, Todtman answered.

"Not good at all," he said. "She stepped through a false door, and that can only mean she is traveling through the afterlife — just as Ren and Alex did to escape the Valley of the Kings. She left the false door in her own tomb to travel to one in New York. In advance of — what did you call it?"

"An undying army," said Alex.

"So wait," said Ren, something occurring to her. "That false door leads to New York?"

Alex knew what she was thinking — and how much she missed home. Todtman nixed the idea immediately. "The door leads to the afterlife, where there are other doors that lead to other places in our world," he said. "But there is danger there, and you must know the way."

"But —" Ren protested.

"But our work still lies in front of us, here in Egypt," said Todtman.

Homesick and stressed, Ren wouldn't let it go: "But if we could —"

She was cut off again, but this time the voice was quieter and the tone softer. It was Alex's mom: "If we don't stop

them, there won't be a New York to go back to. There won't be *any* place to go back to."

Ren looked back at her, stunned. Then her eyes narrowed and she nodded. "Okay," she said.

It was just one word, but Alex didn't doubt the fierce determination behind it. Ren would fight for her home.

Alex would, too. And yet, his feet suddenly felt heavier and his shoulders slumped under the weight of it. Up until now, he'd been concentrating on escape, on getting out of this hole they were in — literally — and getting his mom to safety.

But that was just the first step.

There was only one way to stop The Order now. They needed to recapture the Lost Spells. They needed to use their power to close the portals they'd opened, and to stop the Walkers they'd created. Ten-foot-tall Death Walkers, burning cities, advancing armies . . . It seemed too huge a task for so small and battered a crew. But there was something else he knew all too well: that this had all started when his mom had used those Spells to save him.

He lifted his shoulders and thought back to what he'd heard.

"The leader said he was going to the 'seat of power' to consult the Spells," said Alex, unwilling to say his father's name.

"The seat of power," said Todtman. The phrase seemed to mean something to him, and Alex was relieved. Back in

Peshwar's tomb, the scarab had allowed him to understand the meaning of the words intuitively. But as he was repeating them out loud, he'd felt himself hesitate, unsure whether to say "seat of power" or "seat of the soul." He'd picked the one that made the most sense to him, and he was glad it seemed to make sense to the others, too.

"Do you think he means Cairo?" said Ren. "I mean, that is the capital."

"And the site of The Order's headquarters," said Todtman.

"Wait," said Luke, "isn't this their headquarters?"

"This is where they build their tombs," said Todtman.

Ren clarified: "It's their dead-quarters."

Alex took one last look back at the quiet depths behind them. They were close to the surface now; he could feel it. No one was chasing them out, and no one was stopping them from leaving. The Order was unthreatened: invulnerable monsters leading ruthless men with limitless resources. They didn't seem to think there was any force left on earth that could stop them. But there was one force that was at least willing to try.

There was sunlight up ahead now, and Cairo beyond that.

## Deathquake

As the friends scrambled out of the tunnel mouth, the brutal Egyptian heat pounced on them like a waiting animal. The afternoon sun bore down with laser-beam intensity; after long, dark days underground, no one minded at all.

"Man, do I need this vitamin D!" crowed Luke, spreading his arms and turning his face toward the bright sky.

Alex eyed the sun-scalded landscape. Worn and weathered stone ruins jutted up from the sand. Directly in front of him, a stone foundation was just visible, the building that had once stood atop it lost to the ages. All around the phantom foundation, broken columns and shattered stone rose from the pale sand, like the bones of some great beast.

"They're ruins," said Alex's mom, "but I don't recognize them." Alex could practically hear her mind whirring through a lifetime of scholarship and travel.

"Nor do I," said Todtman. "Recently uncovered, I think."

"Yes," agreed Dr. Bauer. "Under the sand for a very long time. And modest."

"Definitely not a pharaonic site. A temple?"

"Maybe, maybe, but nothing fancy."

"Certainly not. A temple for commoners, then."

The two scholars nodded sagely, and Ren threw in a quick: "That's what I was thinking!"

"Yeah, uh, those sound like some real good points," said Luke. "But maybe we should be looking for a parking lot? You know, cars, roads? So we can get out of here?"

"Yeah," agreed Ren. "Last time we escaped from one of these thingies, there was a parking lot full of cars to steal."

Dr. Bauer gave her a surprised look.

"I mean borrow," said Ren with a shrug.

"This complex was bigger. There must be a lot of entrances," said Alex.

As the group scanned the broken landscape, the ground beneath them began to shake once more. Alex looked over at his mom with wide-open *uh-oh* eyes. The sand around them began to dance like flour tossed in a pan. The other tremors had been quick, beginning to subside almost as soon as they started. But this one kept gaining strength.

As the friends did their best to keep their balance — knees bent, arms out — the stone ruins began to faintly groan. A moment later, a nearby column crashed to the ground.

"I feel like a scrambled egg!" contributed Luke, a half-baked metaphor that somehow proved his point.

Then there was a "Yip!" of pure surprise from Todtman. The German had been knocked to his knees and a broad crack was growing in the sand next to him. He began

crawling away as best he could. But the crack spread, a jagged black opening in the earth that sucked in hundreds of pounds of sand as it grew.

Alex watched in horror as the foundation of the old building began to tip and slide sideways into the ground.

Another jolt knocked Alex and his mom to the ground. Alex felt his body beginning to slide down into the sand as it vibrated all around him. His mom was seated on the ground next to him with her eyes closed and a grimace of pain on her face as she clutched her side. "Mom!" he shouted.

Another crack opened up, closer and spreading outward like a slow smile. Alex was terrified it would swallow him whole.

But almost immediately, everything changed.

It stopped being about what the dancing sand would swallow and became about what it would reveal.

A ragged hand thrust itself out of the ancient earth and into the broad, clear light of day.

The hand clawed at the edge of the spreading black gap. The hand, and then the forearm, and then the elbow appeared and hooked itself over the edge. Falling sand washed over it — catching here and there in the time-yellowed linen that wrapped the arm — but still it kept clawing forward.

Alex was so mesmerized by the sight that he barely noticed the tattered hand breaking through the sand right next to him. It was only when the bony fingers hooked the cuff of his jeans that he snapped out of it.

"What the —" he blurted. He shook his leg, but that just made the thing latch on tighter. Alex grabbed his leg with both hands and tried to tug it free, but the hand tugged right back, using the motion to help pull itself up, a fish that wanted to be caught.

He dropped his calf and reached for the scarab. As soon as his hand closed around it, he sandblasted the mummy's hand free with a whipping lash of desert wind.

As he did, a bright white flash lit his vision like a camera flash. Ren's amulet.

He risked a quick look over, in case she needed help — and that's when he saw it.

He had broken the grip of one hand, but what about the next? And the next? And the thousand after that? Because the entire landscape had transformed from one of sand and stone to one of clawing hands and grasping arms.

Soon, the first heads emerged: time-stained linen pulling free, eyeless sockets staring upward at the sun, and mouths full of jagged brown teeth spitting sand.

Mummies. Everywhere.

The tattered corpses pulled themselves from the earth, grabbing the edges of the old stone blocks, the bases of the old columns, and anything else that seemed solid.

Grabbing anything at all that remained of this commoners' temple. This mass grave.

The undying army had arrived.

# Legions of the Dead

Alex pushed his hand down into the shifting sand — nearly shaking hands with an emerging mummy in the process — and struggled to his feet. He took hold of his mom's wrist. "Ready?" he shouted over the rumbling din.

She nodded, and he leaned back and heaved her to her feet. Her face was stoic and determined despite the pain, and that gave Alex strength, too.

"Here," he said, holding out the scarab. "It's yours, and you're better with it, anyway. Maybe you can hold them off." Alex had seen what his mom could do with the scarab during their last clash with The Order, and it was *awesome*. His mom reached out, but as soon as her hand closed around the ancient artifact, her eyes rolled back in her head and she tipped backward toward the shifting sand.

Alex reached out and grabbed her arm just in time to keep her from falling. Her pulse was racing like a drum solo beneath her skin. The supercharged boost the amulet imparted — the pounding pulse and surging adrenaline —

was too much for his mom's weakened system. The realization that she was hurt even worse than she was letting on hit him like a baseball bat. He reached over and pried the scarab from her hand.

As she recovered from the rush, gasping for breath, Alex hooked his arm around her waist and led her forward gently — or as gently as he could in the rumbling tumult all around. After years of her taking care of him — worrying over every ache and cough and fall — it was his turn. He kept his grip tight and his eyes on the death-torn ground.

"Which way?" shouted Luke, hustling over to help Todtman to his feet.

"There!" called Ren, pointing.

Alex followed her finger and saw sunlight reflecting off a lump of glass and steel in the distance — *a car!*

They hobbled toward it, not walking as much as continually falling forward. All around them, gaps and chasms yawned open in the sand, and leathery hands grabbed at anything solid. Even worse, some of the mummies were beginning to pull themselves out of the ground entirely.

As Alex concentrated on keeping his mom upright, a squat, five-foot human husk turned to stare at him through empty, faintly glowing eye sockets. But the mummy made no move toward Alex and his mom as they labored past. It just stood in the sun, swaying slightly and dripping sand.

"How old do you think these are?" he asked his mom, trying to keep her distracted from the pain.

She assessed the swaying corpse. "Twenty-five hundred years. The first of these mass graves was only discovered recently, but they seem to be mostly from the Late Period."

Alex remembered when the first of the grave sites had been discovered. It was just a few years earlier, right before his shaky health had forced him to start homeschooling — and long before his magical recovery. It had been the talk of the Met break room: the discovery of hundreds of thousands of mummified bodies. They had no treasure or tombs of their own, just the occasional coin or trinket tucked into their wrappings and a big shared hole in the ground.

The friends weaved their way through the legions of the dead, acres of Egypt's former middle class.

"Why aren't they attacking?" called Ren.

"Give 'em time," hollered Luke. "They had a rough trip!"

Alex eyed a wraithlike mummy, its long arms hanging down like willow branches. *Is that it?* he thought. *Are they just recharging, like solar cells in the desert sun?*

Sweat ran down his forehead and into his eyes. His shirt was plastered slickly against his back, and his left arm ached as he tried to carry as much of his mom's weight as possible. Her jagged breathing gave him a sick, worried feeling that lay on top of his own fear like two feet of mud.

The glare from the glass washed across his eyes, snapping him back to attention. What he'd hoped was a parking lot full of sleek getaway cars was, in fact, a single battered old minivan on a small square of cracked pavement.

Todtman limped straight for the driver's-side door. Another jolt rocked the ground, extending the long cracks in the pavement. Alex crouched down low, but the tremors were subsiding now, the earth moving fitfully as it settled.

The entire landscape between them and the tomb exit was now covered with swaying bodies, like a windblown grassland of the dead. Here and there stragglers clawed up from the sand to join them, the mummies already on the surface stooping down to haul them free.

"There must be ten thousand of them," Alex said, his voice soft with awe.

"And it's not over yet," said his mom, pointing out into the desert where still more of the undead were emerging an acre or two at a time.

"They seem to be waiting for something," said Todtman.

He was right. A moment later, the leader — Alex's father — emerged from the same tomb exit they had used.

The raggedly wrapped and mismatched bodies stopped swaying and began to line up in neat rows.

"Groups of twenty," said Ren, counting quickly.

Even across hundreds of yards and with thousands of mummies between them, the leader's massive frame stood out like a park statue. He raised one mighty hand in the air, and the tattered soldiers of the undying army snapped rigidly to attention for their general.

A cold and exposed feeling swept over Alex: the overwhelming sensation of being watched. He couldn't see his

father's eyes at this distance, but he could definitely feel them.

*Fuhhh-SHOOOOP!*

It was the sound of one hundred dry bodies turning as one. The five units closest to the parking lot had simultaneously dug their left heels into the sand and turned crisply toward the gawking friends.

"I think we should go now," said Todtman.

Behind them, one hundred unkillable soldiers rushed forward.

Alex helped his mom across the cracked pavement toward the battered minivan. He gripped her tight and used all his strength to haul her forward. But her injuries had taken their toll. The toe of her left boot caught in a crack as she dragged it heavily over the pavement, and they both went down in a heap.

Alex risked a quick look behind them. The undead were coming. With old bones and dry flesh, most of them were running none too fluidly, either. But there was one moving faster than the rest, fired forward from their ranks like a missile. Alex wrapped his arms around his mom and tried to haul her from the pavement.

Suddenly, strong arms grabbed him. Alex prepared to be torn limb from limb — but it was Luke. He'd come back for

them and was now lifting both his cousin and his aunt to their feet.

"Let's go!" he shouted. "Bauer power!"

They stumbled up and forward. "Watch out," said Alex. With his hands supporting his mom, he couldn't grasp his scarab and could only nod at the lone mummy approaching ahead of the pack.

"I got him," said Luke.

Alex looked at him skeptically. *Maybe if I can get one hand on the scarab . . .*

"Get your mom to the van, man!" shouted Luke. "I said I got this."

As Alex turned and hustled his mom toward the minivan, he could already hear the bony slaps of the sprinting mummy's feet against the pavement.

Todtman and Ren were in the van now, the big side door wide open. "Come on, Mom," he said. "Just a little farther."

Her reply was cut off by a hoarse cry from the onrushing mummy, and Alex turned his head back just as the sprinting corpse crashed into Luke. "No!" gasped Alex.

Instead of avoiding the mummy's grasp, Luke grasped it right back. As he did, he whipped his shoulders around and ducked down, using all of the ragged creature's momentum to toss it over his hip. "Aiyah!" he shouted.

Suddenly, the mummy's dry old bones were bouncing across the cracked pavement — and Alex and his mom were arriving at the minivan. Alex heard the engine start up —

coaxed to life by Todtman's amulet — and saw Ren's hands reach out from the side door to help his mom in. He looked back for Luke, who was bending down to pick up something shiny from the asphalt. Behind him, the first mummy was already climbing back to its feet — and ninety-nine more were rushing onto the lot.

"Get over here!" shouted Alex.

Luke palmed his shiny find and rushed for the door.

Alex climbed in after his mom as the minivan began rolling. Luke leapt into the open door as the lumbering vehicle began a slow turn toward the road. Alex leaned back and did his best to catch his cousin as he thumped down inside.

Ren slammed the door closed and Todtman stomped on the gas.

He ran over two mummies who'd managed to get in front of them. The van rose up and down on its old shock absorbers to a sound track of sickening crunches. But a moment later, they were up to full speed and pulling away from the rest of the pack. Todtman wrestled the lumbering vehicle around a sharp turn and off the lot.

Open road stretched out ahead, and the fields of the undead disappeared in the rearview mirror. Alex helped his mom settle into the bench seat in the back of the van.

"Just need to rest a little," she said.

"I know," he said. Her battered body needed to shut down to heal. Sick for almost his whole life, he knew all

about that. He spied a dusty horseshoe-shaped travel pillow hooked around the armrest and handed it to her. She placed it between her injured ribs and the seat. Soon, her eyes fluttered closed and her ragged breathing calmed slightly.

Alex wiped the first trace of a tear from his eye, exhaled, and returned to the first row of seats. He watched the road disappear under the minivan's wheels. There were other cars on the road now, a freeway entrance up ahead. They were back in the real world.

*Next stop, "the seat of power,"* he thought. Even though The Order members had managed to assume their Stone Warrior forms, the Spells could still end all this, could send the undead back to the afterlife and shut the doors for good. But he knew the mummies and Walkers weren't the only ones who could be undone by the Spells . . .

He shook his head hard, trying to clear the thought away. Then he turned to his cousin. "Thanks, man," he said. "You really came through back there."

Even Ren chimed in. "Yeah, that was pretty cool of you," she admitted. "That mummy was going like a thousand miles an hour."

Luke just shrugged. "Judo, yo," he said. "It's awesome cross-training." His attention was on the shiny object swinging from a rusty chain in his hand.

"Is that what you picked up off the pavement?" asked Alex.

"Yeah," said Luke, still not taking his eyes off it. "It came flying out of that mummy's wrapping when I hip-tossed him. Pretty cool, right?"

Alex nodded. He knew that mummies were often buried with amulets and other charms tucked into their wrappings.

This one was in the form of a cheetah, the world's fastest animal.

# ∩

## Road Worrier

Ren watched Luke as he brushed the last crusty bits of sand and clay from the little bronze cat. *No way it works for him*, she thought. She trusted him more after seeing him put his life on the line to save Alex and his mom. But she still didn't see him as Amulet Keeper material.

"Put it on!" said Alex.

Luke looked down at it. "What, like man jewelry?" he said. He glanced over at the spot where Alex's scarab hung from its fine silver chain. "No offense."

"Whatever," said Alex. "See if it *does* anything."

Luke stared at him.

"Well?" said Alex.

"You tell me," Luke said. "I just tried to hypnotize you."

"Tell me to do something," said Alex.

"Flap your arms like a peacock."

Alex's arms stayed by his sides. He looked down at them, one after the other, and said, "Nothing."

"Maybe it does something else," offered Ren.

Luke squinted at her, as if trying to read the last line of an eye chart. "Not unless you're levitating," he said.

Ren looked down. There was no space between her and her seat, not even a spare centimeter. "Nope."

"Doesn't work," he said, sitting back. "I'll tell you what, though."

"What?" said Alex.

"I do feel pretty . . ." He searched for the right word, giving Alex time to blurt out: "You feel pretty?"

Luke jokingly shook his fist at him. "No, I feel pretty, like, stoked. I was pretty tired from all that . . ." He waved his hand behind them. "That sitting in a cell and then the mummy stuff and everything. But as soon as I put it on, I felt totally pumped."

"Great," said Ren. "Your amulet has the power of a large coffee."

Luke looked down at it. "Good enough for me," he said. "Think I'll call it coffee cat."

Ren sank back into her seat — and into her thoughts. The coffee cat line had reminded her of Pai, the creepy-cute mummy cat who had sacrificed herself to save Ren from an ancient Death Walker in a desert pit. *Was she really gone for good?* she wondered, remembering her little body, battered, bent, and limp. She humored herself with the thought that, if cats had nine lives, Pai had seven left.

Her thoughts shifted to the mission ahead. This was a war now. They'd just seen the army, and its first target was

New York. *Home.* She couldn't let that happen. They had to find the Lost Spells. But even if they could, there was a problem. Alex's mom had gone into hiding with the Spells to try to find a way to undo the magic that had saved his life without undoing him. The Death Walkers and their army had returned to this world, thanks to the Spells — but so had Alex. Sending them back risked sending him back, too. But they'd found his mom before she'd figured out a solution — and led The Order right to her.

Now they were racing toward Cairo, where The Order held the Spells. Trying to recapture them, hoping to use them to save her parents, her city, her everything. Everything except her best friend.

He could be racing toward his grave.

Ren couldn't see any good way to reconcile the two problems. The idea of two problems with two separate and mutually exclusive solutions made her so uncomfortable that she physically squirmed in her torn vinyl seat. She'd faced hard tests before, ones where she had to scrap for partial credit — and extra credit — just to salvage a B+.

But she'd never faced a test that seemed quite so unfair.

The minivan bumped to a stop. Dr. Bauer groaned and shifted in her seat as Ren leaned forward to look out the windshield. Her heart started thumping as she saw a large wooden police barrier with armed men standing on either side. One of them stepped around toward Todtman's window. The guard took one look at Todtman's pale skin and spoke in English.

"You have been stopped because your vehicle matches one we are looking for," said the man.

"Stopped under whose authority?" countered Todtman.

The man smiled. "The Order's, of course," he said, his fingers drumming lightly on the barrel of his gun. "We are the only authority now."

Ren's racing heart did a little backflip, but her mind was oddly clear. *So the conquest wouldn't start in New York, after all*, she thought. She had been underground for too long. *Up here, the conquest was well underway.*

"Out of the vehicle," said the man, his voice rising, his machine gun pointed at Todtman's face. "All of you," he barked. "Get out!"

Alex woke his mom. "We're in trouble," he said softly. "Again."

It seemed like a crime to pry her from the sleep she needed, but it was a crime committed at gunpoint. The gun barrel was inches from Todtman's protruding, slightly frog-like eyes as he slowly opened his door. Still, Alex knew their mentor could slide his hand up to his amulet and scramble the gunman's mind like two eggs at a whisk convention.

The problem was the other three. One of them was coming around now to open the side door of the minivan, but the other two remained far apart on either side of the traffic barrier. Their machine guns were trained on the vehicle.

Alex could take out one of them with a powerful lance of mystic wind, no problem. But by the time he could turn his amulet's power on the second, the bullets would be flying, and his mom was defenseless.

The odds of flooring it and busting through the barricade were no better. You can't make a high-speed escape in a low-speed vehicle.

Still, as they all reluctantly climbed out of the old beater, Alex's mom carrying her threadbare travel pillow like a kid with a teddy bear, he tried to make eye contact with Todtman. Maybe they could coordinate: *You get that one, I'll get this one, and then we, um, duck?*

"Your amulets," said the first guard, his gun barrel dipping from Todtman's froggy face to his avian amulet. "Give them to me."

Alex blinked up into the baking Egyptian sun and groaned. His mind raced: It was now or never.

*PAKKA-PAKKA-PAK!*

The second guard rattled off three shots in the air, making Alex jump.

He fought his racing pulse and slowly slid his hand up toward his scarab.

"Lift them off only by the chains," said the first guard. "Touch the amulets and you die."

So they knew all about the amulets and their power. Out of the corner of his eye, Alex saw one of the guards by the barricade talking low and fast into a cell phone. Alex was

sure the man was reporting the capture to his bosses, and maybe asking if they should take them prisoner or just gun them down on the side of the road.

"What a bummer," said Luke, reaching up for his cheetah. "I just got this thing."

Alex looked over and saw his cousin's hand brush the cheetah on the way up — and then he saw nothing but a swirl of sand and dust in the sunlight.

*SHOOOMP!*

All of a sudden, Luke was in front of Alex, grabbing the gun from the guard who'd fired the warning shots. Alex blinked in disbelief, and in the time it took his eyes to open and close — *WHOOSH!* — Luke was already next to the main guard, smacking him over the head with the butt of the other man's gun. *WHUMP!*

Before that one could even fall to the ground, Luke was somehow all the way over by the barricade, lowering his shoulder into the first guard there. *THUDD!* The man flew through the air and crashed gracelessly to the pavement.

*PAKKA-PAKKA-PAK!*

*Oh no!* The fourth guard was firing at Luke.

But Luke was already gone. Seeing only open air, the guard ceased fire and looked around wildly. Alex saw Luke before the guard did. His cousin, now standing behind the man, tapped him casually on the shoulder. The man swung around — right into a punch that lifted him off his feet.

As the man fell to the ground unconscious —
*SHOOOMP!* — Luke was back by the others, standing next
to the door of the minivan and shaking his hand in mild
pain.

"How —" stammered Alex. "How did you —"

"Don't know, exactly," said Luke, "but as soon as I touched
the amulet, I just felt, like, supercharged."

Alex watched as the first guard — the one Luke had only
disarmed — ran off down the road. The other three were all
in various states of beatdown.

"The amulet must grant some sort of temporary physical
augmentation," mused Todtman.

"The cheetah was a symbol of both strength and power in
dynastic times," added Alex's mom.

"That was *AAAWWESOMME!*" gushed Alex.

Luke, still pale from his underground confinement,
actually blushed as he looked down at his amulet. "Well,
I kind of had an unfair advantage," he admitted. Then he
looked up and smiled. "I guess you could say I'm a cheata."

## A Chaotic Capital

They stayed off the main roads after that. Ren was in the front seat, helping navigate with a crumpled old map, and Luke was conked out in back. As impressive as the cheetah amulet had been, it seemed to take a physical toll on him. After a few more miles, they pulled into a gas station convenience store to get food, gas, and a better map.

When Alex climbed back into the backseat to bring his mom aspirin and water, he was surprised to find her awake again. "You should be resting," he said.

"Not right now," she said, patting the seat next to her. "There's something I need to tell you."

"What?" said Alex. "Is it your side? Should we try to find a hospital?"

She shook her head and answered softly. "It's your father," she said as the old van pulled back out onto the road and headed into the dusk. "You deserve to know."

As Todtman switched on the headlights, Ren puzzled out the new map, and Luke ate half their food, Alex sat

absolutely still and listened to the story of how he came to be.

"We met in Alexandria," she said. "We were both young and both in love: with each other, and with archaeology."

Alex tried to picture the monster he'd met as a young student with a head full of pyramids and hieroglyphs. As a grad student in love.

"We were both so passionate about our work," his mother continued. Amir, your father . . . He was obsessed with finding the Lost Spells even then. I searched with him — and when you were born, you came, too. But the search took us to dark places, searching every secret and forbidden site we could find. These were cursed places no child should have been. I didn't realize until it was too late the toll it was taking — on you, on your health."

Alex couldn't believe it: an entire childhood of pain. Sickness the doctors could never fix. He looked up at his mom, but she was staring straight ahead now, into the past. "That's when you left him?" he said, hoping — almost needing — to hear her say yes.

She shook her head. "That's when I tried," she said. "But he had discovered something else. The mask. Its power fueled his obsession, turned it into something more like madness. He used the mask's power to control me, to keep me close. It wasn't until I discovered something of equal power that I could break free."

"The scarab," said Alex, touching the amulet.

His mom nodded. "The scarab. But by then the damage had been done . . . Honey, I am so sorry. More sorry than you will ever know."

But she was wrong. He knew exactly. He looked up at her, and this time he caught a glimpse of her blue-gray eyes. For the first time, he truly understood the depth behind them. She'd had a life before him, one with triumphs and mistakes of her own. She hadn't understood the damage those dark places were doing to him, but she'd paid the price as much as he had. She'd worried and fretted over him every single day since. She'd cared for and eventually saved him — at great cost to her, at great cost to everyone.

*My mom didn't know the danger*, he thought, *but my dad didn't care*. He couldn't find the words to say any of this to his mom. Instead, he leaned across the seat and wrapped his arms around her as she wrapped hers around him.

After hours of driving, a low glow lit the horizon: city lights caught in a suffocating net of heavy smog.

Cairo.

"Mom, look," he whispered. But she was resting again, her eyes closed, her breathing shallow — and this was no longer the Cairo she had told him about. When he was a kid, she'd made the crazy traffic, wild outside bazaars, and winding side alleys sound like a loud vibrant adventure. No

more. This was a haunted city now, the death-shrouded capital of a country in crisis.

He felt the fear building inside him as they reached the edge of the city and drove toward. The Order's headquarters on the other side of the capital. Alex stared out at the dark streets as the unflappable German drove steadily onward. Alex could already see an open fire burning a few blocks away, flickering flames illuminating a plume of rising smoke. Most of the streetlights were burned out or broken. Todtman slowed down to steer around a car abandoned in the middle of the road. As soon as they cleared it, a pack of stray dogs met them on the other side, barking fiercely. Todtman stepped on the gas, and the mangy mongrels began to chase them, an interchangeable mass of matted fur and snapping teeth.

They lost the dogs and passed the fire, but soon the four-lane road narrowed. Stacked sandbags funneled them into a single lane at the center. Todtman slowed the minivan again, and they all eyed the checkpoint nervously. But there were no armed men this time. No men at all.

It creeped Alex out: Eight million people lived in this city — or used to — and so far they hadn't seen a single soul.

The van rolled slowly through the gap and was suddenly buffeted with bumps and barks and scratches. The dogs had chased them down. Alex looked to his right and saw a large black mutt just below him. It leapt up, scratching at the window. Specks of foamy drool dotted the safety glass as the dog snapped off a quick, hoarse bark.

Todtman cleared the opening and floored it.

The dogs disappeared again into the smoky night.

"Man," said Luke. "Those were some hungry dogs."

"Not hungry," said Ren. "Rabid."

Alex nervously eyed the gobs of virulent drool on the other side of his window as the hot wind outside stretched and dried them.

As they drove deeper into the city, houses and apartment buildings shouldered up from the sidewalks on either side, and Alex was relieved to see the occasional sliver of light slipping through closed blinds.

"Where *is* everybody?" said Ren.

"There's someone!" said Luke, leaning between the seats and pointing. Alex turned and saw a shadowy figure making slow progress across the street. Todtman took his foot of the gas and slowed down as they approached. But as the minivan rolled slowly forward, its headlights hit the figure — and lit its tattered linen.

The mummy swung around and gaped at them, faintly glowing reddish orbs where its eyes should have been. Releasing a ragged, wordless scream, it charged straight at the van's dented hood.

*"Gott im Himmel,"* mumbled Todtman as he stomped the gas and swung the wheel.

The minivan sideswiped the charging mummy as it swerved past — one lumbering old heap striking another — sending the tightly wrapped corpse bouncing up onto the curb.

Alex swung his head around and saw the creature already pushing itself to its feet and setting off after them. Just behind him, he saw the crazed dogs appear at a full run one streetlight back.

There was a loud screech of metal on metal as Todtman rammed the minivan between two more abandoned cars, one in each lane. Alex saw his mom wake up and look around, and he climbed one row back to sit next to her.

"It might be better to travel at night," she said to him. "When Cairo seems too dangerous even for The Order."

Alex nodded and craned his neck to check the time on the dashboard clock: *11:58 p.m.* The problem, of course, was that a city dangerous for The Order was infinitely more dangerous for everyone else. As the clock flicked to 11:59, Ren called out from the front seat: "What is that up there?"

Alex looked where she was pointing and saw a shifting shape on the roof of a low-slung industrial complex, outlined against the moon. At first, he couldn't tell what it was. The image kept shifting. Pieces tore off it and flitted away as other fragments dove in to rejoin it. But as they passed directly underneath, he got a better look.

The shape was that of a large man.

And the pieces tearing free and diving back looked like oversized wasps, purple-black in the moonlight. They grew larger and more defined the farther they flew, but up close they were small. Small and shifting and numerous: hundreds, maybe thousands, of shadowy swarming shapes.

His mom spoke beside him. Her words were so soft that he barely heard them over the rumble of the van. But he didn't really need to. He was thinking the same thing.

*"Death Walker."*

Todtman punched the gas and accelerated out of sight of the grim figure, but the image of swarming evil stayed in Alex's mind as the old van wound deeper into the city's desolate warehouse district.

## Gone

Stiff from the long trip and in various states of injury and exhaustion, the crew crept along the moonlit street like a determined intensive care unit. The Order's secret head-quarters was the last looming structure in a row of dark, deserted warehouses.

· "We're here," whispered Todtman.

"Cool," said Alex, looking up at the blank black windows. "Should we have, like, a plan?"

"We will catch them off guard and move quickly," said Todtman, but he said it while hobbling along with the speed and grace of a three-legged turtle. "We know the Spells are in 'the seat of power.' The last thing they will expect is for us to come straight to them in the middle of the night."

"Yeah, don't sweat it, cuz," added Luke. "I got your back."

Alex looked over at him. Maybe the plan was crazy enough to work: While The Order probably thought they were fleeing for their lives, they'd rush in and grab the Spells. And with Luke's cheetah, they had more firepower than ever. Maybe they had a chance.

As they approached a small side door, Alex pulled his scarab out from under his collar and felt its reassuring weight in his hand. The weight in his other arm was less reassuring. It would be hard to fight while helping his mom stay on her feet.

They reached the door.

"Unguarded," said Ren.

"*Seemingly* unguarded," cautioned Todtman.

But Alex barely heard them. Now that he believed they could succeed, he'd finally asked himself a more complex question: *What if they did?* In a cell or on the run, it had been easy enough to concentrate on escape. But what if the Lost Spells really were in there? The plan was to use them to close the rift between the worlds of the living and the worlds of the dead — to undo the damage that had been done when that doorway had been opened to save his life. The risk — the one no one seemed willing to talk about — was that it would undo him, too.

Alex heard a click as Todtman used his amulet to unlock the door. "Okay," said the scholar. "Carefully now."

Todtman pushed open the door, and Luke ducked inside for a look, but Alex could barely focus on the danger ahead of them. His mind was churning. Back when they were still searching for his mom, he'd blamed himself for all the trouble his second shot at life had caused, and he'd been ready to sacrifice himself to make it right.

But finding his mom had changed things, and the story she'd just told him had changed them more. He'd chewed

over those words in the dark: His father's obsessive search for the Spells was the reason he'd been sick in the first place. The wheels of all this had been set in motion before he could even walk.

And if all that was true, he wasn't the cause of all this trouble. He was the first victim.

Alex wondered, deep down, if maybe he had sacrificed enough. If maybe there was another way. The Spells were so powerful, after all. How close had his mom been to puzzling out a solution with them? Maybe —

"All clear," said Luke, pulling his head back out the dark gap of the open door.

The group slipped inside. Weak moonlight shone gauzily into the huge, hangar-like space from rows of dirty windows twenty feet up. The friends stood silently as their eyes adjusted to the dim light.

"Nothing," whispered Ren. "It's empty."

Todtman knelt down and rubbed the floor with one finger. "Stone dust," he said. "This is where they carved the statues that they now inhabit. I saw the blocks the last time I was here."

Alex felt his mom's weight sink down against his arm and shoulder as she relaxed a little and let out a long, jagged breath. He pushed the toe of one boot along the concrete floor and felt the stony grit. So this was where The Order had begun turning themselves into ten-foot-tall monsters.

"There are doors in the back there," said Luke.

Alex stared where he pointed, but all he saw was blackness.

"Are you sure?" he said.

"Totally," said Luke, and as he turned toward him, Alex saw that his eyes were glowing a soft green. Just like a cheetah's.

"Can you see in the dark?" asked Alex.

"I guess so."

Alex tried to stay quiet as they crept across the floor, but supporting his mom was hard work, and his huffing breath echoed through the cavernous space, mixing with the soft plinks of Todtman's staff.

As they got closer, he saw three doors. The first one was the heaviest, and it seemed to have been blown out from the inside. The heavy steel bar that had once secured it lay bent almost in half on the floor nearby.

Alex saw nothing but blackness inside and stepped aside for Luke to take a look with his cat eyes. "Anything?"

"Nuh-uh," said Luke. "It's like a vault or something. No windows, no nothing."

And the other two rooms were just abandoned offices. Alex heard Ren take a corner too tightly in the dark and slam her shin into the side of a desk.

"Ow!" she huffed, and then: "This is ridiculous!"

She took three quick strides over to the wall. "No, Ren, don't!" hissed Todtman, but it was too late.

She flicked on the lights.

Alex stood blinking in the sudden brightness. When the stars and swirls cleared away, he saw everything there was to see. It wasn't much.

"Empty," said Ren. "This whole place has been cleared out."

Alex's mom settled into an office chair as the others searched around for hidden doorways, passages leading down, anything at all. They even used their amulets to probe the walls and floors. After half an hour, Todtman called a halt to it.

"Nothing," he agreed. "Whatever was in here is gone."

They returned to the main room and looked around the modest old warehouse under the weak electric light.

"This isn't the seat of power anymore, is it?" said Alex.

Todtman smacked the floor angrily with his scuffed staff. "I don't think it ever was."

The Amulet Keepers were quiet for a few moments, and then they heard the banging on the corrugated steel walls of the warehouse. Something was outside — or some things.

Todtman looked up at the old fixtures above them. "The lights have attracted attention," he said. "We should leave."

"But where are we going?" asked Ren as they hustled toward the same door they'd come in.

"To see an old friend," said Todtman. "If he is still alive."

# A Night at the Museum

"There it is," said Alex's mom as a familiar red edifice rose up in front of them.

The battered old minivan had made it back to the city's center. It had even started on the first try — a good thing since there'd been a dozen glowing red eyes approaching its rearview mirror at the time.

A massive brick building loomed above the electric haze of Tahrir Square. Once again, they had returned to the mighty Egyptian Museum.

They parked the stalwart van on a side street and made their way to the museum's massive front doors. No alarm sounded as Alex used the scarab to unlock the heavy double doors. He took one last look behind them as they slipped inside, to see if they'd been followed. All he saw were shifting shadows and dancing moonlight in the eerily empty square.

Inside, the legendary museum was lit only by dim lights from a few display cases and red exit signs. Scattered around these deep shadows, he knew, were some 120,000 exhibits.

What Alex didn't see were any people, or any signs of recent activity at all. Once teeming with a daily army of tourists, the place now felt like an especially epic, million-square-foot attic.

Moving through the first room, Alex's mom had stepped free of his supporting arm, as if the building itself had given her strength. Alex used his suddenly free hand to trace a finger across a glass display case, drawing a track in the thin layer of dust.

"I'm afraid I've let the place go a bit," came a voice. "But we get very few visitors these days."

Alex's heart skipped a beat or three as the words echoed through the hall. But the voice was familiar, and so was the man stepping out of the shadows along the far wall.

Dr. Hesaan — he never had told them his first name — bowed slightly. As surprised as they were by his sudden appearance, he seemed equally surprised to see the new addition to their party. "Dr. Bauer," he said. "It is good to see you . . ." He trailed off before adding "alive."

She managed a quick smile. "You know I can't stay away from this place."

Alex was relieved to not hear quite as much ragged raspiness in her voice this time — and reassured by her friendly rapport with the man. The last time they'd seen the old curator, he'd been attempting to guard the closed museum with only a cricket bat.

"Where's your bat?" asked Alex.

"I don't have much use for it anymore," Hesaan said, shrugging slightly. "Only a lunatic would break in. This museum, like the rest of the city, is now run by The Order."

The friends bristled visibly.

"Relax," said Hesaan. "I hate them just as much as you do."

"But you work for them," said Ren skeptically.

Another shrug. "I work for the museum. I take care of it, as I always have. They simply allow me to."

"Why would they do that?" said Ren, still not convinced. "The last time I saw you, you were charging at them with your cricket bat."

"They allow it because I am the most qualified," he said. "I am the most familiar with this old building — and this much older collection — and its various needs."

Ren signaled she had another question by raising her right hand slightly, but Hesaan kept going. "You have to understand, for you this is a museum: old artifacts and old altars to old gods. To The Order, it is their religion."

Alex looked over at his mom to see what she thought of that. When she nodded in understanding, he did, too. The arrangement seemed clear enough. It was an uneasy truce between enemies, carved out over a small piece of common ground.

"We each have our part to play in this, my old friend," said Todtman to Hesaan. "And I am hoping you might be able to help us find some answers."

"I will do my best," said Hesaan. He stepped toward Todtman and exchanged the sort of quick, awkward hug at which academics have always excelled. "But first, it is late. Let me find you someplace to stay, something to eat. As you can see, I have plenty of extra space." He raised his voice slightly on the final word, and Alex heard it echo through the lacquered wood and polished marble of the empty museum: *space–ace–ace.*

Ren balled up her fist again, not to release a flash of spirit-zapping light this time, but to release . . . what? She was matched off with Luke in a game of rock-paper-scissors. At stake was the third-best sleeping spot in the old employee lounge where they were spending the night. Dr. Bauer and Todtman were the obvious choices for the two couches, and now Ren had her eye on the large woolen rug between them. She'd already defeated Alex, three to two. So far Luke had thrown two straight papers, and she'd cut through them with back-to-back scissors. Now she eyed her opponent carefully. *He wouldn't throw the same thing again . . . would he?*

"One, two," counted Alex. Ren and Luke drew back their hands. "Three!"

Ren threw her hand out, first two fingers V'd into scissors. She looked over at Luke's hand, spread out flat: paper. She smiled. *Of course he would.*

"I thought it had to win sooner or later," muttered Luke, shaking his head.

But there was one last item of business before the group could get some much-needed sleep. A few minutes later, all drowsy eyes were on Ren once again. She took a deep breath and raised her hand toward her amulet.

"Ask it where the Lost Spells are," said Alex.

It had never answered that particular question in the past, and the look she shot him said: *Why would it start now?*

Todtman volunteered an alternative: "Ask it where the seat of power is."

The ibis was an ancient amulet, not Google, and as Ren's hand hovered over the pale stone, she told herself all the things that had helped her get a handle on its power. It didn't offer answers, she reminded herself. It only gave her information: scenes from the past or present, possibilities for the future. And whatever it gave her was more than she had now. *Extra credit.* She formed the familiar, comforting words in her head.

Then she closed her eyes and wrapped her hand around the cool stone. She tried to think the words of Todtman's question as clearly as possible: *Where is the seat —* But before she could finish, another question popped into her head, fully formed and all but screaming for an answer: *Are my parents okay?*

She'd already tried to call home from Hesaan's office phone, but the line had been as dead as the museum's remaining mummies. Now, though, her ibis offered an open line. An image flashed through her mind's eye. The door of their

apartment, seen from the inside, with the chain latched and one of the good chairs from the living room table wedged under the doorknob.

As the scene unfolded the door began to shake, the chain rattled, and the chair wobbled. Something was outside the apartment, not knocking on the door but *beating* on it.

Ren gasped and opened her eyes. Her amulet fell from her hand.

"What did it show you?" said Todtman.

Ren shook her head.

"What?" he insisted.

She looked up at him, blinking away the tears that were just now beginning to appear. "Home," she said. "It showed me home."

Todtman looked at her sternly, but Alex's mom cut in before he could respond. "We're all tired," she said softly. "We'll try again in the morning. Okay, Ren?"

Ren nodded. She was tired: desperately, eye-flutteringly tired after their marathon day. But she also knew how important this was. The world was going up in flames, and they were at a standstill. She would try her best in the morning. She would focus hard and ask the question out loud. Still, she didn't hold out much hope. "It doesn't matter what I ask it," she said softly. "The ibis is in my head. It knows what I want to know."

She stretched out on the heavy rug, her body surrendering to her exhaustion even as her mind continued to pick at what

she'd just seen — *Was it the present, or a future they could still prevent?*

She heard Dr. Bauer shift on the couch above her and looked up to find her looking down. "We are all worried about home," she whispered. "We will fix this."

Ren nodded and tried to stay positive. She fell asleep not to images of destruction but to one of her favorite memories: Alex and his mom and Ren and her parents laughing together at a silly inside joke at the last museum holiday party.

But as the night wore on, her dreams turned dark. She dreamed that New York was under siege and would soon fall to The Order. She dreamed that her parents were in danger. It was the worst nightmare of her life.

And it was all true.

## The Seat of the Soul

Alex rolled over on his small, scratchy rug and groaned. Sunlight was streaming in through the windows. He turned toward his mom's couch. Empty.

He leapt up immediately, sending gift-shop throw pillows flying. But then he spotted her sitting with Todtman and Hesaan at a table by the wall. They were casually dipping flatbread in a beany paste and talking as they ate. Alex's mouth watered at the sight of the food, and he went to join them.

Ren was snoring lightly on the floor. Alex tried to be quiet as he passed, but she coughed up her last snore and her eyes popped open. He waited as she got up to join him.

Luke was still asleep in the corner, a small smile on his face hinting at pleasant dreams of athletic conquest. Alex and Ren let him sleep and headed for the table.

"How are you feeling, Mom?" asked Alex. Now that he was standing close enough, he could see that she was holding a plastic bag of ice against her side.

"Good morning, honey," she said. "I am feeling a little better." She paused and smiled. "Like I was hit by a car instead of a truck."

Beside him, Ren nodded solemnly, waited a respectable few seconds, and then dove for the food. *"Fuul!"* she said, pronouncing it like *fuel*.

*"Fool,"* said Hesaan, correcting her pronunciation.

"Yeah, say it right, fool," said Alex, satisfied that his mom really was feeling better. He picked up a piece of flatbread and dipped it into the dish of stewed fava beans. "What are you guys talking about?" he asked, pulling up a chair.

Todtman shifted over to make space at the table. "We were trying to figure out our mistake," he said. "You told us you heard the leader say that he would consult the Lost Spells in the seat of power . . ."

"And you assumed the seat of power was the old Order headquarters in Cairo," said Hesaan.

"Yes, but the place was abandoned," said Todtman, "cleaned out."

*Wait a second*, thought Alex. His brain was still foggy with sleep, but he tried to remember. *Wasn't there something about that phrase? Something he hadn't been sure of?* He chewed his food and chased the thought through the morning mist as the adults continued talking.

"Yes, why would they be hiding in a warehouse?" said Hesaan. "They have outgrown that little place now. They

have taken over the parliament building, and some others. During the day, they are everywhere in this city."

"Could the seat be the parliament building?" asked Alex's mom.

"Perhaps," said Hesaan skeptically. "But even as arrogant as they are, I would be surprised if they kept something so powerful in such a busy and accessible place. With their international provocations, there is constant talk that the other countries will bomb the place."

"Why don't they?" said Alex.

"They say the leader controls their minds, as needed, and stills their hands. They say that the man has grown immensely powerful."

Hesaan flicked a look over at Alex's mom as he spoke, and Alex wondered if Hesaan knew he was talking about her ex-husband.

"It's true," said Todtman. "But he is a man no longer."

Hesaan nodded gravely, seeming to understand.

Alex remembered the sight. The man who had once been his father, and what he had become: a massive Death Walker in a flickering tomb. He remembered the words rumbling out of his broad chest, Alex's amulet allowing him to understand the ancient dialect — and just like that, the mist lifted. "Wait a second," he sputtered through a mouthful of bean and bread.

The others turned to look at him. He swallowed his *fuul* and cleared his throat. "Okay, so, you guys know I don't speak ancient Egyptian, right? So I have to kind of rely on my amulet for that . . ."

"What is it, hun?" asked his mom, but Todtman was already a step ahead.

"What did he say?" asked the German.

"Well, I thought it was the 'seat of power,' but as I was saying it, I was kind of also thinking —"

"The seat of the soul?" offered Hesaan.

Alex stared at him. "Yeah, but . . . how did you know?"

"There is a word for power," said Hesaan. "An ancient word . . ."

"*Ba*," said Alex's mom. "The pharaoh's power to rule . . ."

Todtman's eyes grew wider, and he stammered excitedly: "Yes, but that word has more than one meaning . . ."

"What do you mean? What other meaning?" interrupted Ren. Alex watched her head spin from one scholar to another and knew she hated to be left out of this.

Alex's mom explained, "*Ba* can mean the soul, too."

"Not the seat of power," said Todtman. "The seat of the *soul*. That's where they have taken the Spells."

"Wait, wait, wait," said Ren. "I seriously hope you are not going to say —"

But the three scholars said it as one: "To the afterlife."

"They have taken the Spells to the one place they are sure no one else can reach them," added Todtman.

"But how is that possible?" said Hesaan, dumbfounded.

Ren looked over at him with a hangdog expression. "Oh, it's possible, all right," she said. "It's just not any fun."

Hesaan looked at her incredulously. "You have been there?"

"We both have," said Alex, remembering their sprint through the treacherous, twilight murk of the Egyptian afterlife. It was a spectral shortcut that had taken them thousands of miles in moments. "It's the amulets that let us do it," he added, trying to explain the inexplicable. "They allow us to go through the false doors."

They all sat silently at the little table, thunderstruck by this new revelation. Footsteps approached. Luke plucked a crumbly white block speckled with blue dots from the breakfast tray. "I sure hope this is cheese," he said, taking a big bite.

"It was cheese a week ago . . ." said Hesaan, staring down at the table.

"It is blue cheese now," said Todtman. "But save some of that for Alex and Ren. They will need their strength today, too."

"Wait, what do you mean?" said Alex.

"Well, you have been there before," said Hesaan, eyeing the lump of Alex's amulet beneath his shirt. "And there are *many* false doors at this museum."

Alex had already finished his breakfast, but he swallowed hard, anyway. His mom put her hand on his shoulder, either seeking to reassure him or concerned he would faint.

He was going back to the afterlife.

He looked over at Ren. She looked like she had seen a ghost.

She was certainly about to.

## To the Afterlife

Alex felt like he was being rushed.

And he was. His mom had offered to make the trip in place of him and Ren, but then she'd barely been able to get out of her chair on her own.

"I'll go with them," said Luke. "I've got one of those gizmos, too." Calling his ancient cheetah amulet a "gizmo" undercut his credibility, but his next statement was more convincing: "You can't just send two nerds to the afterlife alone."

The search party grew to three, and it had been full steam ahead after that.

"You have everything you need now," said Todtman, handing Alex a worn-out backpack rescued from the museum's lost and found room and filled with handpicked artifacts.

Alex slipped it on and felt the bow of an ancient wooden carving of a boat jab him in the back. He shrugged his shoulders to shift the little boat over and heard metal clink against metal at the bottom of the pack.

Then the three could avoid it no longer. They turned to face the false door. It was one of the largest Alex had ever seen, a six-foot-high slab of stone with a rectangular indentation at its center painted a faded red ocher and bordered by raised reliefs of columns. Hieroglyphic writing was carved deep into the ancient stone. It was a symbolic gateway to the afterlife, but in about two steps, it was about to get very real.

Alex pulled the scarab out from under his shirt.

"Be careful, Alex," said his mom. Alex heard something different in her voice, not a torn raspiness but a quiver of deep concern that sounded almost as painful. "You too, Ren . . . And even you, Luke. If you are in danger, come back."

Todtman listened with a just-sucked-lemon look on his face that seemed to say: *Come back? They haven't even left yet!* His actual words were only slightly more diplomatic:

"Yes, be careful, of course — but do not waste time! The world of the living and the world of the dead are very close now. We have seen it ourselves: mummies by the thousands, spirits in the streets. The boundaries are falling, and The Order is getting stronger. Look for signs of The Order when you cross over. Even in the afterlife, they will guard their prize closely. Use your amulets to guide you, if you can. We must find the Lost Spells and repair the damage they're done to our world."

Alex looked away. Todtman could say "we" until he was blue in his froggy face, but he wasn't going. He was staying back: Mission Control to their moon shot, and reinforce-

ments if necessary. Still, Alex knew he was right. The worlds were closer now. His mom had used the Spells to open a gateway between them, to bring him back. Now The Order was using the Spells to tear down the walls — to use the power of the world of the dead to rule the world of the living. The old legend was coming true. The Final Kingdom was almost here.

Almost.

They still had one last, desperate chance.

Alex took a deep breath and one more look at his mom. He opened and closed his mouth, like a guppy, but he couldn't even begin to think of what to say. Instead, he just nodded. Reluctantly, she nodded, too. He looked over at Ren and Luke.

"Let's do this," he said with as much bravery as he could muster. It wasn't much.

Luke gave him a sympathetic look. "Nice try, cuz," he said. "But it goes like this . . ." His next words would've fit right in in a football huddle: "LET'S DO THIS!"

Alex had to admit, it sounded better coming from him. He was even a little fired up by it. Without another word, Alex wrapped his hand around his scarab and stepped toward solid stone.

Beside him, Ren said two words, very softly: "For home." Then she stepped forward, too.

Right behind them, Luke said, "It's go time."

The next thing Alex heard was a loud *POP!*

His vision turned red as he passed through the stone, and he closed his eyes instinctively. When he opened them again, he was in a different world. The washed-out electric lighting of the museum was replaced by a warm amber glow. All around him, deeper veins of red and orange and yellow pooled in the air, coming together and hinting at shapes only to pull apart and drain away. Alex looked down at his feet and saw what appeared to be a well-worn dirt path. He looked back over his shoulder and saw a transparent rose-pink rectangle shimmering in the air: the false door, as seen from the other side. Next to it, Ren and Luke stood washed in the yellow-orange light and blinking incredulously.

"Are you okay?" called Alex over the low, steady hum that seemed to surround them.

All three of them clutched their amulets tightly, like lifelines, but Luke gave him a thumbs-up with his free hand, and Ren called back: "I think so. It's not as scary this time."

Alex nodded. The last time they had traveled through the afterlife, it had been a darker and more frightening place. But now, high above, a fiery object was making slow progress across the golden sky. "It's daytime now," he said.

Luke looked up, shielded his eyes, and said, "The sun is all jacked up."

It was true. It was hard to see through its blazing glow, but the object above them wasn't round. If anything, it looked kind of like a boat. Alex was amazed to realize that it *was*

a boat. As many pictures and carvings as he'd seen of it, his next words sounded crazy, even to him: "It's the sun barque of Amun-Re."

"The *sun god*?" stammered Ren.

Alex could see the idea ricocheting around Ren's orderly mind. He seriously hoped she wouldn't lose it. Instead, she closed her eyes briefly, took a deep breath, and opened them. "Okay, whatever," she said. "Let's just get going."

Alex inhaled the fragrant air, clamped down a little tighter on his scarab, and closed his eyes.

It was the biggest test of his life, and it had only one question. *Could he feel it?*

The scarab could detect the undead and the death magic that created them. It had a strong connection to the Spells, and so did Alex. In Minyahur, the small desert village where his mom had hidden out, studying the Spells, the scarab had nearly burned his hand off when the Spells were close by. And he'd passed out the first time he'd seen them up close. Using the amulet to detect death magic here seemed like a good way to get his hand burned off — this was the *world* of the dead!

But as his eyes closed and his senses stretched out, all he felt — heard, really — was the same buzzing hum getting louder. That's what it was, he realized: the strong, steady signal of the afterlife all around. It was the energy of this strange place, and he didn't need his amulet to hear it.

He relaxed a little more and breathed.

As he relaxed, his senses opened further, and then he *did* sense something. It wasn't a shape or an image as much as a feeling, an almost magnetic pull. The amulet began to heat up in his hand.

He shuffled his feet slightly, turned his shoulders, and then raised his hand.

"The Spells are in that direction," he said. "Somewhere over there."

"Are you sure?" said Ren.

Alex nodded. "I feel a really strong signal. It's almost . . . pulling me there."

He opened his eyes and looked down the length of his arm as if it were the barrel of a gun. He stared into the distance. The air was thick and smelled of earth and water. It still swirled with warm colors and phantom shapes, but the shifting patterns decorated the view more than they obscured it. He could see fields extending outward in every direction, tall stalks of wheat and barley swaying in the wind, washed in golden light. Off in the distance, there were figures moving among the rows of shifting grain, and Alex recognized the timeless, repetitive motions of farmers working the land.

And directly in front of his outstretched arm, past acres of golden fields, was the glittering blue-green band of a river.

The Nile.

As otherworldly as it all seemed, it still made sense to him. The ancient Egyptians believed the dead crossed the Nile on the first leg of their journey into the afterlife. Back at the

museum, they'd prepared for the possibility that they might have to do it themselves.

"So, let me get this straight," said Luke, staring in the direction Alex had pointed. "We're in the land of death, or whatever; there are dudes in these fields, *dead* dudes; something is trying to pull you across a river . . . and you want to *go*?" He lifted his chin toward the riverbank. "You can't even see what's on the other side."

Alex lifted his gaze. The land beyond the winding waterway was obscured by a heavy, fog-like haze. The kingdom of the dead was holding its secrets close.

"We have to," said Alex, trying to sound calmer and more confident than he felt. "I think that's where the Spells are."

Luke considered it for a moment and then shrugged. "You're gonna get us killed," he said. "But at least we're in the right place for it."

"Yeah, let's go," Ren said, eyeing the fieldworkers swaying in the distance. "The faster we find them, the better."

The three friends set off cautiously down the path, the dirt under their feet as black as charcoal. Alex ventured one last look over his shoulder at the fiery vessel inching across the morning sky. He felt its heat on the back of his neck, and when he looked down, he saw his shadow stretching out before him.

They would travel to the west, where the sun died each day.

## To the Nile

They stayed on the path as it cut through a field of waist-high barley. With one hand still wrapped around his scarab, Alex reached out with the other and brushed the top of the nearest stalks. All around them, the light continued to shift and swirl, shapes and colors ornamenting the heavy air. He saw rosy red light pooling in the air ten feet in front of him, forming a perfect circle, like the pupil of an eye. It drained away a moment later, leaving nothing but the vague sensation of being watched.

As his ears adjusted to the steady hum all around, he heard other sounds rise up. Some were faint: airy exhalations that might have been the wind, but sounded more like an old man breathing his last gasp; distant roars that might have been thunder, had the golden sky not been cloudless. Others were louder: A chorus of wailing voices rose up off to their left. Alex whipped his head around, but all he saw was shifting grain.

"Did you guys hear that?" he said, but the voices had already stopped.

"I heard it," said Ren.

Both of them turned to Luke, who shrugged. "I thought it was you two."

Alex turned back toward the fields. Whether or not his ears were playing tricks on him, his eyes were telling a very clear story. The figures working the fields were closer now, the nearest no more than twenty yards away. Their broad backs were slightly stooped and their strong shoulders swung from side to side. Alex couldn't see the blades of the scythes they were carrying, but he knew they were harvesting the grain. Golden stalks disappeared with each swing.

*Shesh shesh shesh* went the blades.

"Are they dangerous?" asked Ren, walking a little closer.

Alex shook his head. "I don't think so," he said. The figures hadn't so much as glanced in their direction.

"So those guys are, like, one hundred percent dead, right?" hissed Luke. "And that's why they look like that?"

They were close enough to see them clearly now. Some had skin the color of stone, but most were shades of blue. They wore simple clothes but regal headdresses that seemed oddly out of place in the sun-washed fields.

"They're shabti," said Alex.

"Yeah," agreed Luke. "They're definitely shabby."

"Shab*ti*," corrected Ren. Then she turned toward Alex and added: "But, uh, you better tell us — I mean Luke — what those are again."

Alex managed half a smile. He knew that Ren liked to know what was going on, and that a little information might help keep her calm in this strange world. Still, he pretended he was explaining it for Luke's benefit.

"The ancient Egyptians believed that the afterlife was just, like, an extension of everyday life. There was no sickness or death, I mean, obviously. But you still had to work, to grow crops and stuff. So they put these little statues in their tombs. They're called shabti, or answerers. Each day, when the dead were called to work, they could send out one of their shabti to answer for them."

Alex told the story as they passed by the first of the silent laborers. *Shesh shesh shesh*. He could see the long, sharp, curved blades of their scythes now, but still the enchanted laborers ignored them. Alex concentrated on keeping his voice calm and steady and willed his feet not to break into a panicked run.

Soon, they passed by the shabti. Now the fields on either side of them were cut low, piles of barley awaiting collection on the ground and little bits of it floating lightly in the golden air.

*Chooo!*

Ren sneezed and Alex jumped. She didn't make fun of him, like she normally would have, though. He knew she was way more freaked out by all this than he was. "Your mom taught you really well," she said instead. "I mean, about the shabti and stuff."

"Thanks," he said. With the fields cut low, they could see the river ahead clearly.

"Why are you thanking me?" said Ren. "I was complimenting your mom."

Alex snorted out half a laugh, and that seemed so crazy that he snorted out a full one. Who would've thought it: laughing in the afterlife.

"I was just kidding," said Ren, too freaked out to laugh but clearly wanting to join in the good mood. "You did a good job learning."

"The thing is," said Alex, "I didn't realize I was learning. It's just that every story she told, I was right there, listening. Every exhibit she worked on, I was right there watching. And . . . I . . ."

His voice trailed off. He was lost in both memory and realization. He had learned so much as a sick kid trailing after his mom in the museum, and now he was using it on his own. He'd chased after her when she disappeared, and then moped when he thought she'd abandoned him. And now he was here leading this mission. Not abandoned, but independent. She'd given him what he needed to navigate this strange world. At least, he hoped so . . .

"Anyway," said Ren, snapping him out of it, "I'm glad you know so much about it."

"Me too," he said. "That reminds me. See all this black dirt we're walking on? That's where the Nile flooded and then pulled back. That's how Egyptians lived for thousands

of years, farming the floodplains of the Nile. Before the big dams were built and the Nile stopped flooding."

"Uh, no offense, dude," said Luke. "I mean, I know you two are having like a nerd moment or whatever — but who cares about dirt?"

Alex didn't deny being a little nerdy around the edges, but he still didn't like to hear it from his cool jock cousin. "I was about to mention the crocodiles," he said. "And the snakes. Those came with the floodwaters, too. Lots of 'em."

Luke and Ren looked all around, their eyes suddenly a little wider.

Alex kept his eyes forward, staring at the massive expanse of the Nile, a legendary river flowing through two worlds at once.

## The Kingdom of the Dead

Ren eyed the edge of the river warily. She'd seen enough nature documentaries to know that that's where crocodiles ambushed their prey. Up close, the current was coffee-colored and thick with sediment, the kind of water that made it very hard to spot crocodiles, and impossible to spot snakes.

"Oh wow!" said Alex.

Ren reluctantly lifted her eyes from the river's murky surface and gasped in astonishment.

The far shore, which had been hidden in haze as they walked, now revealed itself. More fields filled the floodplain on the other side, but beyond them, a vast kingdom stretched to the horizon. White stone temples, majestic houses, and even a few colossal pyramids glowed and shimmered in the golden light. It was a scene from out of a history book, a museum painting come to life.

And moving along the broad avenues, just visible from where she stood, people walked, alone or in small groups. As Ren watched, not blinking and barely remembering to

breathe, she even saw a glittering, horse-drawn chariot, looking like a tiny toy in the distance. It kicked up a plume of dust and sand behind it before turning a corner and disappearing.

*The kingdom of the dead.*

She nearly fainted.

"Let's get that boat," said Alex.

"Uhhh," said Luke, and Ren thought that summed it up pretty well.

She looked at Alex, incredulous. "How are you not freaked out by all this?" She pointed across the water. "By all of *them*?"

"I *am* freaked out," said Alex, and a slight tremble in his voice confirmed it. "But dead doesn't necessarily mean evil. These are the good ones, I think. And, anyway, we have work to do."

"The *good* ones," said Luke. "What, like . . . Casper the Friendly Ghost?"

Instead of answering, Alex shrugged his backpack off and lowered it to the ground. He unzipped it and carefully pulled out the small wooden carving of a boat. It was a little more than a foot long and a little less than three thousand years old. They'd taken it from a storeroom in the museum. Its edges worn down and its paint worn off, it was one of thousands of items that didn't quite merit display space.

But the little boat was about to earn its keep now.

"I don't see how we're supposed to get across this huge river in a toy," said Luke. "What is that, a boat for ants?"

"They put these in the tombs so the spirits could cross the Nile," said Alex. He walked over to the river's edge. Ren

followed a step behind and watched as he knelt down and placed the little boat on the gently rippling surface.

Immediately, the boat's frame pushed up and out, quickly reaching the height of Ren's shoulders. As she and Alex both jumped back to avoid getting knocked over by the bow, Ren thought of the packet of little sponge dinosaurs her dad had given her once, the ones that expanded when you dropped them in water.

By the time the little boat stopped growing, it was a real boat big enough for three. It was made not of wood but of bundled reeds that rose up to a high point on each end. All Ren managed to say was "Whoa."

And then it occurred to her that she was supposed to get in this thing now — and to travel to the other side. Where so many of the dead were. Suddenly, the possibility seemed all too real. "I don't know . . ." she said.

"We have to, Ren," said Alex, stepping forward and gingerly touching the reedy side of the craft. "I am getting such a strong signal from over there."

Ren looked at him. There was something wrong with what he had just said, a hole in the logic, but she couldn't place it. Her brain was too full of wonder and fear.

A moment later, it got worse.

"That is not your vessel," she heard. "The one it was made for has already crossed over." The voice was strong and steady. And it did *not* belong to Alex or Luke. "Where did you get this boat?"

Ren wheeled around to see who the voice belonged to.

Who, or *what*.

He was tall and muscular and dressed in ancient garb. A white-and-yellow shendyt kilt was wrapped around his waist, and a wide, ornate collar necklace hung from his neck. Thickly woven straps crisscrossed his broad chest, meeting at a massive, perfectly round ruby. He held a long, thin staff in one hand. But who could possibly care about any of that when his head — the head talking to them right now — was that of a jet-black jackal?

As she stared in disbelief, he turned to meet her eyes. Her knees felt like jelly, and her punch-drunk brain had its finger on the light switch.

*Talking dog*, she thought vaguely. *Good talking dog man. Don't bite.*

*Anubis.*

The guardian of the underworld.

Not just an ancient Egyptian god but, as Alex's mom would say, one of the big ones.

"I asked you a question," said the deity, the daggerlike tips of two huge white canine teeth appearing as he spoke. "Where did you get this boat? And answer carefully. The afterlife is a perilous place for tomb raiders."

Alex gulped in just enough air to squeak out: "In a museum."

Anubis's jackal ears swung toward the small sound. He looked at Alex, considering. Alex's heart hammered hard in his chest.

Out of the corner of his eye, he saw Ren swaying on her feet. He wanted to run over and help her, but he didn't dare move. He had the distinctly unpleasant feeling that he was being judged. Luke was standing beside her, staring at the ancient god in wide-eyed, slack-jawed wonder. *Please don't say anything stupid*, thought Alex.

"I will accept your answer," said Anubis, and Alex relaxed just a little. Even Ren seemed to stop wobbling. Luke's mouth closed and opened again silently, like a goldfish's. "Your museums empty our tombs just as surely as the thieves do, but at least they take good care of what they find."

Anubis paused and then added cryptically, "And then, too, you have been vouched for." His jackal head looked off to a spot farther up the bank. "It is funny, in a way."

Alex had no idea what any of that meant. *Vouched for? Funny? Did gods like jokes?* He had zero chance of mustering a polite laugh at the moment, so he stuck to what he knew. "Thank you," he said, bowing slightly. "We're sorry about the boat, but we need to cross . . ."

"You may not," said Anubis, suddenly striding forward.

The three friends scrambled to get out of his way. Alex turned to see the deity raise his staff and tap the bow of the boat. As the boat shrank and shriveled, Alex dropped his

head in defeat. A moment later, he saw the little wooden carving once again bobbing like a bath toy on the river. All three of them watched silently as the current caught it and it began to float away.

"We needed that," said Alex to his own feet.

"Why is that?" said Anubis.

Alex looked up slightly, still not daring to make direct eye contact with the deity. "Because we are looking for something," he ventured. "Something important."

"All hope would seem to be lost, then," said Anubis.

And there was something about the way he said it: almost playful. *Is he teasing me*, wondered Alex, *or mocking me?* "The people — well, the things — we're after are *evil*," he protested. "Our world is in *danger*."

Anubis sized him up with glowing green eyes, and Alex was afraid he had gone too far. *Would the next thing he felt be those dagger-like teeth? That battle staff?*

And then . . . Anubis smiled. He smiled in the way dogs do sometimes. It would have been cute, if he weren't a seven-foot-tall death god. "I know they're evil," he said. "That's why I did not let them cross, either."

A hundred questions flooded Alex's mind, but Anubis was already walking away. "I take no part in this conflict, other than to protect my realm," said the ancient guardian of the afterlife. "What you seek and the ones you fear are here on the borderlands. But hurry, for this land is no place for the living, especially at night."

As the god headed up the bank, Alex turned to look at the others. "That really just happened, right?" he said. "You heard all that?"

"Oh, that happened all right," said Luke. "That Snoopy-looking dude was hella real."

"That was Anubis, wasn't it?" said Ren. "I've seen his, like, statues."

Alex nodded and turned back for one more look.

But Anubis was gone.

As soon as Ren registered that fact, she let Alex have it. "I can't believe you were going to magic-boat us over to the *city of the dead* for no reason! The Death Walkers aren't even over there!"

Alex looked at his amulet. "But I got such a strong signal," he protested, his voice breaking slightly.

"Yeah," said Ren, "because that thing detects *spirits*, too." She pointed to the endless city on the far shore. "And, I mean, *hello*, the *kingdom* of the dead?"

"Oh yeah," said Alex.

He looked down at his feet, embarrassed. He saw his shadow stretching out behind him. *Behind him* . . . He looked up. The fiery vessel had crossed over the river and begun its descent.

"Um, we should really get going," he said, reaching down to pick up his pack.

"Yeah," said Luke. "Let's get out of here before the rest of the zoo shows up."

As they walked quickly back up the bank, Alex picked over what Anubis had said: *Did not let them cross . . .* Something big occurred to him.

"The gods are more powerful than the Death Walkers," he said, and as soon as he heard the words out loud, he knew they were true. Back in the Egyptian desert, Sekhmet had obliterated a Death Walker their amulets had been powerless against. Anubis had stared down The Order's stone warriors and turned them back.

"Yeah," said Ren. "Obviously. They're gods. It's kind of in the definition."

Alex knew there was some greater significance to that fact, something he wasn't quite getting. Amazingly, Luke was the one to put his finger on it.

"It would be cool if the gods could put the beatdown on The Order," he said. "Instead of leaving it up to three middle schoolers from Manhattan." Then he quickly added: "Not that we're not awesome."

Alex stared at his cousin. It was a statement so obvious that it had taken Luke to say it. "That *would* be cool," said Alex. "So cool."

As they neared the top of the bank, Ren came up next to him. "You know," she said, "if the gods did that we wouldn't need to use the Spells."

He nodded. His best friend was just as worried about what might happen to him if they used the Spells as he was. She wanted him to live, too — even if she did yell at him sometimes.

"Of course," she added, "that's a pretty big *if*."

He knew she was right about that, too. Relying on the divine intervention of ancient, animal-headed deities wasn't much of a plan — it was like planning to win the lottery as a career goal. It was a nice thought, but the time for daydreaming was over. Now they needed to figure out how to do it for themselves. Alex scanned the ground near the top of the bank. Anubis had said that what they were looking for was on this side of the bank. *But where?*

He scanned the bank in both directions, and then looked down at his feet. There in the dark dirt of the timeless Nile he saw a scattering of small footprints. He huffed out a little laugh. "I think I figured out who vouched for us back there," he said, pointing down.

The others gathered around. "Are those . . . cat prints?" said Luke.

"Anubis was right," said Alex. "It is kind of funny. Imagine being saved from a dog-headed god . . . by a little cat."

"Pai!" exclaimed Ren, dropping to her knees and tracing the tracks with her fingers.

"It must've been her," said Alex.

They looked all around, but there was no sign of Ren's undead BFF, and the tracks vanished into the harder dirt higher up the bank.

Ren stood up and brushed her hands on her jeans. "Okay, Pai did her part," she said. "I guess it's time I did mine."

She took a deep breath and reached for her ibis.

# A Dangerous New Direction

Ren tried to calm her thoughts. The last time she'd used the ibis, it had shown her a fearful scene from home. Now she was worried about what it might show her, and what it might not. She took hold of the ancient amulet, closed her eyes, and made her question as clear and focused as possible. It was a question the ibis had never answered before, but maybe now it would. Now that they were so close . . .

"Where are the Lost Spells?" she said out loud.

Instantly, a series of images flashed through her mind.

The first: the little wooden boat bobbing along the current near the shore.

The second: a frightening and familiar figure standing near the riverbank. His face and neck were swollen with stings, his body was wrapped in crimson robes, and there was a huge scorpion stinger where his left hand should have been. It was the first Death Walker they'd faced, the Stung Man. In the river behind him, bobbing lazily along, was the little boat.

Finally, she saw a long line of men. They were dressed in ancient garb, but as the first man in line stepped into a glowing portal in the air, his features changed. He aged three thousand years in one step and his outfit was replaced by the ragged wrappings of a mummy as he disappeared through the false door.

Ren's eyes fluttered open.

"What did you see?" said Alex. "Anything?"

She described each image carefully. "It seems like it wants us to follow the boat along the river."

"We need to go north," Alex said.

"That's right," she said. She remembered now: Unlike most U.S. rivers, the Nile flows north, out of Africa and up to the Mediterranean Sea. So that's the way it would carry the little boat. "But why do you think it showed me the Stung Man?" she said.

Back in New York, at the start of all this, they'd used the ancient Egyptian Book of the Dead and Alex's amulet to send him back to the afterlife. But that wouldn't work this time: They were already in the afterlife!

"I don't know," said Alex. "He could be guarding the Spells. We'll have to try to avoid him or at least hold him off until we can find them."

*Hold him off?* thought Ren. *He has a scorpion stinger the size of a desktop printer — and usually about a thousand actual scorpions with him, too.* But she had another concern that was even bigger. "What about the men — I mean mummies?"

she asked. "Do you think those are the ones heading to New York?"

Alex nodded grimly. "Yeah," he said. "Pretty sure."

It made sense to Alex that the mummies would look like the people they'd once been while they were still in the afterlife. Then they'd be mummies again when they stepped back into the world of the living. And he knew The Order's first target was NYC, a high-profile demonstration of their abilities, meant to strike fear into the rest of the world.

But he had a bigger concern, too. Ren had asked the ibis where the Spells were. He'd heard her with his own ears. But he also knew that her attention was divided by her homesickness and concern about her parents. And the ibis knew it, too. The last time she'd tried to ask it about their mission, it had shown her home instead.

*Was this time different?* he wondered as they headed north along the riverbank. *Or were they chasing the wrong thing?*

"So that portal, or false door or whatever," she said, "it leads to New York?"

"Man," said Luke. "I would love to get back to NYC."

"Guys!" Alex snapped. "We need to concentrate on what we're doing here, okay?"

"I know," said Luke. "I'm just, like, seriously missing my PlayStation."

They walked on wordlessly for a while, keeping their eyes and ears open and doing their best to move quietly, though the ground had grown so muddy that their footsteps made small squelches. The three of them were spread out in a line, with Ren farthest up the bank, Alex in the middle, and Luke closer to the river. Together, their six feet were making a chorus of burpy sounds in the soggy soil. Alex turned to the others to tell them to step softly, but as he did, he saw a man in black robes slip silently out from behind a palm tree and step in front of Ren. "Watch out!" he blurted.

But she'd already stopped cold.

She saw the knife, too.

Alex and Luke both grabbed for their amulets, but the man held the knife just under Ren's chin. "There is no need for that," he said. "I just came to see who passes along my bank."

Alex didn't dare unleash a burst of wind with the knife so close to Ren, but the amulet did allow him to understand the man's ancient tongue. "*Your* bank?" he said, trying to keep the fear and concern from his voice.

"I maintain it," said the man.

Luke moved a few squelches closer to Alex and whispered, "I could get him."

Alex shook his head slowly and whispered back, "Not yet. Can't risk it." If Luke hit this guy at top speed, the impact could drive the knife right into Ren.

The man paid no attention to the hushed conversation and continued to talk about maintaining the bank. "If it weren't for me, it would be a swamp. There is a spring — and many snakes. But I keep it nice. Nice for you to pass."

"Uh, thanks?" said Ren, who had quietly taken hold of her amulet, too. She said it through her teeth to avoid opening her mouth too wide and cutting herself on the blade.

"You are welcome!" said the man grandly, lowering his knife just a touch. Then he seemed to remember something sad and shook his head ruefully. "But such work is not easy. I am afraid I must ask —"

"For a small contribution?" volunteered Alex eagerly, suddenly understanding. "Just a reasonable toll, perhaps?"

The man smiled broadly. "I am glad you understand me! Clearly you are a very intelligent boy."

*And you're a bandit and a thief*, thought Alex, but what he said was: "Hold on."

Once again, Alex swung the pack from his back. He stuck his hand in and began rifling through the bottom. Soon he felt the old, cold gold clinking under his hand.

"No tricks," said the man.

Alex pulled his hand out of the pack and held up three ancient coins — another gift from the overstocked museum. "Of course not," he said. "Just a small, um, appreciation."

Thousands of years had dulled the luster of the coins, but the man eyed them greedily as Alex walked them over to him, spread out on his outstretched palm. The man lunged for

them with his free hand, but Alex pulled back and pocketed one of the coins. "We will give you this one when we cross 'your bank' safely on the way back."

The bandit smiled and grabbed the two remaining coins with the quickness of a cobra striking. Alex felt the man's ragged nails scratch across his palm. Then the bandit lowered his knife and began to back away, bowing slightly. "You truly are a smart boy," he said. "And these are fine coins. So I will give you one last bit of information. Beware, strange children, for the borderlands are unsettled. There is discord between the world of the living and the world of the dead."

"Uh, no offense," said Ren, no longer needing to talk through her teeth. "But we kind of know that already."

"Smarter than I thought, then," said the thief, pocketing the coins and sheathing his knife. "But did you know that Ammit herself prowls these lands now, upset by the imbalance?"

"Ammit?" said Alex. "The devourer of souls?" Alex had seen Ammit's strange image many times, carved into the walls of tombs and painted on the scrolls of the Book of the Dead. A demigod with the head of a crocodile, the body of a lion, and the hindquarters of a hippo, she had one grim job: to devour the hearts — and souls — of those who failed the weighing of the heart ceremony.

"Yes," said the man, looking both ways nervously as he stepped back alongside the thick old tree. "The pull of the far shore is strong, but I have stayed on this side for long

ages to avoid her fearsome jaws. Now she has come to the borderlands!"

"Uh, okay," said Ren, clearly ready to be done with this man. "We'll keep our eyes open."

"Your ears," he said. "You will know the devourer by her cry."

And then, without another word, he stepped toward the tree and disappeared completely. Not behind it but, somehow, inside.

"Good thing Todtman thought of giving us those old coins," said Ren, glaring at the old tree. "That guy could've killed me."

"Oh, I don't know," said Alex, giddy with relief to see his best friend still alive. He knocked on the tree trunk as they walked past. "His bark is worse than his bite."

Ren groaned at the pun, and Alex slung the pack back over his shoulder. It was lighter now, without the boat and coins. He felt a few old scrolls, protective spells from the Book of the Dead, rolling around inside.

Luke led the way, high-tech sneakers on timeless soil, as they angled back down the bank and followed the river around a wide corner. New knowledge jumbled together in Alex's head like puzzle pieces in a box:

*Ammit herself prowls the borderlands . . .*

*The gods are stronger . . .*

# Against the Grain

"There it is!" said Luke, pointing toward the river.

The little wooden boat was lying on its side on the river-bank. Alex looked back over his shoulder as they walked toward it. He couldn't say exactly how far it had come — or they had come — since they'd first set this thing in the water. All he knew was that the golden light was starting to fade, and the colors swirling in the air were getting darker and more ominous, bloodreds replacing rosy pinks, blues edging toward black. The growls and groans and huffs and wails that had sounded far-off before seemed louder now, closer. Alex didn't like any of it, and the darkening world wasn't his only concern. "We need to be careful." he said as Ren bent down to pick up the boat. "If the boat's here, the Stung Man could be, too."

Kneeling in the sand with her hand a few inches from the boat, Ren paused and looked back toward him. "Maybe we got here first," she said. "Maybe I was wrong."

As she spoke, Alex saw a large black scorpion scamper up

from the little pocket of shade under the boat's hull. "Ren!" he gasped.

"What?" she said, her fingers just inches from the scorpion's flexed tail, the curved stinger twisting into position for a strike.

"Scorpion!" shouted Luke.

Ren jumped up and back as the angry arachnid struck out at empty air.

"Where did that come from?" said Ren. "Do you think it's one of *his*?"

The first Death Walker had faced a grisly demise from scorpion stings thousands of years earlier, and back in New York, the venomous insects had been a surefire calling card of the Stung Man. But here, in between palm trees and the Nile, the little creepy-crawler seemed to fit right in. "Maybe not?" Alex said hopefully.

"Uh, what about those ones?" she said, her voice suddenly shaky.

Alex turned and saw why. The bank was suddenly dotted with scorpions. Some were large and black and others were small and pale, but all of them were packing potent venom and heading down the bank, their exoskeletons clicking and clacking softly.

"This place is really starting to bug me," muttered Luke.

Alex grabbed his amulet, planning to clear a path through the arachnid army with a gust of desert wind. Instead, he got a warning. A sharp pulse, like a radar signal bouncing off a

mountain, rang in his mind. Alex spun around. And there he was.

"I was hoping we'd meet again," said the Stung Man. He stood just up the bank, no more than twelve feet away.

"Oh no," breathed Ren, grabbing for her own amulet.

The Stung Man advanced toward them with long, confident strides, and the scorpions scurrying all around him.

"What happened to his face?" whispered Luke. Alex realized it was his cousin's first encounter with this Walker and the swollen, discolored flesh of his eternally unhealing wounds. But there was no time for explanation — only action.

Ren raised her hand and delivered a blinding white flash that caught the Stung Man by surprise. He closed his eyes too late and grunted in annoyance.

Meanwhile, Alex delivered a whipping, whistling lance of wind that scattered dirt and scorpions as it cut up from the bank to the line of palm trees. "Go!" he shouted, and the friends took off running toward the tree line. There was nothing to be gained from fighting the Stung Man out in the open, before they'd ever located the Spells, and the only plan that made sense was escape.

As they raced up the bank, Alex pictured the massive stinger that took the place of the Stung Man's left hand. He could almost feel it shooting forth and piercing his back with its cruel, curved point. He ran faster as Luke whooshed past him in a cheetah-powered blur. Half a step behind him, Ren's feet slapped dirt. "Come on, come on!" he called over his shoulder.

Luke was at the crest of the bank. Moving at hyper-speed, he had already molded the dark soil of the floodplain into a dozen perfectly round dirt balls. Now he delivered the first one down the slope in a high-kicking baseball pitch.

A dull *THOKK!* of exploding dirt gave way to an indignant shout from the Walker.

Alex didn't need to turn around to know that Luke's first pitch was a strike. Instead, he eyed the fields just beyond his cousin. The grain was higher here, as if unharvested for some time — perfect for hiding three kids!

"Into the field!" he called.

Luke whipped one more major league dirtball down the slope as Alex and Ren reached the top of the bank and sprinted straight past him. Luke turned and followed, immediately overtaking the others. Their own frantic footsteps mixed with the beat of the Stung Man's sandals slapping the dirt behind them. As the sound of the Walker's pursuit grew closer — hoarse shouts and muttered curses mixing with heavy footfalls — Alex tensed up, preparing for the terrible pain of the massive stinger piercing his back.

And then he felt it.

The rough slap of tall sprouts of barley hitting his face as they burst into the field. "Keep going!" he said as the Stung Man roared his disapproval behind them.

Alex crashed through the tall ripe stalks, his vision just a whirl of green and gold and tan. His heart pounded and he gasped for breath, feeling like he was sucking in nearly as much grain and dust as air.

For a few chaotic moments he lost track of the others and panicked. *Had Ren fallen? Had Luke been brought down by the stinger?* But then he heard Ren. "This is going to be murder on my allergies!" she huffed from right behind him. The crash of stalks laid low in front of him told Alex his cousin was still at full speed.

But if he could hear his friends, so could the Stung Man. "Slow down!" he gasped. "We have to be quiet if we want to lose him."

The crashing subsided. "Okay," Ren said softly from beside him.

"Good plan," said Luke from a few yards ahead.

Alex took the lead as they snaked their way through the field single file. The grain grew taller the deeper they went, and soon even Luke could stand up straight with no fear of being seen.

"Okay," whispered Alex. "Let's stop for a second."

They stood still, catching their breath and listening carefully. The only sound Alex could hear was the wind gently rustling the grain. He took hold of his amulet and searched, but the intense radar signal was gone. All he felt was the same general buzzing hum as before. "I think we lost him," he said. "I'm not getting any signal from the amulet."

"None?" said Ren. "Not the Lost Spells, either?"

Alex shook his head. "I think they must be hidden again," he said. They knew it was a possibility. When The Order had captured the Spells from his mom's desert hideout, they'd

**125**

also captured the ancient cloaking spells she'd wrapped them in.

"We'll never find them now," said Ren angrily, punctuating the thought with a small sneeze. *Choo!*

"Not cool," said Luke.

*Had they really come all this way — into another world! — only to come up short?* Alex refused to believe it. "Wait," he said as the three knelt down next to each other in the sea of swaying grain. "We did see the first thing the ibis showed you. And then we ran into the Stung Man."

"Okay, so what does that mean?" asked Luke.

"We banished him here. But Todtman said that if The Order got the Spells, the Walkers we'd banished would be able to come back," Alex explained. "So if the Stung Man's still hanging around here, then maybe it means he's helping to guard the Spells."

"Okay, maybe," said Ren. "But they're not going to hide the most powerful spells in the world in some field. Remember what else Todtman said, right before we left? 'Even in the afterlife they will guard their prize closely.' They wouldn't just leave them out in the open."

Alex considered it. "Right . . . so we're looking for some kind of building, and we know it's on this side of the river and that we're probably pretty close."

"Not many buildings around here," said Luke, plucking a stalk of barley from the ground. "It's not exactly midtown."

*Midtown . . . Skyscrapers . . .* It gave Alex an idea. He looked up at the sky, cut into sections above him by the waving grain. "We need to get up high and look."

Ren looked back the way they'd come. "Maybe if we climbed one of those trees by the river?"

"We can't risk going back," said Alex. "The Stung Man could still be there."

Luke eyed the top of the grain. "I might be able to, like, high-jump it," he mused. "For, like, a second."

Alex pictured his cousin jack-in-the-boxing up over the fields, getting a quick glimpse at most. Then he had a better idea. Better . . . and worse. He dropped his head. "Oh, this bites," he said. He'd seen kids do this at the pool at the YMCA. He'd always been too sick and weak to join in, and the lifeguards always blew their whistles to stop it, anyway. He looked up at his undersized friend. He was so much stronger and healthier since his mom had used the Spells to save him — but he still couldn't believe what he was about to say.

"What?" said Ren.

Alex sighed. "Do you know what a chicken fight is?"

## Guard Crocs

Alex boosted Ren up on his shoulders. Luke was the obvious choice for the job — taller and stronger — but the big jock had balked. "This is seriously all you," he'd said, putting his hands up and backing up a step.

Alex did his best, but it was more of a launch than a lift. As soon as Ren was more or less in position, Alex lurched up and forward. Ren wobbled and rose, and rose and wobbled. Luke reconsidered slightly, helping to steady her. But five seconds later, it all came crashing down. Ren toppled from Alex's shoulders, taking him with her. And when Luke tried to catch them, he wound up on the ground, too. The three fell in a heap among some crushed stalks of barley.

"Did you see anything?" asked Alex from the bottom of the pile.

"I saw some roofs!" crowed Ren.

Alex pumped his fist: *Yes.* "Let's go," he said. And as the first skittering, chittering sounds of scorpions advancing through the tall grasses reached their ears, Ren and Luke didn't argue.

Alex and Luke followed Ren's lead. They kept low and tried to disturb the tall stalks as little as possible, easily outpacing their tiny, tail-heavy pursuers. Soon, they came to the edge of the field. They stopped just short, peering through the last few rows of barley.

Ren's sense of direction had been unerring: A complex lay before them. Three square stone buildings were arranged in a triangular formation. And at its point stood Ta-mesah. As an Order operative, he'd nearly finished off Alex and Ren in London. Now, as a hulking, ten-foot-tall Death Walker with the head of a huge crocodile, he stood sentry in front of the largest building.

In front of the other two buildings, two enormous crocodiles basked in the late-day sun. "They've got to be twenty feet long," said Luke.

Alex peered through the thin veil of barley as it swayed in a light breeze. The air was dark gold now, and it swirled and glimmered with shifting shapes, but as he watched, he saw three glowing rectangles hold firm.

He pointed them out to the others. "Portals," he said. "More false doors, like the one we came in through."

"This is like the Grand Central Terminal of the afterlife," Ren whispered.

Suddenly, Ta-mesah's gaze shifted and he scanned the edge of the field. Alex's breath caught. *Had he heard them?* he wondered. *How was that even possible? Crocodiles barely have ears!*

But then Alex's own ears picked up a rustling to their left. The friends sank a little farther back into the stalks

and watched as the Stung Man emerged from the field and approached Ta-mesah. The two conversed briefly. The new Death Walker was so much larger than the old one — thanks to his mammoth stone statue — that the exchange looked like a father and son talk.

*Father.*

The thought hit Alex hard. *His own father had caused all this: a father he had never known, a father he never would . . .* He shook his head hard to clear it and then turned to the others. "I'm pretty sure I can guess what they're talking about," he said.

"So much for the element of surprise," said Ren.

Alex took hold of his amulet and felt his pulse race with ancient energy. He leaned in and tried to pick up at least some of what they were saying. It was no use. At this distance, their words were just a low mumble. A moment later, the Stung Man walked past Ta-mesah and into the tall open archway of the central stone building.

"That's got to be the one with the Spells," whispered Ren. "It's bigger, and guarded by Death Walkers. The other two are just guarded by reptiles."

Luke eyed them. "Those are some Jurassic Park–looking reptiles."

"Yeah, but crocodiles are dumb as mud. They've got brains the size of walnuts. And most of that is for hunting."

"That's the part that worries me!" hissed Luke.

Alex eyed the formidable stone structure. It was the size of a small house but built like an old bank. It had one

visible entrance, which was currently blocked by a ten-foot-tall undead ambush predator. And at least one more Death Walker was already inside.

"What do we do?" said Ren.

"I don't know," answered Alex, eyeing the long shadows stretching out behind the buildings. "But whatever it is, we have to do it fast."

"Maybe if one of us, like, lures him away," Luke offered. "And the others sneak inside . . ."

"And straight into a giant scorpion stinger?" countered Ren.

"Okay," he said. "What's your big idea?"

Ren's mouth opened, but nothing came out.

Suddenly, a huge sound filled the air. It was as loud as thunder and sounded like a combination between a roar and a low, rumbling growl.

"What the what?" blurted Luke.

Ta-mesah flinched visibly and then froze. A few moments later, he slowly lifted his long snout to sniff the air. Alex realized that what had been a crocodile mask in life had now become the Death Walker's head. Even more amazing: This ten-foot-tall, croc-headed undead powerhouse was very clearly *scared*.

On either side of their master, the two massive crocodiles called back in response. Their low, huffing growls sounded like layers peeled off from the original sound. Suddenly, Alex understood where that thunderous roar had come from — and why even Ta-mesah was afraid. He remembered the old thief's words: *You will know the devourer by her cry . . .*

**131**

He turned to others, wide-eyed. "It's Ammit."

Ren had just removed her hands from her ears and nodded. She knew the legend, too. It was fear of Ammit's jaws at the weighing of the heart ceremony that caused the Death Walkers to flee the afterlife in the first place. And as the roar split the sky again, Alex recognized it as the angry product of a croc's mouth and a lion's lungs.

Ta-mesah recognized it, too. Alex watched him slink back toward the building and disappear inside the open mouth of its doorway. *The gods are stronger . . .* The crocs called back once again and then fell silent. Alex sized up the sinister sentries. They were big, but their legs looked short and stubby. "This is our chance to get inside," he said.

After arguing earlier, Ren and Luke were suddenly on the same page. "Are you nuts?" they said simultaneously.

"Now they're both in there!" said Ren.

"Maybe they're hiding?" ventured Alex.

"Maybe they're *waiting!*" she countered.

"It's our only chance," he said. "Once he comes back out, we'll be stuck here till dark — and then it will be just as dangerous outside."

Luke looked around. "Those spooky voices are definitely getting louder," he admitted. "It's like a ghost concert out here — and I don't like the sound of that roar, either."

Ren still looked unconvinced, though, and Alex played the only card he had left. He pointed to the nearest portal, hanging in the air. "Somewhere nearby, there's another of

these that an army of the dead is marching through to New York."

Ren's expression shifted quickly from skeptical to resolute. She looked back toward the buildings. "Okay," she said, "but what about the crocodiles?"

Alex sized them up one last time. The animals were at least sixty feet from the doorway. Here at the edge of the field, the friends were half as far away — and with legs twice as long. "Don't worry about them," he said.

"Yeah, they look even slower than you two," said Luke. "And that's saying something."

Ren glared at the menacing crocs. "We've come a long way for this," she said. "What's thirty more feet?"

As the crocs settled back onto their bellies to bask in the last rays of sun, Alex realized how true that was. They really had come a long way. He had gone from a life on the sidelines to one in the thick of the action. From a kid too fragile for gym class to one preparing for a life-or-death sprint straight toward danger. Kneeling next to him, the cousin who had betrayed them in the desert was now an Amulet Keeper himself.

And Ren? As Alex gathered his legs underneath him and crouched down low, he took one last look over at his best friend. She'd struggled to come to terms with a world of magic and mummies, secret signs and changing rules. From London to Luxor, she'd struggled mightily with her ibis. But here in this strange otherworld, she had harnessed its

power to lead them right where they needed to go. And she was preparing to sprint straight toward the unknown.

Ren turned and caught him looking. "What?" she said.

"Nothing," said Alex.

"Whatever," said Ren. "Now, what's your plan for the Walkers?"

"We'll catch them by surprise or sneak around them," he said. "We'll use our amulets, if we have to. We've done this before."

Ren gave him a deeply skeptical look. "Not with two . . ."

"Okay, fine," said Alex. "I just came up with a new plan. It comes in three parts."

He crouched down deeper and relayed the first part: "On your mark . . ."

He touched his hands to the ground in front of him.

"Get set . . ." He raised up into a sprinter's stance. Beside him, Luke did the same. The two boys clearly had the same plan. Which was . . .

"Go!" blurted Alex as he and Luke took off running.

"Wait, what? That's it?" called Ren, but she took off right behind them.

In a blink — much faster than Alex had imagined possible — the two huge crocs took off running, too.

It was dinnertime.

# Light in the Darkness

Ren's legs pumped furiously as the huge carnivores converged on the friends from either side, rushing toward them in a brisk, improbable gallop.

"How are they so fast?" Alex yelped.

"I saw them gallop like this in a nature documentary once," called Ren. "I assumed it was on fast-forward!"

As the crocs closed in, Ren saw Luke reach up toward his amulet and disappear in a blur. *Fast-forward indeed*, she thought. He reappeared a moment later, under the stone archway at the building's entrance.

Now it was just her and Alex left on the menu. She had two choices: rush straight forward toward two waiting Death Walkers or stop and be eaten. *He called this a plan?* She was so angry at Alex that she almost wished he'd trip. She turned that anger to energy, edging past him despite his longer legs. The open doorway was just up ahead now, ten feet away. Luke waved them forward from inside: *Come on! Come on!* The crocs were coming from either side, maybe twenty feet away. She did the math.

They would make it. She eased up ever so slightly — as Alex went sprinting past Luke into the dark open mouth of the building.

Behind them, the massive crocs collided with a sound like two thick T-bone steaks being slapped together. Ren rushed inside, and Luke reached out to slow her down. "Thanks," she said. She scanned the dark entryway: no immediate sign of the Walkers. She felt a brief flash of relief, but it vanished as she turned back toward the entrance and realized their croc troubles weren't over yet. Either of the creatures could fit inside the archway, filling the entry with snapping jaws and blocking off all escape.

The two beefy beasts untangled themselves from their collision. Then slowly and in perfect unison, they turned their big beady eyes toward the entrance — and the tender little morsels inside.

"They're going to come in here, aren't they?" said Luke. "And then we're pretty much done for."

"Yep."

The larger of the two behemoths took a step toward the entrance, a string of saliva hanging from its slightly open mouth. Luke whispered, "I can't believe I'm doing this."

"Wait," said Ren. "Don't go out there. We'll figure something out in here, hide in the dark or something."

"Nah," said Luke. "You two do your thing. I'll hold off these things. I'm not the smartest guy — but you said it yourself: Crocodiles are dumb as mud."

**136**

He touched his amulet and disappeared back into the daylight. A split second later, he appeared in front of the monstrous crocs. "Here, lizard, lizard, lizard!" he called.

The closest one lunged. Ren held her breath — but Luke was already gone.

She exhaled and turned back into the darkness. She hoped he'd be able to distract the cold-blooded killers for long enough — and she hoped he wouldn't get eaten in the process. All of which meant one thing: She trusted him again. She even kind of liked him. Risking your life repeatedly for someone tends to have that effect.

It was the other one she was still mad at.

"Alex?" she hissed, heading down the dark tunnel of the entryway, her wide-open eyes desperately searching the darkness for friend and foe alike.

There was no response for a few steps, and then she heard his voice: "I'm here."

She flinched with fear and then swatted out blindly at him.

"Where's Luke?" he said.

"Saving our bacon," she answered, slapping what felt like his shoulder. "Great plan, by the way: *On your mark, get set, go!*"

"It worked, didn't it?" he said.

As glib as his words were, his voice told her that he was scared. His voice and common sense: Anything could be in here with them. *Would the next voice in her ear rise from the lifeless lungs of a Death Walker?* She lowered her hand, sucked

in a deep breath, and waited for her eyes to adjust to the darkness.

Slowly, the fading light filtering in from the open entry-way revealed a high-ceilinged hallway. It ended five feet from them in a massive stone door. "That thing looks like it weighs a ton," Ren whispered. "Like, literally, a ton."

"At least we know where the Spells are," said Alex.

"Yeah, and the Death Walkers," said Ren. This was bad. No light or sound escaped from inside, so there was no way to know what awaited them, and she was sure the big stone slab would grind loudly against the floor if they opened it. She wondered if they even could. She glanced over at Alex's shadowy silhouette. *Maybe he can push it open with his amulet*, she thought. *But what then?*

She looked down at her own amulet, glowing softly in the murk. She still hadn't been able to move heavy objects with it the way Alex and Todtman could. The ibis was a symbol of Thoth. He was the ancient Egyptian god of wisdom, writing, and moonlight, and apparently he didn't do manual labor. Still, the ibis had its own unique abilities.

Standing there in the dark, she got a bright idea.

Alex could hear his heart beating as he crouched down on one side of the door. Ren was barely visible on the other side, and he dearly hoped she knew what she was doing.

Finally, the moment they'd been waiting for — and dreading — arrived.

Stone ground loudly against stone, drowning out even Alex's racing heart, as the door began to open inward. Flickering firelight leaked out into the hall, only to be eclipsed by a massive figure.

Ta-mesah's reputation preceded him — and so did his snout. Before he'd even pushed his toothy visage all the way into the hall, a second figure appeared directly behind him. In the wash of firelight Alex would see the glossy venom bulb at his side.

*Now, Ren*, he thought.

He closed his eyes tightly as she sprang to her feet.

*FWOOOP!*

Even through his eyelids, the blinding white flash lit Alex's vision.

Ta-mesah grunted in pain and surprise, and the Stung Man once again covered his eyes too late, nearly stinging his own face in the process.

Unnoticed, Alex slipped quietly past them, through the door, and inside the chamber.

The room was half lit by a small stone pool with yellow-orange flames dancing on its surface. Alex desperately searched the deep shadows.

Speed was key now. The rapid-fire slap of Ren's footsteps had already disappeared down the hallway. Taking a page from Luke's playbook, she was trying to lure at least one of

the dazzled Death Walkers into pursuit. But there was no guarantee they would take the bait.

Alex's thoughts were interrupted by movement. A shadowy blur buzzed past his ear. Turning to get a better look at it, he saw a second shape fill his vision: dark purple in the faint firelight and the size of a Thanksgiving turkey. He ducked and it flew inches over his head, tearing out half a dozen strands of hair as it went.

Alex gasped from the pain, but the sound was drowned out by an angry buzzing that grew louder with each passing second, as if he'd just stepped on a hornets' nest.

*Hornets*, he thought. *Oh no.* An image flashed through his mind: a ragged figure, teeming and torn, on a rooftop in Cairo.

Suddenly, the deafening buzz fell silent. A hollow, desolate voice that rose up in its place, and a nightmare stepped clear of the shadows, revealing itself in the flickering glow.

$$\longleftarrow\!\!+\!\!+\!\!+\!\!\longrightarrow$$

Ren bolted out of the dark entryway as if shot from a gun. There was no need to adjust to the daylight. Dusk had come to the land of the dead. She looked around desperately for any sign of approaching croc jaws. Instead, she saw Luke literally grabbing one of the toothy beasts by the tail. It seemed like the definition of a bad idea, but Luke caught sight of her and shouted an explanation. "They were giving up on

trying to catch me," he shouted. "Just trying to keep their attention!"

"Look out!" Ren shouted in response.

The croc swung its big head around but couldn't reach him. The second croc gave it another go, lunging at him from nearby. But before it could even sniff Nikes, Luke vanished in a blur. In his sudden absence, the crocs turned toward Ren and eyed her greedily. Ren swallowed hard. She didn't know if she looked more appetizing, but she was sure she looked slower. They sprinted toward her.

Behind her, she could hear heavy footfalls echoing through the entry hall. Two sets. Both Death Walkers were in pursuit — and close. She was in between a croc and a hard place. *Would she be torn apart? Stung to death? Something worse?*

She took off running, putting everything she had into one quick burst of speed.

Her legs strained, her head pounded, her lungs burned — and her plan worked.

The two crocodiles shot like rockets toward the spot where she'd been standing, just outside the entrance to the building. The closest one lunged for her, just missing her left leg as she scooted past it and into the clear. Even with walnut-sized brains, the crocs knew better than to collide again. But it hadn't occurred to them not to block the exit. The second croc lunged at Ren, too, partially climbing over the other one's back to do it. Together they formed a wide wall of twisting reptilian flesh just outside the entryway.

The Walkers hit the brakes, stopping just short of the living roadblock. Ta-mesah released a hoarse, huffing growl. He grabbed the big beasts by the backs of their necks and tossed them aside with mindboggling strength.

Before the crocs even landed, Ren hit the wall of barley like an arrow, disappearing inside.

"Nice move," she heard. The voice came from right beside her, and she jumped nearly as high as the tall grain. But it was only Luke. She shushed him and grasped her amulet tight so that she could understand the Walkers' words.

"Forget her," rumbled Ta-mesah, scanning the wall of grain and slowing to a walk. "She is just trying to lure us away from the boy."

Still trying, Ren reached out with her free hand and rustled the stalks all around her. The Walkers ignored the desperate gesture.

"True," said the Stung Man. "And he is dead by now. Let us go see if there's anything left of him."

Ren's blood ran cold. *The crocs, the Stung Man, Ta-mesah — they were all right here — but he was confident Alex was dead. Had she let her best friend run straight into a trap? Was there something else lying in wait inside? Something even worse?*

## Facing the Founder

Alex wasn't dead. Not yet, anyway.

The bizarre figure before him was toying with him, as a cat would a mouse. "I founded The Order long ago, when civilization itself was still young and Egypt was new."

The founder paused, his rasping voice winding down like a buzz saw. Alex stared at him, horrified and transfixed. A churning swirl of purple and black enveloped him like a thick, liquid suit. Now and then an insect's eye or a translucent wing appeared in the mix, only to be sucked back into the maelstrom. Large, wasp-like bodies bubbled up and disappeared. Sometimes a gap appeared and Alex caught a glimpse of the founder's desiccated body beneath. Alex understood now that this was the very first Death Walker.

"I see you have met my friends," said the founder. He plunged one bony, clawlike hand into his own swirling chest and plucked one of the ghostly wasps. Free from the teeming mix, it grew from the size of a sparrow to the size of an eagle and snapped at the air with jagged needle-sharp teeth.

Without even looking at it, the founder plunged it back in. "They started as spirits — human souls. They were drawn to me, because my spirit was stronger. But over the centuries, I have taken over those spirits. We have become a sort of hive. Now they hunger for other souls to consume." He paused. "As you will see in a moment."

Alex knew that the founder would soon devour him, body and soul. He knew he should fight, but the idea seemed absurd. *What could I possibly do to this ancient creature?* Right now it was one being, more or less. Blasting it with wind or launching some object at it would just scatter the hive — which would pick him clean in seconds.

Alex's heart raced with fear and sank with despair at the same time. Because the real pity of it was that he had come so close to his goal. So very close.

On a raised stone platform directly beside the founder lay the Lost Spells of the ancient Egyptian Book of the Dead. They were covered over with the thin linen of the concealment spells, but he knew they were there. They had given him a second life, and he could feel them in his blood.

"Yes, the Spells," said the founder, following his eyes. "For so long we searched for them: a power far greater than our own, a power beyond imagination. And now they are ours. Perhaps I should thank you, but you have caused us trouble as well. So instead, you will die."

Alex searched his mind desperately for some escape. He was too far into the room to sprint for the door. There was

nothing substantial to hide behind. Even if fighting was futile, he would have to try.

Alex heard heavy footsteps at the door behind him. He didn't dare turn around, but he knew that the other Walkers had returned.

The founder smiled. Vain in the way powerful men have always been, he'd simply been waiting for an audience. He raised one hand, and the hive began to grow there, like a grotesque, inflating fist. Wings sprouted, buzzing loudly; eyes appeared.

But Alex clung tightly to something the Death Walker had just said: *A power far greater than our own.*

The founder was more powerful than him. Ta-mesah was more powerful than him. Even the Stung Man, whom he'd defeated before, was beyond harm here. But none of them were the most powerful thing in this room.

As the leader lowered his churning arm toward him, Alex used the power of the scarab for the smallest of tasks.

He flipped aside the light, age-yellowed linen of the con-cealment spells.

A wave of power spread through the room like a ripple on smooth water. It was barely visible — just a brief wink and bend to the firelight — but the effect was profound.

The founder held his vengeful spirits as he turned to look at the powerful ancient text. The other two Death Walkers, who'd been hovering near the door to avoid being caught in the carnage, took a step back.

Alex was barely aware of any of it. His head swam and his knees nearly buckled. All he could do was stare at the Spells that had brought him back. As he did, the ancient scroll's ink-black text began to glow a soft gold.

*This is your chance*, he told himself. *Your last chance.*

For a moment, no one moved. Even the swarming spirits fell nearly still. And then, his legs wobbly and his vision lit by stars and phantom symbols, Alex teetered forward.

The founder took a step to block him, but Alex willed his dazzled eyes to focus and his breathless lungs to speak. "Get back!" he managed. "I have activated the Spells!"

"You can't wield this power," said the founder. He punctuated his words with a dismissive snort. But he didn't take another step.

Alex wobbled forward like a baby deer on ice. "Of course I can," he said, his voice little more than a pained gasp.

"He's used the Book of the Dead before," said the Stung Man. "He banished me here before the doors were fully opened."

The founder looked at the Stung Man carefully. "The Book is one thing," he said. "The Lost Spells are another." He turned back to Alex and repeated himself: "You can't wield this power!"

Alex stumbled past him, passing mere feet from the deadly swarm. "Why not?" he mumbled. With the Spells so close, he felt like he was speaking underwater, but he poured

everything he had left into his next words. "My mother used them . . . *And my father.*"

The founder glared at him. "Enough. I will destroy you."

The words formed clearly in Alex's troubled mind: *The gods are stronger . . .*

"No!" he shouted. "With a word, I can summon the Devourer! Her ancient name glows at the top of this page. Don't you see it?"

It was a bluff. A total bluff. The top line could have said Cheez Whiz for all he knew. He could barely see the walls with all the stars swirling in his eyes, much less read a scroll. With one last lurch, he stumbled toward the stone platform. Just inches from the Spells, his blood ran hot and his head went blank. He flung his free hand up gracelessly, but it worked. The concealment spells flapped upward like a wing and then fell across the face of the scroll.

Alex's head cleared slightly, and he scooped the ancient texts up against his chest: the thin, gauzy concealment spells and the heavy old scroll they guarded. It felt like hugging an electric eel, but he held on tight.

"One word!" he blurted, doubling down on his bluff.

Then he turned unsteadily and lurched out of the room.

With hate in their eyes, his stunned enemies let him pass.

Out in the hallway, he pulled the linen veil tight over the old scroll and took off running.

## The Sensation of Flight

As soon as Alex began to run, the Walkers realized he'd been bluffing and came after him. Alex bolted out the short hallway at full speed and rushed between the crocs, now lying motionless on their backs. He heard Ta-mesah's heavy footsteps slap the stone floor of the hallway and then soften as they hit dirt. *He was right behind him!*

"Over here!" Ren called from somewhere in the field.

Alex angled toward the sound and grimaced as Luke added: "Don't look back, cuz!"

He did his best to protect the ancient Spells with his arms as he ducked his head and rammed into the barley. Luke and Ren were waiting a few rows in.

"I have them!" Alex gasped. "We need to get back to the portal where we came in!"

"Okay," said Ren, already turning to run. "We can head to the riverbank and follow it back!"

The three friends crashed and stomped through the tall, fragile stalks.

With his friends beside him, their long-sought prize in his arms, and the concealing crops all around, a wave of hope washed over him. The Spells had saved his life twice now — and he'd just gotten a glimpse of their power. Three unstoppable Walkers had been held hostage by the mere threat of it.

But it wasn't just the Spells they feared: It was Ammit. The gods really were stronger. Anubis had turned the Walkers back at the river. He was the guardian of the afterlife, and his word was law here. But Ammit was the enforcer of that law, and her jaws brought oblivion.

As Alex ran, the stalks stinging his face, a wild thought occurred to him: *Maybe they could win.*

*And if they did* . . . This whole time, he'd been almost as afraid of finding the Spells as of not finding them. They could save his world, but they could also end his life. He'd been willing to risk it before.

But now? Knowing that this plot began long before him, that his mom had never abandoned him, and that the Spells in his arms scared his enemies stiff . . . He still wanted to win, but feeling the wild elation of escape, the sensation of flight as he ran alongside his friends, he knew something else. He wanted to live, too. *But how?*

A sound much louder than three grain-stomping kids rose up behind them. Alex looked back over his shoulder and saw the barley bend forward in a massive wave. As it did, Alex felt a swift slap strike his whole body at once. "Guh!" he blurted, stumbling onto one knee.

Ren was knocked to the ground beside him. Only Luke managed to keep his balance. All around them, acres of slender stalks were pushed to the ground as they were overrun by the invisible wave. Regaining his balance and turning once again, Alex saw the source. The hulking frame of Ta-mesah stood in the twilit distance. His arms were extended and his palms thrust outward.

He had used his formidable powers to flatten the grain.

The three Amulet Keepers were suddenly out in the open. Movement caught Alex's eye and he raised his gaze to the gray sky, which was turning a deep, bruise-like purple behind them, clouding over with a swarm of fast-flying shapes.

Ren scrambled to her feet, eyes darting back at the rows of flattened grain and up at the swarm of hungry spirits. "The portal's too far away," she said. "We'll never make it!"

"We have to try," called Luke, reaching down to help Ren up. He alone had the speed to escape, but he wouldn't do it without them.

They turned and ran across the flattened field.

Ta-mesah had flattened the grain all the way to the edge of the field, and Ren squinted into the dim distance as she ran.

And there it was: an army on the march.

An uninterrupted line of men appeared out of a glowing gateway in the air at one end, only to march steadily forward

and disappear into the air at the other. Ren had seen this before, when her amulet had shown it to her. She knew they were stepping out of one false door and into another, traveling from Egypt to New York by a macabre shortcut through the afterlife.

An odd feeling washed over her overheated system. As the infernal buzzing grew louder and closer and as the Death Walkers closed in, she stared at the spot where the undead soldiers were disappearing. *New York*, she thought. *At least I'll die close to home.*

The fading gray twilight was filled with darkening swirls and whorls and streaks. Wails and growls and disembodied gasps filled her ears. Soon this would be the menacing nighttime world she'd seen on her first trip to the afterlife — if she lived that long. She turned her attention to the uneven ground in front of her. As she did she saw a faint but familiar glow hanging in the gray air just up ahead. Her muscles burning and her legs pumping, she looked a little closer.

"*PUH!*" she gasped as she felt a hard, sharp push from behind.

She stumbled forward, falling through the spectral light and into darkness.

## Back Where It All Started

Sure, Alex felt bad about pushing his best friend through the glimmering portal. And maybe he felt a little weird about grabbing his cousin by the hand and tugging him through. But he felt worse about tripping over Ren once he leapt through himself, and worse still when Luke fell through on top of him.

"Duh-off!" he blurted as his foot caught Ren's leg, and he blurted something worse when Luke sandwiched him onto the hard floor. He did his best to land on his shoulder and protect the ancient Spells from the impact.

As Luke rolled free, Alex shot a look back to make sure nothing was coming through the portal after them. *Had they lost them in the dim light and distance?* he wondered desperately. *And if so, for how long?*

He turned to examine their new surroundings. They could be anywhere there was a false door, including some old tomb deep beneath the ground. As he looked around, he realized that they *were* in a tomb. But the mix of natural and electric light told him that this tomb was in a museum.

"Why does it look so —" Ren began.

"Familiar," said Alex. He was sure now: the immaculately restored old stone, the little silver information plaques, the lights burning softly overhead . . . He turned back to the others, unable to keep the smile from his face. "We're at the Met," he said. "We're home!"

They were in the big, reconstructed tomb at the entrance to the Egyptian wing, the one that always had a line snaking through it in the summer. Alex peered out of the tomb mouth and saw the back of the north-side ticket booths. Beyond that, huge banners hung down from the ceiling of the Great Hall. Sunlight streamed in the museum's high windows. It had been twilight in Egypt, but it was still midday in New York.

"Finally," said Ren, her voice breaking with emotion.

The three climbed to their feet, grunting and groaning as their bumps and bruises required. Alex carefully refolded the concealment spells. His head swam, and a hot, static energy tingled through his fingers as he touched the scroll beneath them, but he felt better again as soon as he pulled the linen veil tight. He removed his old backpack and stuffed the bundle deep inside, putting the old scrolls already in there on top to pin the protective linen in place.

"I'll take that," said Ren. "I know they make you kind of swoony."

Alex didn't argue — they did make him swoony. He handed over the pack, and she put it on.

Alex looked out into Room 100 of The Metropolitan

Museum of Art, a place as familiar to him as the lobby of his own apartment building. The lights were low, and the room was empty. The museum was closed tight in the middle of the day. Alex edged out of the tomb mouth.

"See anything?" asked Ren, a few steps behind him.

"Hear anything?" added Luke, a few steps behind her.

"Nothing," he said, turning back to them. They were quite a sight. Ren's nose was running from her allergies, and tears from her watering eyes had carved tracks through the thick layer of dirt and grain dust on her cheeks. Luke looked like the "Before" picture in a laundry detergent ad.

"How did you know this portal led back to New York?" asked Ren.

"I didn't," Alex admitted, lowering his voice as they eased silently out of the room and toward the ticket booths. "But I figured that's where all those mummies were headed, and this one was close by. Plus, you know, we were about to get torn into a million pieces by those wasp things."

Ren nodded, satisfied with his deductive reasoning.

"Good call," added Luke.

They edged past the empty ticket booths and looked out into the grand marble expanse of the museum's entrance hall. The huge old building felt solid and familiar, but far from safe. Just up ahead, near the center of the hall, flashing red light washed in through the tall glass doors and painted the walls and floors. The friends rushed toward it.

"It looks like a war zone," said Ren once they reached the big glass doors.

**154**

Alex could only nod. Wooden barricades and stacked sandbags lined the streets in front of the museum. The flashing lights came from two NYPD cruisers parked on Fifth Avenue, bookending two large, blocky armored personnel carriers with thick knobby tires. Alex craned his neck to look up East 82nd Street. He saw a cloud of thick gray-and-black smoke billowing up in the distance. Somewhere nearby, a fire was raging.

Silhouetted figures shifted inside the police cruisers, but there was no traffic and the normally packed sidewalks were deserted. A city of millions was on lockdown. The only sound was the rumble of the army vehicles' idling engines purring through the safety glass. *Police, military, open fires, and empty streets* . . . He could hardly believe this was the same bustling city where he'd grown up.

"My parents," moaned Ren. "I hope they're okay."

"I'm with you on that," said Luke solemnly. And Alex thought of his well-meaning aunt and uncle, and all that Luke had suffered to keep them safe.

"Yeah," Alex said, "but before we find our families —"

"I know, bro," said Luke. "What's the plan?"

"Call Cairo," Alex said, the red lights washing over his dirt-smeared face. "I can't use these Spells — they knock me for a loop — but my mom can. And then she can, you know, save the world."

"Yeah, that part sounds important," agreed Luke.

The friends took one more look out at the war zone where they'd grown up and then headed toward the main office.

**155**

"So how did you escape from all those Death Walkers back there, anyway?" Ren asked Alex.

Alex managed half a smile. "I told them Ammit was on the way."

"They are really scared of that dude, huh?" said Luke.

"She's a lady," said Alex. "Sort of. But yeah: really scared."

They walked quietly for a while and then Ren leaned in toward Alex and said a few hesitant words: "I was thinking . . ."

Alex smiled at her. "That doesn't surprise me."

She got to the point. "The Walkers are afraid of the gods. And the gods definitely don't seem to like the Walkers. Did you hear the way Anubis talked about them? He *knew* they were evil . . ."

"They don't exactly keep that a secret," said Alex.

"Don't you get it?" she said. "What if the gods could do something more than scare them? What if they could do *what they're scared of*? They're afraid of that ceremony, the weighing of the heart. They're afraid of being *judged*. What if there was someway to, I don't know, put them on trial?"

"That would be *awesome*," said Alex. It was as if his best friend had read his mind — and then taken his thoughts a step further. The two had known each other nearly their entire lives, and their thoughts often ran along the same lines, like two trains on parallel tracks, with Ren's maybe half a length ahead. But all tracks still led to the same ques-

tion that had stopped Alex before. "But how do we get the gods to do it?" he said.

"Yeah," Ren answered. "That's the thing."

A few minutes later, they were in Alex's mom's office. Alex had the emergency cell phone she kept in her bottom drawer pressed to his ear. His finger shook as he held it steady next to a line midway down the *H*s in his mom's address book: "Dr. Hesaan, Cairo."

Now they had to hope that one flickering bar of service — Alex imagined one last stubbornly functional cell tower somewhere in the Bronx — would be enough to connect two crisis-crippled cities six thousand miles apart.

The phone rang: once, twice, three — "Who is this?"

The connection was weak, but the voice was familiar. Alex exhaled mightily and put the phone on speaker for the others. "Hey, Dr. Hesaan," he said. "It's Alex. Can I talk to my mom, or Todtman?"

"So they have telephones in the afterlife now," said Hesaan. "Strange days . . . But they are both here. Just a second."

It was Todtman who came on the line. He listened carefully to what Alex had to tell him. "New York?" he said.

"Yeah," breathed Alex, hardly believing it himself. "Right back where it all started."

Todtman was silent, thinking.

"Where it started and where it will end," he said at last. "You must stay where you are. We will come to you."

Alex could only imagine how long that would take. "What if they find us first? They're going to figure out where we went sooner or later."

"Then let us hope it is later. We are on the way. Stay out of sight, and keep the Spells safe."

Ren grabbed the phone from Alex's hands and got right to her point. "I can't stay here," she said. "I have to go home and check on my parents. It's not far."

"I am sorry, Ren, but you must stay there. We will need you for this. We will need everyone. You have been away from home a long time, but the risk is too great. Peshwar and her army control most of the city by now."

"But —" she protested.

"Please, Ren, stay safe," pleaded Todtman. "This will all be over soon . . . One way or the other."

The line went dead.

But outside the office, a stronger buzz was already growing.

## Company

Alex rushed toward the door and closed it as quickly and quietly as he could. He listened closely as the noise grew louder and angrier. "It's coming from the hall," he whispered.

"It's one of those bugs, isn't it?" said Luke.

Alex tried to think of something — anything — else it could be. But he couldn't. He nodded slowly, his eyes on the frosted glass panes alongside the door.

The buzzing grew louder, closer.

A shadowy shape flashed past out in the hallway, and Alex gasped. He looked over at Ren, asking the question with his wide-open eyes: *Did it see us?*

The buzzing grew softer and then, very suddenly, louder. Alex turned back toward the door — where a dark shape was hovering on the other side of the frosted glass. The spirit wasp flew back a few inches and then rammed its body into the pane. *WHUMP!*

Alex's hand fumbled beneath his shirt for his amulet.

*WHUMP! WHUMP!*

It tried two more times to break the glass, but then seemed to reconsider. For a long moment, it just stared in at them with dark, malevolent eyes. Then it turned and disappeared back down the hallway.

"Oh no," said Ren.

"What?" said Alex. "Isn't it a good thing it went away?"

Ren shook her head. "It's a scout," she said. "It found us."

"Oh, snap!" said Luke. "It's going back to snitch."

The three friends took off after it, but by the time they reached the hallway, they'd lost the speeding spirit.

"We have to stop it before it goes back through the portal!" said Alex urgently.

With his amulet, Luke was more than fast enough to catch the bug as it bugged out — but he didn't know his way around the museum. Instead, he ran alongside the others as they navigated the twisty interior, taking every shortcut they knew. They finally caught sight of the thing in the Great Hall. "There!" called Alex.

"Give me something to throw over it!" called Luke. But they had nothing. Luke tried to strip off his Under Armour top while at a full run and wiped out on the slick tile, sliding across the polished floor with his shirt over his head.

It darted through the ticket booths, utterly ignoring the "suggested donation" sign.

A few moments later, Alex and Ren sprinted into Room 100 just in time to see the infernal bug enter the big tomb.

Ren tried to blast it with her ibis, but the bug was already inside the stone entryway.

"No!" cried Alex as the thing flew full speed into the false door. The buzzing disappeared instantly.

*Whoomp!* Luke appeared by their side, holding his shirt in one hand and his amulet in the other. "Where'd it go?"

Alex lifted his chin toward the ancient portal.

The only sound in the quiet room was the three friends, breathing hard.

"I think we're going to have company," huffed Alex.

A man's voice boomed through the room: "Oh, but you already do."

## The Day Turns Red

"Gah! Todtman!" huffed Ren as Alex clutched his chest. "Don't scare us like that!"

"*Tut mir leid,*" said the German, leaning on his walking stick. "I am sorry. But I am more sorry that we could not stop that pest. I had just turned the corner when I saw it flash by."

As if to demonstrate the process, Dr. Bauer rounded the corner. Alex rushed over to hug her. "Careful, hun!" she said, and he pulled up short and did his best to hug her healthy side. She reached down and ruffled his hair. Then he did a double take. "Wait, where did you two come from?"

Todtman flashed his quick, sly smile and said, "There are many false doors in this museum."

"But you only have one amulet," said Ren.

"I'm an Amulet Keeper, too, though," said Dr. Bauer. "And I held on *very* tight."

Todtman waved away the pleasantries and scanned the three kids quickly. "Where are the Spells? Are they safe?"

Ren swung the backpack off. Todtman clucked once in disapproval. "They are thousands of years old, irreplaceable. They are not . . . a math workbook."

"Actually, they're surprisingly durable," said Dr. Bauer, taking the backpack from Ren. "Strong magic makes for strong scrolls."

Alex watched his mom gracefully shift the backpack from one hand to the other.

"You're moving a lot better," he said.

She turned and smiled. "I am full of Hesaan's arthritis medication."

"Is that safe?" said Ren, and it occurred to Alex just what a good doctor she would make.

"None of this is safe," said Alex's mom, unzipping the pack and peering inside. "But it does numb the pain."

Alex watched her pluck out the extra scrolls and lower them to the floor. There was only one scroll that mattered now, in the pack and in the world. "Mom," said Alex, hesitating, unsure of what exactly he was asking. "Can the Lost Spells do . . . other things?"

"Yeah," added Ren. "Can they, like, talk to the gods?"

Dr. Bauer looked from one to the other. She knew when they were up to something. "All Egyptian spells invoke the old gods in some way," she said. "But it's not a conversation. It's more like calling out a name and hoping for an echo. And the Lost Spells are quite specialized. They deal with the afterlife, its gateways and guardians."

"Guardians?" said Alex and Ren together.

"Enough questions," said Todtman. "We must use the Spells immediately. The Death Walkers and their army will be here in moments, too many and too powerful to oppose. We must repair the rift *now*."

He turned toward Dr. Bauer, put his hand on her arm, and looked her in the eyes. "Maggie," he said. "Can you use the Spells here, now? We have little time."

She took one more look inside the pack, then glanced into the dark entryway of the tomb. "In there," she said. "We should be close to a portal for this, within sight. It will have more effect that way. And if we close one, we close them all."

They filed back inside the old tomb. Before they made it halfway down the entryway, a huge crashing noise thundered out of the inner sanctum, followed by the brittle screech of cracking stone. All around them, the big stone structure began to rumble and shake. Something was coming through the portal. Something *big*.

"Let's get out of here!" called Alex.

"There's another portal in the Temple of Dendur," said Alex's mom. "We can use that!"

They hustled out of the shaking structure toward the familiar temple. It was housed in the largest room in the museum, even bigger than the Great Hall. It had always been Alex's favorite place at the Met. He'd spent days gazing out of the room's soaring glass wall into Central Park, peering into its midnight black reflecting pool, or looking

up at the ancient temple itself, brought over from Egypt and reconstructed block by block here.

A heavy stone block crashed to the floor behind the friends as they headed deeper into the Egyptian wing. They wound their way through the maze of half-lit rooms, past grand granite statues and cases of glittering jewelry of gold, carnelian, turquoise, and lapis lazuli. A carving of the cow-headed goddess Hathor gazed out at them with big, sad eyes as they rushed by. A quick glance was enough for Alex to recognize each exhibit. He'd spent his childhood here, and many of the items were as familiar to him as the decorations in his own bedroom. *Would it all end here as well?*

He shook his head hard to clear it, but the thought would not be cleared.

They reached the temple quickly, but it was not the safe haven they'd hoped for. Daylight streamed through the panes of the soaring three-story glass wall, and just outside a battalion of mummies swayed in sun.

"There are like a brillion of them!" said Luke.

It looked more like a few hundred to Alex, a small fraction of the overall army, but it was still more than enough to tear the Keepers limb from limb. "What are they waiting for?" said Ren.

The answer came in a brilliant flash of crimson light outside the windows. As the day turned red, Alex swung around and saw the leader of the undead strike-force. The lioness-headed Peshwar stood at the front of her troops,

supersized in death just as Ta-mesah had been. In her long, clawlike hand was a crackling crimson energy dagger.

"Take cover!" shouted Todtman.

As the Death Walker whipped her hand up and forward, the friends ducked behind the row of statues just inside the double doors. An explosion shook the room as the energy dagger blew a huge hole in the massive glass wall.

The mummies began clambering clumsily inside, pausing only to allow their leader to step gracefully through the jagged opening.

"We have to get out of here," called Todtman. But as he turned toward the door, Alex saw him stop cold. Todtman began to slowly back up as Ta-mesah dipped his fearsome head through the doorway. A moment later, the Stung Man appeared, and a fierce buzzing grew in the room behind him

"Over here," called Dr. Bauer. "This way."

Not daring to take their eyes off the approaching enemies, the group followed her voice toward the southeast corner of the hangar-like room.

"You cling to your lives like you cling to those Spells," rumbled Ta-mesah, leveling his lifeless gaze at the huddled friends. "And soon, you will have neither."

But Dr. Bauer knew the great museum well, and she'd chosen this corner for a reason. A small side door there connected back to the western edge of the Egyptian wing.

Alex knew it, too. And he knew they didn't need to conquer their enemies. All they needed to do was protect his

mom long enough for her to use the Spells. He tightened his left hand around the scarab. "Go!" he shouted as hurricane force wind shot out from his right hand.

He formed his fingers into a tight spear, concentrating the wind, and aimed it right for Ta-mesah's face. The force had little effect on the massive Walker — but at least Alex couldn't hear what the big creep was saying anymore.

A handful of mummies, their formerly bone-dry corpses half-soaked from wading through the reflecting pool, attempted to scramble around Ta-mesah's hulking frame. Alex dialed back the mystic wind and let them. Then he redirected the blast low, mowing the mummies down like bowling pins.

With the powerful wind no longer blasting his face, Ta-mesah charged forward, but his thick legs got tangled with the squirming mummies on the floor in front of him. Trying to kick free, he snapped one of mummies nearly in half and went down in a heap on top of the others.

The Amulet Keepers took advantage of the opening and darted through the side door, into darkness.

## Sacrifices

The rooms on the western side of the wing had no windows, and were lit only by a few Exit signs. Alex blinked into the ruddy murk in time to see the others filing quickly into the next room. As he rushed to catch up, Alex could hear the shuffling stampede of bony feet behind him.

As the group cleared the next room, Alex yanked the glass door closed behind them. *That ought to hold them . . .* he thought. *For about three seconds.* Empty eye sockets were already gaping at him as he locked the door with his amulet. Leathery hands were already pounding on the glass as he turned to run.

They just needed a few quiet minutes within sight of a portal for his mom to use the Spells. So close to their goal, he got a wild, cornered feeling, knowing that the Spells could kill him. His mom knew that, too. She'd had the Spells for weeks and been unwilling to take that chance. His feelings a jumble, he both hoped and feared she'd risk it now.

He looked up at his mom, one hand clutching the Spells, the other grasping her injured side. He wanted to run along-

side her — she'd sacrificed so much for him — but he stayed a few steps behind instead. He wanted even more to protect her.

Behind them, the glass door exploded under some massive, unseen force. The friends ducked their shoulders and entered Room 100 from the opposite side of where they'd left it. Pursued by a wave of mummies and Death Walkers, they could do nothing but rush straight past the last of the portals. Alex exhaled when he saw no sign of the founder as they passed the ruined temple — but he simply hadn't been looking hard enough. From one shadowy corner, a hovering member of the hive began to beat its wings furiously. The buzz rose to a high-pitched whine.

"Zap it, Ren!" called Alex.

*FWOOP!*

White light washed the corner clean of shadow and seemed to stun the wasp spirit. It dipped in the air, the outer layer of its body turning to purple vapor. The urgent whine fell back to a buzz, but it was too late. Another wasp turned the corner to join it, and then a dozen more.

Ren let out one more burst of mystic light as covering fire as the friends rushed out of the room. As the thundering stampede of mummies began to merge with the angry hum of swarming spirits, Alex closed and locked the big glass double doors behind them.

They rushed back through the ticket booths, but in front of them lay the wide-open expanse of the Great Hall.

"We'll never make it across," said Todtman. "They'll tear us apart before we get halfway."

"Behind there," said Dr. Bauer, pointing to the long counter along the wall where the museum sold memberships and event tickets.

Ren turned and, running backward, released two more blinding flashes at the bodies and souls massing behind the heavy safety-glass doors. If their pursuers saw them slip behind the counter, it was all over.

A moment later, they were all crouched behind the tall, dark counters.

"We need a plan," said Ren in an insistent, hissy whisper. "We can't just keep running and hiding."

"If we stop running and hiding, we're dead," said Luke.

The pounding on the big glass doors was turning to a brittle crackling as Todtman crept up alongside Alex and his mom. "You two stay here," he said.

"What?" said Alex as his mom said, "No!"

He ignored them both. "The nearest portal is right behind you. We will lead them away. Stay quiet and perfectly still until we are gone. Then move fast — and do not fail!"

"But it's me they're looking for," said Dr. Bauer. "Me and the Spells."

"I know," said Todtman. He closed his hand around his amulet. His eyes closed and his face reddened with effort. Two shimmering shapes appeared beside him: a boy and a woman, rough approximations of Alex and his mom.

"Whoa," gasped Alex. He reached out to touch his phantasmal twin, but his hand passed through.

**170**

"It is only in your mind," said Todtman.

*Prr-KRISH!* The big double doors exploded outward. The crimson light washing the walls left no doubt as to the cause. As bits of safety glass rained down on the tile, the others sprang into action.

"Good luck," whispered Ren, before slipping out from behind the counter and into harm's way.

Alex was too stunned to respond and only managed to gasp "Ren" at the spot where she had been. It took everything he had, and his mom's reassuring hand on his shoulder, to stay still as the others risked their lives leading The Order forces across the Great Hall and into the vast museum beyond.

"Over here!" Alex heard Luke call as he used his speed to lure the lurching mummies and their deathly leaders as far away as possible. "No, over *here!*" he called as he zoomed farther down the hall.

The strobe-light flash of Ren's amulet washed the walls, followed by a crimson response from Peshwar. There was a loud explosion, but Alex exhaled as he saw a second flash, this one farther away. He knew that most of The Order's forces would chase Todtman and his phantoms. He could only hope the old man could stay out of their deadly range.

Just feet away, on the other side of the counter, mummies lurched and spirits buzzed. The big Death Walkers followed in turn, like tanks taking the field after the infantry. But after a few loud and terrifying minutes, the Great Hall fell silent. The others had succeeded in luring the enemies

farther into the museum, up its marble stairs and into its masterpiece-filled galleries.

Ren, Todtman, and Luke . . . They were all risking their lives for this. Alex felt overwhelmed by their bravery, but more than that, he felt an obligation to do his part.

"Let's go," he said, helping his mom to her feet.

They had one more shot — bought at great cost — and they could not waste it.

His mom nodded and rose. Their feet crunched through the shattered glass as they approached the first tomb, the stone cracked from where the Walkers had come through. It was dark and quiet inside Room 100. Except for . . . an ominous and all-too-familiar buzzing.

The founder was still inside the fractured tomb. The oldest Walker had released some of his hive to the chase, but the man himself had found his new nest.

Slowly, very slowly, Alex and his mom backed away from the entrance.

"Where now?" whispered Alex.

"Dendur," answered his mom.

Eyes wide-open for any more stragglers, they hurried back toward the Temple of Dendur.

Ta-mesah took one more swipe at Alex's image only to see his massive hand pass harmlessly through it. He released a ruffled huff that flared his croc nostrils.

"They are illusions," hissed Peshwar. "Tell us where the real ones are, old man."

Todtman stood in the shadowy back corner of the room, breathing hard, blood trickling from his nose and split lower lip. All around him, Greek statues bore silent witness to a brave man's last stand.

Cut off from the exit by two massive Death Walkers, he could run no more. "They are right here," said Todtman, gesturing to the two phantom figures next to him. "Don't you see them?"

"I see your crude trick," rumbled Ta-mesah, eyeing the shimmering shells. "The simple work of a street magician."

The flickering images vanished, and the smallest of smiles creased Todtman's froggy features. "Not such a crude trick," he said as a red glow lit up the room, turning the pale marble statues a garish pink.

The energy dagger grew long and wicked in Peshwar's hand. Todtman was certain his next words would be his last. "After all," he said, "it has kept you both here, so far from where you need to be, for so very long."

Peshwar snarled as she whipped the deadly dagger straight toward him. Todtman tried to leap to the side, but his crippled leg betrayed him one last time. The crackling crimson dagger sank deep into his chest, and a heart that had begun beating some six decades earlier in a small village in Bavaria convulsed and fell still.

His body crumpled to the cold tile floor.

# The Lost Spells

Alex and his mom were inside the shallow alcove of the Temple of Dendur. The Lost Spells were spread out across the floor, and the letters of the ancient text glowed softly as she chanted the first few lines in a rhythmic, almost trance-like voice. The power of the Spells had saved him once, but now it was taking a heavy toll. His vision was speckled with stars and phantom symbols, and his head was woozy. He sat gracelessly, legs straight out, shoulders against the side of the temple for support.

Suddenly, his mom stopped chanting and looked up. The glow began to fade, and Alex's head began to clear ever so slightly. "I can't do it," she said.

Alex struggled to understand her through the slowly lifting fog in his mind. "You need the scarab," he said, reaching for the chain around his neck with clumsy fingers.

"No," she said. "It's not that. The scarab lets you read the language, understand the spells — that's how it lets you use the Book of the Dead. But I already read this

language and understand these spells. It's . . . you. Alex, you're my son."

As overwhelmed as his mind was, he knew exactly what she meant. But he also remembered the sacrifice the others were making to buy them this time. "I know, but —"

She cut him off. "If I close these doorways, if I undo the damage that I did . . ."

She didn't have to finish. Alex knew the rest all too well: She could snuff him out like a birthday candle. How could he convince his own mother to risk his life? "But if you don't . . ." he began. He didn't need to finish that sentence, either. They both knew how it ended: in a death-shadowed world ruled by madmen.

He met her eyes through the nebula of tiny stars that lit his vision.

"I am proud of you," she said, "and I love you, and . . . I will try."

He saw a single tear roll down her cheek, and then he saw a huge figure looming up behind her.

"Oh no," he gasped, but it was already too late. The leader reached down and plucked the woman who had once been his wife from the floor by her shoulder.

She screamed and kicked back at him with her boots. It was useless. "Alex," she called. "The amulet."

*Yes*, he thought. He'd seen her use it before and knew she was a more experienced and powerful Amulet Keeper than he was. But as he reached up for the chain once again,

the leader spared a quick glance for his son. He flicked his free hand in Alex's direction, and an invisible wave of force slammed Alex back into the temple wall. Alex's head bounced off stone with the sound of a coconut considering cracking. A jolt of pain shot through him, and he fought to stay conscious. As his eyes fluttered half closed, he saw his mom tossed across the tile platform in front of the temple. She landed on her injured side and slid like a broken toy.

"No!" he called weakly.

He struggled to stand, but battered from the blow and woozy from the Spells, he was like a boxer who couldn't peel himself from the canvas. His legs twitched and jerked but refused to gather underneath him. One numb hand pawed his chest, managing only to push the scarab around, not grasp it.

His mom's body was still now, and as he stared at it, hoping for any sign of movement, the room began to fill up behind her. He caught snatches of it through his peripheral vision. The hulking figures of Ta-mesah and Peshwar, the ornate robes of the Stung Man, the sea of ragged wrapping as the mummies followed, the growing buzzing in the air. He didn't know if they'd been called back by their leader or if their chase was simply over.

Finally, he saw his mom's hand twitch open and closed. Her legs straightened out and she flopped over onto her back. Alex could let himself breathe again.

Meanwhile, The Order's forces had massed beneath the temple's raised platform, staring up at their leader. Alex saw

something move out of the corner of his eye and turned to see Ren and Luke rush into the room last, following the forces they'd been trying to lead away, still trying to get their attention. They stopped cold inside the entrance, just short of the undead army in front of them.

Alex saw the look of shock on Ren's face as she spotted his mom's crumpled body. Then he saw her face collapse as she spied him slumped inside the alcove.

"It is over, Amulet Keepers," called the leader, his booming voice echoing through the massive space.

Ren's small voice rose up in response: "Then give us our friends and we'll leave."

A layer of mummies moved in between his friends and the door they'd come through, sealing off any escape. "You will get nothing," said the leader, "and you will go nowhere."

Alex tried again to stand but succeeded only in flopping back to the floor — and attracting Peshwar's attention. "The boy is alive, and near the Spells," she hissed from her place near the edge of the platform. "Kill him now."

The leader looked back. "He can't even rise to his feet in the presence of the Spells," he said. "Much less give voice to the chants. He is no danger to us."

"Your weakness for the boy puts us in danger," said Peshwar.

The leader stared down at her. "Are you challenging me?"

She bowed her head, pointing the empty sockets of the lioness skull at the floor, but still she spoke. "Kill them all," she said. "It's easy. Like this."

She tossed something toward the platform. As it clattered to a stop at the leader's feet, Alex recognized Todtman's walking staff.

The realization that Todtman was dead hit him like a punch to the heart. But under Peshwar's cruel gaze, he felt that sorrow turn to something else. Anger and loyalty and loss mixed in his battered body — and it gave him strength. His fingers found his amulet and finally closed around its familiar form. The ancient energy flowed through him. He looked over at the Lost Spells. He pulled himself closer.

His father was right: He couldn't stand in their presence or chant their words. But as he edged closer to the old scroll, he thought he just might be able to read them. The Spells were specialized, his mom had said. They dealt with the afterlife, with its gateways and guardians.

As Alex's vision filled with fresh pinpricks of light and his head lolled limply on his neck, he looked for the name of one guardian in particular.

"Behind you!" called Peshwar.

"The boy!" growled Ta-mesah.

Alex knew the leader was turning toward him, knew he had only seconds left, but he dared not look up — and there it was! The name he was looking for.

With all his remaining strength and all the breath left in his lungs, he called that name. Just one word, but he filled it with all the anger and sadness and helplessness he felt. His enemies had broken the rules, not just the laws of this world,

but the laws of life and death. And they had done so cruelly and for the basest of all reasons: power. As full of stars as his vision was, it was hard to tell, but he thought the word might even have glowed a little, flickered on the page, as he said it.

A moment later, a fresh wave of force from the leader sent Alex flying backward across the tile. He slammed hard into the back of the alcove. He managed to protect his head this time, but he felt something crack in his chest.

*Just like my mom*, he thought as he once again teetered on the edge of consciousness. He peered out of the alcove and saw his father staring in. The Spells were between them, ten feet away. It might as well have been ten miles.

The room was quiet, save for the buzz of the spirits, and still, save for the gentle swaying of the mummies.

"He has failed," Peshwar hissed into the calm.

The reply came almost immediately, but it wasn't from the leader or any of the other Walkers. It wasn't from any of the Keepers, either. It wasn't in words at all, in fact. Peshwar got her answer in the form of a great and terrible roar. The cry shook the room.

Part lion.

Part crocodile.

Part thunder.

Alex leaned his battered frame back against the temple wall and smiled.

His call had been answered.

# The Devourer

Alex never saw the great beast enter the room. Turning his head toward the source of the terrible roar, she was simply there. She was the size of a truck and as terrifying as she was improbable. Her huge crocodile head dwarfed that of Ta-mesah and gave the Walker no more than a glance as she swept her vision across the room.

Alex's head swam and fresh pain stabbed him deep inside. He was terrified for his mom, who was still lying helplessly on the platform. He had called Ammit in desperation, but had no way of knowing what this otherworldly presence might do.

Ammit was the ultimate enforcer of good and evil in ancient Egypt, the one who devoured the souls of the unworthy, destroying them forever. But now the rules had been cheated, the boundaries between the worlds torn open, and this much was clear: Ammit was mad.

She released another roar, so fearsome and so close, that Alex could do nothing but cover his ears. Then, with slow, deliberate steps, she began to move toward the platform. Her

enormous front paws, those of a massive lion, pushed forward with the fluid ease of a jungle cat, while her huge back feet, those of a hippo, plodded forward to join them.

As she moved, she brushed by rows of swaying mummies. At the slightest touch, they disintegrated into clouds of dust and scraps of linen. Two more steps and she had reached the platform. With surprising grace, she pulled herself up.

Suddenly, there were only two people left in her path. Once again, the leader reached down and plucked Alex's mom up by the shoulder. This time she could offer no resistance, but from his perch inside the temple, Alex saw her eyes flutter open. She stared at the strange creature and breathed her name in awe: "Ammit . . ."

The beast came a few steps closer and seemed to examine her.

A jolt of fear shot through Alex's system. His mom was in danger: direct, immediate danger.

Surrounded by The Order forces, the creature's paralyzing presence had seemed a reprieve. But now he understood how stupid he'd been. This was the devourer, and she was here for a reason.

Alex gasped a word of his own: "Mom . . ."

But it was the other half of the family tree that responded. The leader thrust Alex's mom forward toward Ammit. She pried uselessly at his powerful fingers. Alex managed to get his legs underneath him. He desperately wanted to rush over and help her. But what could he do? Even with his amulet,

he'd be little more than another pair of hands prying use-
lessly at a death grip.

"Yes," called the leader. "Take her. She is the one you want.
She opened the portals. *She* started all of this. We merely
responded to these changes, traveled between the worlds as
a floating leaf would follow a river."

Alex glared at him. But the words still stung. She *had*
opened the portals, but she'd done it for him. She didn't
know what would happen, but she had risked everything.

He looked at his mom, twisting in the grip of a madman.

He looked down at Todtman's staff.

He looked across the room at Ren, who had risked so
much for friendship. He saw Luke still standing next to her,
with the speed to escape but the loyalty to stay.

"No!" Alex called out from his sheltered stone alcove.
"It's because of me. The portals were opened to let me back.
Don't take her." He rose slowly to his feet. "Take me."

"No, Alex, don't," called Ren.

But the words were already out.

Ammit turned her head, and one cold crocodilian eye
fell on Alex. He saw the vertical slit in the center narrow
as it focused on him. She turned her body toward him
now, golden lion fur rippling. Alex put his hand out to
steady himself as he walked past the spot where the Spells
lay and toward the avenging demigod. He felt the pain
in his side and tasted the blood in his mouth, but he kept
walking.

"Yes, take the boy," purred the leader. "He's the cause."

**182**

Ammit paused. Her head swung back and faced the leader. Her strong, huffing breaths rippled his robes as they looked at each other. Alex's mom hung an arm's length away, and Alex was nearly out of the temple now.

Ammit looked over at him one more time, and then back at his mom.

Then, with a speed Alex would not have imagined possible, Ammit's head swung back. Her jaws flashed open, extending all the way down to the floor and revealing rows of huge white teeth.

Alex heard a huge gulp of air as the devourer pulled her prey toward her.

Alex's heart stopped and his eyes closed as the enormous jaws snapped shut.

Quiet.

Alex slowly opened his eyes. His mom was still there. The leader's arm began to fall limply from her shoulder.

Just his arm.

The rest of him was gone.

He had been devoured in one swift bite, by a creature who had seen so many hearts weighed and so many souls judged that she was quite capable of doing it herself.

"Yes!" shouted Ren.

"In your face!" added Luke.

Alex's heart started again. He breathed.

The leader's arm hit the floor with a soft thud. No longer the size of a small tree trunk, it was just a human arm again, tightly wrapped in strips of linen.

Alex's mom wobbled on her feet, and Alex wanted to rush over to help her. But he could still barely stand himself.

Ammit swung around and took a few plodding steps toward the edge of the platform. She opened her mouth again, not to devour but to roar. Ammit's cry shook the room. When it was done, she stood firm at the front of the platform, in between Alex and his mom and The Order's forces. The meaning seemed clear: protection.

Alex's mom walked unsteadily back toward the temple — and the Spells inside.

"Are you okay?" Alex said, stumbling out to help her.

"No," she said. "But I know what I need to do. I looked into Ammit's eyes, and I saw something there. I think I understand her."

As Alex's mom knelt down over the Spells, the ancient text began to glow once more. She took her time now, confident in the protection afforded her.

*Would the Death Walkers dare attack Ammit to try to stop this?* Alex wondered. His answer came in a crackling of crimson energy and the rising buzz of a purple swarm, but that was the last he saw. As the ancient words rose on the air, his head swam and his knees buckled. He knelt on the cool tile as his vision filled with light and color. Behind him, he knew, his mom was reciting the rest of her chosen spell.

A minute later, Alex's head cleared. *I'm still here!* He understood now: His mom wasn't the only one under Ammit's protection. Somewhere in front of him, he heard the creature give one last satisfied huff. The swirling colors faded from

his vision as he stood, but he still didn't believe his eyes. All around, the mummies lay like dominoes on the floor, their bodies curling in on themselves stiffly.

It was a sight both gruesome and glorious, because there were new mummies among them, as well. Alex wheeled around and found each one in turn. Ta-mesah and Peshwar were merely mummies in masks, their bodies no larger than they'd been during their hateful lives. The Stung Man was a mummy, too, albeit a much older one, as timeworn and leathery as any of the others. And oldest of all, the founder, who was now little more than a skeleton wrapped in ragged yellow cloth in the far corner of the room.

Alex looked back toward Ammit, but she was gone. She had vanished just as mysteriously as she had appeared, although with far fewer witnesses.

"I don't under —" he began, but suddenly arms wrapped around him from behind. His mom. They hugged each other softly, both injured now. A moment later, two more arms wrapped around them. Ren had no intention of missing out on the victory party.

Alex turned his head to take a breath. Through vision clouded not by mystic stars but by the first hint of tears, he saw Luke standing a few steps farther back. Not much of a hugger, Luke gave his cousin a big thumbs-up. "Bauer power," he said.

The others hugged for a while, though.

"Todtman," Ren said, and Alex could feel her shoulders heave with a small sob.

"I know," said Alex's mom. "He was a good man."

But that wasn't good enough for Ren. "He was a *great* Egyptologist," she said.

And that did it for Alex — a sob shot through him, too, as happy tears and sad tears rolled down his cheeks. The tears mixed there softly, joining together and continuing on, like the waters of the mighty blue Nile.

Finally, the group hug pulled apart.

"What happened to them all?" asked Ren, sniffling and gesturing around the room. "To the Death Walkers, I mean."

Dr. Bauer looked around the room, counting the fallen. "We sent them to the ceremony," she said.

"The weighing of the heart?" said Alex.

His mom nodded. "Yes, they can't avoid it any longer."

Ren shook her head. "That is one test they are *not* ready for."

"That's okay," said Alex. "I'm pretty sure Ammit has already decided on their grades."

Even amid the sorrow and loss, the friends managed to exchange a few soft laughs. Even Luke, who pretended he knew what they were talking about.

# Epilogue: The Business of Living

Cairo had always been a somewhat chaotic place — ask anyone who's ever rented a car there — and so it was back to something like normal when the friends arrived for Todtman's funeral. His final wish was to have his ashes scattered in the waters of the Nile as it rolled north to the sea. It was done from the deck of a large, slow-moving boat, among a few rows of stoic Germans and what seemed to be about half the world's museum curators. Alex and Ren leaned over the side to watch the ashes scatter and fall.

*"Auf wiedersehen,"* whispered Ren, who had decided to learn German in Todtman's honor.

Alex already spoke some, but he stayed silent and just watched. This time, his tears really did mix with the waters of the Nile.

And what was there to do after that but get back to the business of living? Alex's mom and Ren's dad were busier than ever, trying to get the Met's battered Egyptian wing up and running again. There was, for obvious reasons, a surging

public interest in ancient Egypt. At night, Dr. Bauer studied the Spells, making sure everything was as it should be.

The wider world did its part: picking up the pieces, reburying the dead. Eventually, things returned to something like normal. Even for the families at the center of the maelstrom, who found themselves at a dinner party at the Durans' place a month later.

Alex's mom and Ren's mom and dad talked about the things parents talk about, Luke helped himself to seconds, and Alex and Ren chattered on about the school where they were once again classmates.

Alex felt something brush against his ankle and flinched. His nerves were, to be honest, still a little on edge.

"Oh, don't worry about her," said Ren, reaching down and scooping up a sleek black cat.

"You got a cat?" said Alex.

Ren's dad looked over, finished chewing, and said, "Or she got us. Just showed up on the doorstep. Pretty weird considering we're on the fourteenth floor. Anyway, she wouldn't leave until Ren got home."

"And then we couldn't get her to let the cat go," added Ren's mom.

Alex looked at the cat's golden eyes and coat of elegant jet-black fur as it purred softly in Ren's arms. There was something so familiar about it all. "What's her name?" he said, leaning in to pet the newest addition to the Duran family.

Ren leaned in, too. "Don't you know?" she whispered.

Alex looked from her to the cat and back again. "No way," he said. "Pai?"

The cat looked up at him, centuries of wisdom in her golden eyes. "Mmuh-Rack!"

Alex shook his head. He'd always heard that cats had nine lives. He had no doubt this former mummy would enjoy her second one.

He looked around the table at his family and friends. He was pretty sure he would, too.

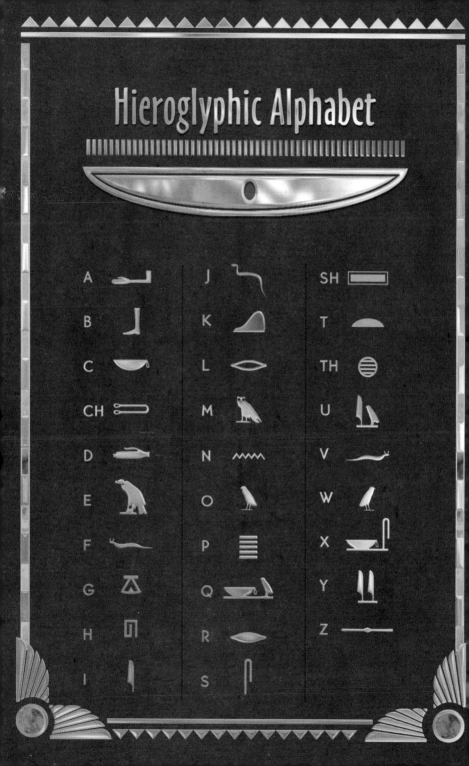

# TOMBQUEST

## THE FINAL KINGDOM

X

# MICHAEL NORTHROP

SCHOLASTIC INC.

## Deathquake

As the friends scrambled out of the tunnel mouth, the brutal Egyptian heat pounced on them like a waiting animal. The afternoon sun bore down with laser-beam intensity; after long, dark days underground, no one minded at all.

"Man, do I need this vitamin D!" crowed Luke, spreading his arms and turning his face toward the bright sky.

Alex eyed the sun-scalded landscape. Worn and weathered stone ruins jutted up from the sand. Directly in front of him, a stone foundation was just visible, the building that had once stood atop it lost to the ages. All around the phantom foundation, broken columns and shattered stone rose from the pale sand, like the bones of some great beast.

"They're ruins," said Alex's mom, "but I don't recognize them." Alex could practically hear her mind whirring through a lifetime of scholarship and travel.

"Nor do I," said Todtman. "Recently uncovered, I think."

"Yes," agreed Dr. Bauer. "Under the sand for a very long time. And modest."

"Definitely not a pharaonic site. A temple?"

"Maybe, maybe, but nothing fancy."

"Certainly not. A temple for commoners, then."

The two scholars nodded sagely, and Ren threw in a quick: "That's what I was thinking!"

"Yeah, uh, those sound like some real good points," said Luke. "But maybe we should be looking for a parking lot? You know, cars, roads? So we can get out of here?"

"Yeah," agreed Ren. "Last time we escaped from one of these thingies, there was a parking lot full of cars to steal."

Dr. Bauer gave her a surprised look.

"I mean borrow," said Ren with a shrug.

"This complex was bigger. There must be a lot of entrances," said Alex.

As the group scanned the broken landscape, the ground beneath them began to shake once more. Alex looked over at his mom with wide-open *uh-oh* eyes. The sand around them began to dance like flour tossed in a pan. The other tremors had been quick, beginning to subside almost as soon as they started. But this one kept gaining strength.

As the friends did their best to keep their balance — knees bent, arms out — the stone ruins began to faintly groan. A moment later, a nearby column crashed to the ground.

"I feel like a scrambled egg!" contributed Luke, a half-baked metaphor that somehow proved his point.

Then there was a "Yip!" of pure surprise from Todtman. The German had been knocked to his knees and a broad crack was growing in the sand next to him. He began

crawling away as best he could. But the crack spread, a jagged black opening in the earth that sucked in hundreds of pounds of sand as it grew.

Alex watched in horror as the foundation of the old building began to tip and slide sideways into the ground.

Another jolt knocked Alex and his mom to the ground. Alex felt his body beginning to slide down into the sand as it vibrated all around him. His mom was seated on the ground next to him with her eyes closed and a grimace of pain on her face as she clutched her side. "Mom!" he shouted.

Another crack opened up, closer and spreading outward like a slow smile. Alex was terrified it would swallow him whole.

But almost immediately, everything changed.

It stopped being about what the dancing sand would swallow and became about what it would reveal.

A ragged hand thrust itself out of the ancient earth and into the broad, clear light of day.

The hand clawed at the edge of the spreading black gap. The hand, and then the forearm, and then the elbow appeared and hooked itself over the edge. Falling sand washed over it — catching here and there in the time-yellowed linen that wrapped the arm — but still it kept clawing forward.

Alex was so mesmerized by the sight that he barely noticed the tattered hand breaking through the sand right next to him. It was only when the bony fingers hooked the cuff of his jeans that he snapped out of it.

"What the —" he blurted. He shook his leg, but that just made the thing latch on tighter. Alex grabbed his leg with both hands and tried to tug it free, but the hand tugged right back, using the motion to help pull itself up, a fish that wanted to be caught.

He dropped his calf and reached for the scarab. As soon as his hand closed around it, he sandblasted the mummy's hand free with a whipping lash of desert wind.

As he did, a bright white flash lit his vision like a camera flash. Ren's amulet.

He risked a quick look over, in case she needed help — and that's when he saw it.

He had broken the grip of one hand, but what about the next? And the next? And the thousand after that? Because the entire landscape had transformed from one of sand and stone to one of clawing hands and grasping arms.

Soon, the first heads emerged: time-stained linen pulling free, eyeless sockets staring upward at the sun, and mouths full of jagged brown teeth spitting sand.

Mummies. Everywhere.

The tattered corpses pulled themselves from the earth, grabbing the edges of the old stone blocks, the bases of the old columns, and anything else that seemed solid.

Grabbing anything at all that remained of this commoners' temple. This mass grave.

The undying army had arrived.

# Legions of the Dead

Alex pushed his hand down into the shifting sand — nearly shaking hands with an emerging mummy in the process — and struggled to his feet. He took hold of his mom's wrist. "Ready?" he shouted over the rumbling din.

She nodded, and he leaned back and heaved her to her feet. Her face was stoic and determined despite the pain, and that gave Alex strength, too.

"Here," he said, holding out the scarab. "It's yours, and you're better with it, anyway. Maybe you can hold them off." Alex had seen what his mom could do with the scarab during their last clash with The Order, and it was *awesome*. His mom reached out, but as soon as her hand closed around the ancient artifact, her eyes rolled back in her head and she tipped backward toward the shifting sand.

Alex reached out and grabbed her arm just in time to keep her from falling. Her pulse was racing like a drum solo beneath her skin. The supercharged boost the amulet imparted — the pounding pulse and surging adrenaline —

was too much for his mom's weakened system. The realization that she was hurt even worse than she was letting on hit him like a baseball bat. He reached over and pried the scarab from her hand.

As she recovered from the rush, gasping for breath, Alex hooked his arm around her waist and led her forward gently — or as gently as he could in the rumbling tumult all around. After years of her taking care of him — worrying over every ache and cough and fall — it was his turn. He kept his grip tight and his eyes on the death-torn ground.

"Which way?" shouted Luke, hustling over to help Todtman to his feet.

"There!" called Ren, pointing.

Alex followed her finger and saw sunlight reflecting off a lump of glass and steel in the distance — *a car!*

They hobbled toward it, not walking as much as continually falling forward. All around them, gaps and chasms yawned open in the sand, and leathery hands grabbed at anything solid. Even worse, some of the mummies were beginning to pull themselves out of the ground entirely.

As Alex concentrated on keeping his mom upright, a squat, five-foot human husk turned to stare at him through empty, faintly glowing eye sockets. But the mummy made no move toward Alex and his mom as they labored past. It just stood in the sun, swaying slightly and dripping sand.

"How old do you think these are?" he asked his mom, trying to keep her distracted from the pain.

She assessed the swaying corpse. "Twenty-five hundred years. The first of these mass graves was only discovered recently, but they seem to be mostly from the Late Period."

Alex remembered when the first of the grave sites had been discovered. It was just a few years earlier, right before his shaky health had forced him to start homeschooling — and long before his magical recovery. It had been the talk of the Met break room: the discovery of hundreds of thousands of mummified bodies. They had no treasure or tombs of their own, just the occasional coin or trinket tucked into their wrappings and a big shared hole in the ground.

The friends weaved their way through the legions of the dead, acres of Egypt's former middle class.

"Why aren't they attacking?" called Ren.

"Give 'em time," hollered Luke. "They had a rough trip!"

Alex eyed a wraithlike mummy, its long arms hanging down like willow branches. *Is that it?* he thought. *Are they just recharging, like solar cells in the desert sun?*

Sweat ran down his forehead and into his eyes. His shirt was plastered slickly against his back, and his left arm ached as he tried to carry as much of his mom's weight as possible. Her jagged breathing gave him a sick, worried feeling that lay on top of his own fear like two feet of mud.

The glare from the glass washed across his eyes, snapping him back to attention. What he'd hoped was a parking lot full of sleek getaway cars was, in fact, a single battered old minivan on a small square of cracked pavement.

Todtman limped straight for the driver's-side door. Another jolt rocked the ground, extending the long cracks in the pavement. Alex crouched down low, but the tremors were subsiding now, the earth moving fitfully as it settled.

The entire landscape between them and the tomb exit was now covered with swaying bodies, like a windblown grassland of the dead. Here and there stragglers clawed up from the sand to join them, the mummies already on the surface stooping down to haul them free.

"There must be ten thousand of them," Alex said, his voice soft with awe.

"And it's not over yet," said his mom, pointing out into the desert where still more of the undead were emerging an acre or two at a time.

"They seem to be waiting for something," said Todtman.

He was right. A moment later, the leader — Alex's father — emerged from the same tomb exit they had used.

The raggedly wrapped and mismatched bodies stopped swaying and began to line up in neat rows.

"Groups of twenty," said Ren, counting quickly.

Even across hundreds of yards and with thousands of mummies between them, the leader's massive frame stood out like a park statue. He raised one mighty hand in the air, and the tattered soldiers of the undying army snapped rigidly to attention for their general.

A cold and exposed feeling swept over Alex: the overwhelming sensation of being watched. He couldn't see his

father's eyes at this distance, but he could definitely feel them.

*Fuhhh-SHOOOOP!*

It was the sound of one hundred dry bodies turning as one. The five units closest to the parking lot had simultaneously dug their left heels into the sand and turned crisply toward the gawking friends.

"I think we should go now," said Todtman.

Behind them, one hundred unkillable soldiers rushed forward.

Alex helped his mom across the cracked pavement toward the battered minivan. He gripped her tight and used all his strength to haul her forward. But her injuries had taken their toll. The toe of her left boot caught in a crack as she dragged it heavily over the pavement, and they both went down in a heap.

Alex risked a quick look behind them. The undead were coming. With old bones and dry flesh, most of them were running none too fluidly, either. But there was one moving faster than the rest, fired forward from their ranks like a missile. Alex wrapped his arms around his mom and tried to haul her from the pavement.

Suddenly, strong arms grabbed him. Alex prepared to be torn limb from limb — but it was Luke. He'd come back for

them and was now lifting both his cousin and his aunt to their feet.

"Let's go!" he shouted. "Bauer power!"

They stumbled up and forward. "Watch out," said Alex. With his hands supporting his mom, he couldn't grasp his scarab and could only nod at the lone mummy approaching ahead of the pack.

"I got him," said Luke.

Alex looked at him skeptically. *Maybe if I can get one hand on the scarab . . .*

"Get your mom to the van, man!" shouted Luke. "I said I got this."

As Alex turned and hustled his mom toward the minivan, he could already hear the bony slaps of the sprinting mummy's feet against the pavement.

Todtman and Ren were in the van now, the big side door wide open. "Come on, Mom," he said. "Just a little farther."

Her reply was cut off by a hoarse cry from the onrushing mummy, and Alex turned his head back just as the sprinting corpse crashed into Luke. "No!" gasped Alex.

Instead of avoiding the mummy's grasp, Luke grasped it right back. As he did, he whipped his shoulders around and ducked down, using all of the ragged creature's momentum to toss it over his hip. "Aiyah!" he shouted.

Suddenly, the mummy's dry old bones were bouncing across the cracked pavement — and Alex and his mom were arriving at the minivan. Alex heard the engine start up —

coaxed to life by Todtman's amulet — and saw Ren's hands reach out from the side door to help his mom in. He looked back for Luke, who was bending down to pick up something shiny from the asphalt. Behind him, the first mummy was already climbing back to its feet — and ninety-nine more were rushing onto the lot.

"Get over here!" shouted Alex.

Luke palmed his shiny find and rushed for the door.

Alex climbed in after his mom as the minivan began rolling. Luke leapt into the open door as the lumbering vehicle began a slow turn toward the road. Alex leaned back and did his best to catch his cousin as he thumped down inside.

Ren slammed the door closed and Todtman stomped on the gas.

He ran over two mummies who'd managed to get in front of them. The van rose up and down on its old shock absorbers to a sound track of sickening crunches. But a moment later, they were up to full speed and pulling away from the rest of the pack. Todtman wrestled the lumbering vehicle around a sharp turn and off the lot.

Open road stretched out ahead, and the fields of the undead disappeared in the rearview mirror. Alex helped his mom settle into the bench seat in the back of the van.

"Just need to rest a little," she said.

"I know," he said. Her battered body needed to shut down to heal. Sick for almost his whole life, he knew all

about that. He spied a dusty horseshoe-shaped travel pillow hooked around the armrest and handed it to her. She placed it between her injured ribs and the seat. Soon, her eyes fluttered closed and her ragged breathing calmed slightly.

Alex wiped the first trace of a tear from his eye, exhaled, and returned to the first row of seats. He watched the road disappear under the minivan's wheels. There were other cars on the road now, a freeway entrance up ahead. They were back in the real world.

*Next stop, "the seat of power,"* he thought. Even though The Order members had managed to assume their Stone Warrior forms, the Spells could still end all this, could send the undead back to the afterlife and shut the doors for good. But he knew the mummies and Walkers weren't the only ones who could be undone by the Spells . . .

He shook his head hard, trying to clear the thought away. Then he turned to his cousin. "Thanks, man," he said. "You really came through back there."

Even Ren chimed in. "Yeah, that was pretty cool of you," she admitted. "That mummy was going like a thousand miles an hour."

Luke just shrugged. "Judo, yo," he said. "It's awesome cross-training." His attention was on the shiny object swinging from a rusty chain in his hand.

"Is that what you picked up off the pavement?" asked Alex.

"Yeah," said Luke, still not taking his eyes off it. "It came flying out of that mummy's wrapping when I hip-tossed him. Pretty cool, right?"

Alex nodded. He knew that mummies were often buried with amulets and other charms tucked into their wrappings.

This one was in the form of a cheetah, the world's fastest animal.

## Road Worrier

Ren watched Luke as he brushed the last crusty bits of sand and clay from the little bronze cat. *No way it works for him*, she thought. She trusted him more after seeing him put his life on the line to save Alex and his mom. But she still didn't see him as Amulet Keeper material.

"Put it on!" said Alex.

Luke looked down at it. "What, like man jewelry?" he said. He glanced over at the spot where Alex's scarab hung from its fine silver chain. "No offense."

"Whatever," said Alex. "See if it *does* anything."

Luke stared at him.

"Well?" said Alex.

"You tell me," Luke said. "I just tried to hypnotize you."

"Tell me to do something," said Alex.

"Flap your arms like a peacock."

Alex's arms stayed by his sides. He looked down at them, one after the other, and said, "Nothing."

"Maybe it does something else," offered Ren.

Luke squinted at her, as if trying to read the last line of an eye chart. "Not unless you're levitating," he said.

Ren looked down. There was no space between her and her seat, not even a spare centimeter. "Nope."

"Doesn't work," he said, sitting back. "I'll tell you what, though."

"What?" said Alex.

"I do feel pretty . . ." He searched for the right word, giving Alex time to blurt out: "You feel pretty?"

Luke jokingly shook his fist at him. "No, I feel pretty, like, stoked. I was pretty tired from all that . . ." He waved his hand behind them. "That sitting in a cell and then the mummy stuff and everything. But as soon as I put it on, I felt totally pumped."

"Great," said Ren. "Your amulet has the power of a large coffee."

Luke looked down at it. "Good enough for me," he said. "Think I'll call it coffee cat."

Ren sank back into her seat — and into her thoughts. The coffee cat line had reminded her of Pai, the creepy-cute mummy cat who had sacrificed herself to save Ren from an ancient Death Walker in a desert pit. *Was she really gone for good?* she wondered, remembering her little body, battered, bent, and limp. She humored herself with the thought that, if cats had nine lives, Pai had seven left.

Her thoughts shifted to the mission ahead. This was a war now. They'd just seen the army, and its first target was

New York. *Home.* She couldn't let that happen. They had to find the Lost Spells. But even if they could, there was a problem. Alex's mom had gone into hiding with the Spells to try to find a way to undo the magic that had saved his life without undoing him. The Death Walkers and their army had returned to this world, thanks to the Spells — but so had Alex. Sending them back risked sending him back, too. But they'd found his mom before she'd figured out a solution — and led The Order right to her.

Now they were racing toward Cairo, where The Order held the Spells. Trying to recapture them, hoping to use them to save her parents, her city, her everything. Everything except her best friend.

He could be racing toward his grave.

Ren couldn't see any good way to reconcile the two problems. The idea of two problems with two separate and mutually exclusive solutions made her so uncomfortable that she physically squirmed in her torn vinyl seat. She'd faced hard tests before, ones where she had to scrap for partial credit — and extra credit — just to salvage a B+.

But she'd never faced a test that seemed quite so unfair.

The minivan bumped to a stop. Dr. Bauer groaned and shifted in her seat as Ren leaned forward to look out the windshield. Her heart started thumping as she saw a large wooden police barrier with armed men standing on either side. One of them stepped around toward Todtman's window. The guard took one look at Todtman's pale skin and spoke in English.

"You have been stopped because your vehicle matches one we are looking for," said the man.

"Stopped under whose authority?" countered Todtman.

The man smiled. "The Order's, of course," he said, his fingers drumming lightly on the barrel of his gun. "We are the only authority now."

Ren's racing heart did a little backflip, but her mind was oddly clear. *So the conquest wouldn't start in New York, after all*, she thought. She had been underground for too long. *Up here, the conquest was well underway.*

"Out of the vehicle," said the man, his voice rising, his machine gun pointed at Todtman's face. "All of you," he barked. "Get out!"

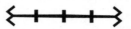

Alex woke his mom. "We're in trouble," he said softly. "Again."

It seemed like a crime to pry her from the sleep she needed, but it was a crime committed at gunpoint. The gun barrel was inches from Todtman's protruding, slightly frog-like eyes as he slowly opened his door. Still, Alex knew their mentor could slide his hand up to his amulet and scramble the gunman's mind like two eggs at a whisk convention.

The problem was the other three. One of them was coming around now to open the side door of the minivan, but the other two remained far apart on either side of the traffic barrier. Their machine guns were trained on the vehicle.

Alex could take out one of them with a powerful lance of mystic wind, no problem. But by the time he could turn his amulet's power on the second, the bullets would be flying, and his mom was defenseless.

The odds of flooring it and busting through the barricade were no better. You can't make a high-speed escape in a low-speed vehicle.

Still, as they all reluctantly climbed out of the old beater, Alex's mom carrying her threadbare travel pillow like a kid with a teddy bear, he tried to make eye contact with Todtman. Maybe they could coordinate: *You get that one, I'll get this one, and then we, um, duck?*

"Your amulets," said the first guard, his gun barrel dipping from Todtman's froggy face to his avian amulet. "Give them to me."

Alex blinked up into the baking Egyptian sun and groaned. His mind raced: It was now or never.

*PAKKA-PAKKA-PAK!*

The second guard rattled off three shots in the air, making Alex jump.

He fought his racing pulse and slowly slid his hand up toward his scarab.

"Lift them off only by the chains," said the first guard. "Touch the amulets and you die."

So they knew all about the amulets and their power. Out of the corner of his eye, Alex saw one of the guards by the barricade talking low and fast into a cell phone. Alex was

sure the man was reporting the capture to his bosses, and maybe asking if they should take them prisoner or just gun them down on the side of the road.

"What a bummer," said Luke, reaching up for his cheetah. "I just got this thing."

Alex looked over and saw his cousin's hand brush the cheetah on the way up — and then he saw nothing but a swirl of sand and dust in the sunlight.

*SHOOOMP!*

All of a sudden, Luke was in front of Alex, grabbing the gun from the guard who'd fired the warning shots. Alex blinked in disbelief, and in the time it took his eyes to open and close — *WHOOSH!* — Luke was already next to the main guard, smacking him over the head with the butt of the other man's gun. *WHUMP!*

Before that one could even fall to the ground, Luke was somehow all the way over by the barricade, lowering his shoulder into the first guard there. *THUDD!* The man flew through the air and crashed gracelessly to the pavement.

*PAKKA-PAKKA-PAK!*

*Oh no!* The fourth guard was firing at Luke.

But Luke was already gone. Seeing only open air, the guard ceased fire and looked around wildly. Alex saw Luke before the guard did. His cousin, now standing behind the man, tapped him casually on the shoulder. The man swung around — right into a punch that lifted him off his feet.

As the man fell to the ground unconscious —
*SHOOOMP!* — Luke was back by the others, standing next
to the door of the minivan and shaking his hand in mild
pain.

"How —" stammered Alex. "How did you —"

"Don't know, exactly," said Luke, "but as soon as I touched
the amulet, I just felt, like, supercharged."

Alex watched as the first guard — the one Luke had only
disarmed — ran off down the road. The other three were all
in various states of beatdown.

"The amulet must grant some sort of temporary physical
augmentation," mused Todtman.

"The cheetah was a symbol of both strength and power in
dynastic times," added Alex's mom.

"That was *AAAWWESOMME!*" gushed Alex.

Luke, still pale from his underground confinement,
actually blushed as he looked down at his amulet. "Well,
I kind of had an unfair advantage," he admitted. Then he
looked up and smiled. "I guess you could say I'm a cheata."

## A Chaotic Capital

They stayed off the main roads after that. Ren was in the front seat, helping navigate with a crumpled old map, and Luke was conked out in back. As impressive as the cheetah amulet had been, it seemed to take a physical toll on him. After a few more miles, they pulled into a gas station convenience store to get food, gas, and a better map.

When Alex climbed back into the backseat to bring his mom aspirin and water, he was surprised to find her awake again. "You should be resting," he said.

"Not right now," she said, patting the seat next to her. "There's something I need to tell you."

"What?" said Alex. "Is it your side? Should we try to find a hospital?"

She shook her head and answered softly. "It's your father," she said as the old van pulled back out onto the road and headed into the dusk. "You deserve to know."

As Todtman switched on the headlights, Ren puzzled out the new map, and Luke ate half their food, Alex sat

absolutely still and listened to the story of how he came to be.

"We met in Alexandria," she said. "We were both young and both in love: with each other, and with archaeology."

Alex tried to picture the monster he'd met as a young student with a head full of pyramids and hieroglyphs. As a grad student in love.

"We were both so passionate about our work," his mother continued. Amir, your father . . . He was obsessed with finding the Lost Spells even then. I searched with him — and when you were born, you came, too. But the search took us to dark places, searching every secret and forbidden site we could find. These were cursed places no child should have been. I didn't realize until it was too late the toll it was taking — on you, on your health."

Alex couldn't believe it: an entire childhood of pain. Sickness the doctors could never fix. He looked up at his mom, but she was staring straight ahead now, into the past. "That's when you left him?" he said, hoping — almost needing — to hear her say yes.

She shook her head. "That's when I tried," she said. "But he had discovered something else. The mask. Its power fueled his obsession, turned it into something more like madness. He used the mask's power to control me, to keep me close. It wasn't until I discovered something of equal power that I could break free."

"The scarab," said Alex, touching the amulet.

His mom nodded. "The scarab. But by then the damage had been done . . . Honey, I am so sorry. More sorry than you will ever know."

But she was wrong. He knew exactly. He looked up at her, and this time he caught a glimpse of her blue-gray eyes. For the first time, he truly understood the depth behind them. She'd had a life before him, one with triumphs and mistakes of her own. She hadn't understood the damage those dark places were doing to him, but she'd paid the price as much as he had. She'd worried and fretted over him every single day since. She'd cared for and eventually saved him — at great cost to her, at great cost to everyone.

*My mom didn't know the danger*, he thought, *but my dad didn't care.* He couldn't find the words to say any of this to his mom. Instead, he leaned across the seat and wrapped his arms around her as she wrapped hers around him.

After hours of driving, a low glow lit the horizon: city lights caught in a suffocating net of heavy smog.

Cairo.

"Mom, look," he whispered. But she was resting again, her eyes closed, her breathing shallow — and this was no longer the Cairo she had told him about. When he was a kid, she'd made the crazy traffic, wild outside bazaars, and winding side alleys sound like a loud vibrant adventure. No

more. This was a haunted city now, the death-shrouded capital of a country in crisis.

He felt the fear building inside him as they reached the edge of the city and drove toward. The Order's headquarters on the other side of the capital. Alex stared out at the dark streets as the unflappable German drove steadily onward. Alex could already see an open fire burning a few blocks away, flickering flames illuminating a plume of rising smoke. Most of the streetlights were burned out or broken. Todtman slowed down to steer around a car abandoned in the middle of the road. As soon as they cleared it, a pack of stray dogs met them on the other side, barking fiercely. Todtman stepped on the gas, and the mangy mongrels began to chase them, an interchangeable mass of matted fur and snapping teeth.

They lost the dogs and passed the fire, but soon the four-lane road narrowed. Stacked sandbags funneled them into a single lane at the center. Todtman slowed the minivan again, and they all eyed the checkpoint nervously. But there were no armed men this time. No men at all.

It creeped Alex out: Eight million people lived in this city — or used to — and so far they hadn't seen a single soul.

The van rolled slowly through the gap and was suddenly buffeted with bumps and barks and scratches. The dogs had chased them down. Alex looked to his right and saw a large black mutt just below him. It leapt up, scratching at the window. Specks of foamy drool dotted the safety glass as the dog snapped off a quick, hoarse bark.

Todtman cleared the opening and floored it.

The dogs disappeared again into the smoky night.

"Man," said Luke. "Those were some hungry dogs."

"Not hungry," said Ren. "Rabid."

Alex nervously eyed the gobs of virulent drool on the other side of his window as the hot wind outside stretched and dried them.

As they drove deeper into the city, houses and apartment buildings shouldered up from the sidewalks on either side, and Alex was relieved to see the occasional sliver of light slipping through closed blinds.

"Where *is* everybody?" said Ren.

"There's someone!" said Luke, leaning between the seats and pointing. Alex turned and saw a shadowy figure making slow progress across the street. Todtman took his foot of the gas and slowed down as they approached. But as the minivan rolled slowly forward, its headlights hit the figure — and lit its tattered linen.

The mummy swung around and gaped at them, faintly glowing reddish orbs where its eyes should have been. Releasing a ragged, wordless scream, it charged straight at the van's dented hood.

*"Gott im Himmel,"* mumbled Todtman as he stomped the gas and swung the wheel.

The minivan sideswiped the charging mummy as it swerved past — one lumbering old heap striking another — sending the tightly wrapped corpse bouncing up onto the curb.

Alex swung his head around and saw the creature already pushing itself to its feet and setting off after them. Just behind him, he saw the crazed dogs appear at a full run one streetlight back.

There was a loud screech of metal on metal as Todtman rammed the minivan between two more abandoned cars, one in each lane. Alex saw his mom wake up and look around, and he climbed one row back to sit next to her.

"It might be better to travel at night," she said to him. "When Cairo seems too dangerous even for The Order."

Alex nodded and craned his neck to check the time on the dashboard clock: *11:58 p.m.* The problem, of course, was that a city dangerous for The Order was infinitely more dangerous for everyone else. As the clock flicked to 11:59, Ren called out from the front seat: "What is that up there?"

Alex looked where she was pointing and saw a shifting shape on the roof of a low-slung industrial complex, outlined against the moon. At first, he couldn't tell what it was. The image kept shifting. Pieces tore off it and flitted away as other fragments dove in to rejoin it. But as they passed directly underneath, he got a better look.

The shape was that of a large man.

And the pieces tearing free and diving back looked like oversized wasps, purple-black in the moonlight. They grew larger and more defined the farther they flew, but up close they were small. Small and shifting and numerous: hundreds, maybe thousands, of shadowy swarming shapes.

His mom spoke beside him. Her words were so soft that he barely heard them over the rumble of the van. But he didn't really need to. He was thinking the same thing.

"Death Walker."

Todtman punched the gas and accelerated out of sight of the grim figure, but the image of swarming evil stayed in Alex's mind as the old van wound deeper into the city's desolate warehouse district.

## Gone

Stiff from the long trip and in various states of injury and exhaustion, the crew crept along the moonlit street like a determined intensive care unit. The Order's secret headquarters was the last looming structure in a row of dark, deserted warehouses.

· "We're here," whispered Todtman.

"Cool," said Alex, looking up at the blank black windows. "Should we have, like, a plan?"

"We will catch them off guard and move quickly," said Todtman, but he said it while hobbling along with the speed and grace of a three-legged turtle. "We know the Spells are in 'the seat of power.' The last thing they will expect is for us to come straight to them in the middle of the night."

"Yeah, don't sweat it, cuz," added Luke. "I got your back."

Alex looked over at him. Maybe the plan was crazy enough to work: While The Order probably thought they were fleeing for their lives, they'd rush in and grab the Spells. And with Luke's cheetah, they had more firepower than ever. Maybe they had a chance.

As they approached a small side door, Alex pulled his scarab out from under his collar and felt its reassuring weight in his hand. The weight in his other arm was less reassuring. It would be hard to fight while helping his mom stay on her feet.

They reached the door.

"Unguarded," said Ren.

"*Seemingly* unguarded," cautioned Todtman.

But Alex barely heard them. Now that he believed they could succeed, he'd finally asked himself a more complex question: *What if they did?* In a cell or on the run, it had been easy enough to concentrate on escape. But what if the Lost Spells really were in there? The plan was to use them to close the rift between the worlds of the living and the worlds of the dead — to undo the damage that had been done when that doorway had been opened to save his life. The risk — the one no one seemed willing to talk about — was that it would undo him, too.

Alex heard a click as Todtman used his amulet to unlock the door. "Okay," said the scholar. "Carefully now."

Todtman pushed open the door, and Luke ducked inside for a look, but Alex could barely focus on the danger ahead of them. His mind was churning. Back when they were still searching for his mom, he'd blamed himself for all the trouble his second shot at life had caused, and he'd been ready to sacrifice himself to make it right.

But finding his mom had changed things, and the story she'd just told him had changed them more. He'd chewed

over those words in the dark: His father's obsessive search for the Spells was the reason he'd been sick in the first place. The wheels of all this had been set in motion before he could even walk.

And if all that was true, he wasn't the cause of all this trouble. He was the first victim.

Alex wondered, deep down, if maybe he had sacrificed enough. If maybe there was another way. The Spells were so powerful, after all. How close had his mom been to puzzling out a solution with them? Maybe —

"All clear," said Luke, pulling his head back out the dark gap of the open door.

The group slipped inside. Weak moonlight shone gauzily into the huge, hangar-like space from rows of dirty windows twenty feet up. The friends stood silently as their eyes adjusted to the dim light.

"Nothing," whispered Ren. "It's empty."

Todtman knelt down and rubbed the floor with one finger. "Stone dust," he said. "This is where they carved the statues that they now inhabit. I saw the blocks the last time I was here."

Alex felt his mom's weight sink down against his arm and shoulder as she relaxed a little and let out a long, jagged breath. He pushed the toe of one boot along the concrete floor and felt the stony grit. So this was where The Order had begun turning themselves into ten-foot-tall monsters.

"There are doors in the back there," said Luke.

Alex stared where he pointed, but all he saw was blackness.

"Are you sure?" he said.

"Totally," said Luke, and as he turned toward him, Alex saw that his eyes were glowing a soft green. Just like a cheetah's.

"Can you see in the dark?" asked Alex.

"I guess so."

Alex tried to stay quiet as they crept across the floor, but supporting his mom was hard work, and his huffing breath echoed through the cavernous space, mixing with the soft plinks of Todtman's staff.

As they got closer, he saw three doors. The first one was the heaviest, and it seemed to have been blown out from the inside. The heavy steel bar that had once secured it lay bent almost in half on the floor nearby.

Alex saw nothing but blackness inside and stepped aside for Luke to take a look with his cat eyes. "Anything?"

"Nuh-uh," said Luke. "It's like a vault or something. No windows, no nothing."

And the other two rooms were just abandoned offices. Alex heard Ren take a corner too tightly in the dark and slam her shin into the side of a desk.

"Ow!" she huffed, and then: "This is ridiculous!"

She took three quick strides over to the wall. "No, Ren, don't!" hissed Todtman, but it was too late.

She flicked on the lights.

Alex stood blinking in the sudden brightness. When the stars and swirls cleared away, he saw everything there was to see. It wasn't much.

"Empty," said Ren. "This whole place has been cleared out."

Alex's mom settled into an office chair as the others searched around for hidden doorways, passages leading down, anything at all. They even used their amulets to probe the walls and floors. After half an hour, Todtman called a halt to it.

"Nothing," he agreed. "Whatever was in here is gone."

They returned to the main room and looked around the modest old warehouse under the weak electric light.

"This isn't the seat of power anymore, is it?" said Alex.

Todtman smacked the floor angrily with his scuffed staff. "I don't think it ever was."

The Amulet Keepers were quiet for a few moments, and then they heard the banging on the corrugated steel walls of the warehouse. Something was outside — or some things.

Todtman looked up at the old fixtures above them. "The lights have attracted attention," he said. "We should leave."

"But where are we going?" asked Ren as they hustled toward the same door they'd come in.

"To see an old friend," said Todtman. "If he is still alive."

# A Night at the Museum

"There it is," said Alex's mom as a familiar red edifice rose up in front of them.

The battered old minivan had made it back to the city's center. It had even started on the first try — a good thing since there'd been a dozen glowing red eyes approaching its rearview mirror at the time.

A massive brick building loomed above the electric haze of Tahrir Square. Once again, they had returned to the mighty Egyptian Museum.

They parked the stalwart van on a side street and made their way to the museum's massive front doors. No alarm sounded as Alex used the scarab to unlock the heavy double doors. He took one last look behind them as they slipped inside, to see if they'd been followed. All he saw were shifting shadows and dancing moonlight in the eerily empty square.

Inside, the legendary museum was lit only by dim lights from a few display cases and red exit signs. Scattered around these deep shadows, he knew, were some 120,000 exhibits.

What Alex didn't see were any people, or any signs of recent activity at all. Once teeming with a daily army of tourists, the place now felt like an especially epic, million-square-foot attic.

Moving through the first room, Alex's mom had stepped free of his supporting arm, as if the building itself had given her strength. Alex used his suddenly free hand to trace a finger across a glass display case, drawing a track in the thin layer of dust.

"I'm afraid I've let the place go a bit," came a voice. "But we get very few visitors these days."

Alex's heart skipped a beat or three as the words echoed through the hall. But the voice was familiar, and so was the man stepping out of the shadows along the far wall.

Dr. Hesaan — he never had told them his first name — bowed slightly. As surprised as they were by his sudden appearance, he seemed equally surprised to see the new addition to their party. "Dr. Bauer," he said. "It is good to see you . . ." He trailed off before adding "alive."

She managed a quick smile. "You know I can't stay away from this place."

Alex was relieved to not hear quite as much ragged raspiness in her voice this time — and reassured by her friendly rapport with the man. The last time they'd seen the old curator, he'd been attempting to guard the closed museum with only a cricket bat.

"Where's your bat?" asked Alex.

"I don't have much use for it anymore," Hesaan said, shrugging slightly. "Only a lunatic would break in. This museum, like the rest of the city, is now run by The Order."

The friends bristled visibly.

"Relax," said Hesaan. "I hate them just as much as you do."

"But you work for them," said Ren skeptically.

Another shrug. "I work for the museum. I take care of it, as I always have. They simply allow me to."

"Why would they do that?" said Ren, still not convinced. "The last time I saw you, you were charging at them with your cricket bat."

"They allow it because I am the most qualified," he said. "I am the most familiar with this old building — and this much older collection — and its various needs."

Ren signaled she had another question by raising her right hand slightly, but Hesaan kept going. "You have to understand, for you this is a museum: old artifacts and old altars to old gods. To The Order, it is their religion."

Alex looked over at his mom to see what she thought of that. When she nodded in understanding, he did, too. The arrangement seemed clear enough. It was an uneasy truce between enemies, carved out over a small piece of common ground.

"We each have our part to play in this, my old friend," said Todtman to Hesaan. "And I am hoping you might be able to help us find some answers."

"I will do my best," said Hesaan. He stepped toward Todtman and exchanged the sort of quick, awkward hug at which academics have always excelled. "But first, it is late. Let me find you someplace to stay, something to eat. As you can see, I have plenty of extra space." He raised his voice slightly on the final word, and Alex heard it echo through the lacquered wood and polished marble of the empty museum: *space-ace-ace*.

<del>&lt;—+—+—+—&gt;</del>

Ren balled up her fist again, not to release a flash of spirit-zapping light this time, but to release . . . what? She was matched off with Luke in a game of rock-paper-scissors. At stake was the third-best sleeping spot in the old employee lounge where they were spending the night. Dr. Bauer and Todtman were the obvious choices for the two couches, and now Ren had her eye on the large woolen rug between them. She'd already defeated Alex, three to two. So far Luke had thrown two straight papers, and she'd cut through them with back-to-back scissors. Now she eyed her opponent carefully. *He wouldn't throw the same thing again . . . would he?*

"One, two," counted Alex. Ren and Luke drew back their hands. "Three!"

Ren threw her hand out, first two fingers V'd into scissors. She looked over at Luke's hand, spread out flat: paper. She smiled. *Of course he would.*

"I thought it had to win sooner or later," muttered Luke, shaking his head.

But there was one last item of business before the group could get some much-needed sleep. A few minutes later, all drowsy eyes were on Ren once again. She took a deep breath and raised her hand toward her amulet.

"Ask it where the Lost Spells are," said Alex.

It had never answered that particular question in the past, and the look she shot him said: *Why would it start now?*

Todtman volunteered an alternative: "Ask it where the seat of power is."

The ibis was an ancient amulet, not Google, and as Ren's hand hovered over the pale stone, she told herself all the things that had helped her get a handle on its power. It didn't offer answers, she reminded herself. It only gave her information: scenes from the past or present, possibilities for the future. And whatever it gave her was more than she had now. *Extra credit.* She formed the familiar, comforting words in her head.

Then she closed her eyes and wrapped her hand around the cool stone. She tried to think the words of Todtman's question as clearly as possible: *Where is the seat —* But before she could finish, another question popped into her head, fully formed and all but screaming for an answer: *Are my parents okay?*

She'd already tried to call home from Hesaan's office phone, but the line had been as dead as the museum's remaining mummies. Now, though, her ibis offered an open line. An image flashed through her mind's eye. The door of their

apartment, seen from the inside, with the chain latched and one of the good chairs from the living room table wedged under the doorknob.

As the scene unfolded the door began to shake, the chain rattled, and the chair wobbled. Something was outside the apartment, not knocking on the door but *beating* on it.

Ren gasped and opened her eyes. Her amulet fell from her hand.

"What did it show you?" said Todtman.

Ren shook her head.

"What?" he insisted.

She looked up at him, blinking away the tears that were just now beginning to appear. "Home," she said. "It showed me home."

Todtman looked at her sternly, but Alex's mom cut in before he could respond. "We're all tired," she said softly. "We'll try again in the morning. Okay, Ren?"

Ren nodded. She was tired: desperately, eye-flutteringly tired after their marathon day. But she also knew how important this was. The world was going up in flames, and they were at a standstill. She would try her best in the morning. She would focus hard and ask the question out loud. Still, she didn't hold out much hope. "It doesn't matter what I ask it," she said softly. "The ibis is in my head. It knows what I want to know."

She stretched out on the heavy rug, her body surrendering to her exhaustion even as her mind continued to pick at what

she'd just seen — *Was it the present, or a future they could still prevent?*

She heard Dr. Bauer shift on the couch above her and looked up to find her looking down. "We are all worried about home," she whispered. "We will fix this."

Ren nodded and tried to stay positive. She fell asleep not to images of destruction but to one of her favorite memories: Alex and his mom and Ren and her parents laughing together at a silly inside joke at the last museum holiday party.

But as the night wore on, her dreams turned dark. She dreamed that New York was under siege and would soon fall to The Order. She dreamed that her parents were in danger. It was the worst nightmare of her life.

And it was all true.

## The Seat of the Soul

Alex rolled over on his small, scratchy rug and groaned. Sunlight was streaming in through the windows. He turned toward his mom's couch. Empty.

He leapt up immediately, sending gift-shop throw pillows flying. But then he spotted her sitting with Todtman and Hesaan at a table by the wall. They were casually dipping flatbread in a beany paste and talking as they ate. Alex's mouth watered at the sight of the food, and he went to join them.

Ren was snoring lightly on the floor. Alex tried to be quiet as he passed, but she coughed up her last snore and her eyes popped open. He waited as she got up to join him.

Luke was still asleep in the corner, a small smile on his face hinting at pleasant dreams of athletic conquest. Alex and Ren let him sleep and headed for the table.

"How are you feeling, Mom?" asked Alex. Now that he was standing close enough, he could see that she was holding a plastic bag of ice against her side.

"Good morning, honey," she said. "I am feeling a little better." She paused and smiled. "Like I was hit by a car instead of a truck."

Beside him, Ren nodded solemnly, waited a respectable few seconds, and then dove for the food. *"Fuul!"* she said, pronouncing it like *fuel*.

*"Fool,"* said Hesaan, correcting her pronunciation.

"Yeah, say it right, fool," said Alex, satisfied that his mom really was feeling better. He picked up a piece of flatbread and dipped it into the dish of stewed fava beans. "What are you guys talking about?" he asked, pulling up a chair.

Todtman shifted over to make space at the table. "We were trying to figure out our mistake," he said. "You told us you heard the leader say that he would consult the Lost Spells in the seat of power . . ."

"And you assumed the seat of power was the old Order headquarters in Cairo," said Hesaan.

"Yes, but the place was abandoned," said Todtman, "cleaned out."

*Wait a second*, thought Alex. His brain was still foggy with sleep, but he tried to remember. *Wasn't there something about that phrase? Something he hadn't been sure of?* He chewed his food and chased the thought through the morning mist as the adults continued talking.

"Yes, why would they be hiding in a warehouse?" said Hesaan. "They have outgrown that little place now. They

have taken over the parliament building, and some others. During the day, they are everywhere in this city."

"Could the seat be the parliament building?" asked Alex's mom.

"Perhaps," said Hesaan skeptically. "But even as arrogant as they are, I would be surprised if they kept something so powerful in such a busy and accessible place. With their international provocations, there is constant talk that the other countries will bomb the place."

"Why don't they?" said Alex.

"They say the leader controls their minds, as needed, and stills their hands. They say that the man has grown immensely powerful."

Hesaan flicked a look over at Alex's mom as he spoke, and Alex wondered if Hesaan knew he was talking about her ex-husband.

"It's true," said Todtman. "But he is a man no longer."

Hesaan nodded gravely, seeming to understand.

Alex remembered the sight. The man who had once been his father, and what he had become: a massive Death Walker in a flickering tomb. He remembered the words rumbling out of his broad chest, Alex's amulet allowing him to understand the ancient dialect — and just like that, the mist lifted. "Wait a second," he sputtered through a mouthful of bean and bread.

The others turned to look at him. He swallowed his *fuul* and cleared his throat. "Okay, so, you guys know I don't speak ancient Egyptian, right? So I have to kind of rely on my amulet for that . . ."

"What is it, hun?" asked his mom, but Todtman was already a step ahead.

"What did he say?" asked the German.

"Well, I thought it was the 'seat of power,' but as I was saying it, I was kind of also thinking —"

"The seat of the soul?" offered Hesaan.

Alex stared at him. "Yeah, but . . . how did you know?"

"There is a word for power," said Hesaan. "An ancient word . . ."

"Ba," said Alex's mom. "The pharaoh's power to rule . . ."

Todtman's eyes grew wider, and he stammered excitedly: "Yes, but that word has more than one meaning . . ."

"What do you mean? What other meaning?" interrupted Ren. Alex watched her head spin from one scholar to another and knew she hated to be left out of this.

Alex's mom explained, "Ba can mean the soul, too."

"Not the seat of power," said Todtman. "The seat of the soul. That's where they have taken the Spells."

"Wait, wait, wait," said Ren. "I seriously hope you are not going to say —"

But the three scholars said it as one: "To the afterlife."

"They have taken the Spells to the one place they are sure no one else can reach them," added Todtman.

"But how is that possible?" said Hesaan, dumbfounded.

Ren looked over at him with a hangdog expression. "Oh, it's possible, all right," she said. "It's just not any fun."

Hesaan looked at her incredulously. "You have been there?"

"We both have," said Alex, remembering their sprint through the treacherous, twilight murk of the Egyptian afterlife. It was a spectral shortcut that had taken them thousands of miles in moments. "It's the amulets that let us do it," he added, trying to explain the inexplicable. "They allow us to go through the false doors."

They all sat silently at the little table, thunderstruck by this new revelation. Footsteps approached. Luke plucked a crumbly white block speckled with blue dots from the breakfast tray. "I sure hope this is cheese," he said, taking a big bite.

"It was cheese a week ago . . ." said Hesaan, staring down at the table.

"It is blue cheese now," said Todtman. "But save some of that for Alex and Ren. They will need their strength today, too."

"Wait, what do you mean?" said Alex.

"Well, you have been there before," said Hesaan, eyeing the lump of Alex's amulet beneath his shirt. "And there are *many* false doors at this museum."

Alex had already finished his breakfast, but he swallowed hard, anyway. His mom put her hand on his shoulder, either seeking to reassure him or concerned he would faint.

He was going back to the afterlife.

He looked over at Ren. She looked like she had seen a ghost.

She was certainly about to.

## To the Afterlife

Alex felt like he was being rushed.

And he was. His mom had offered to make the trip in place of him and Ren, but then she'd barely been able to get out of her chair on her own.

"I'll go with them," said Luke. "I've got one of those gizmos, too." Calling his ancient cheetah amulet a "gizmo" undercut his credibility, but his next statement was more convincing: "You can't just send two nerds to the afterlife alone."

The search party grew to three, and it had been full steam ahead after that.

"You have everything you need now," said Todtman, handing Alex a worn-out backpack rescued from the museum's lost and found room and filled with handpicked artifacts.

Alex slipped it on and felt the bow of an ancient wooden carving of a boat jab him in the back. He shrugged his shoulders to shift the little boat over and heard metal clink against metal at the bottom of the pack.

Then the three could avoid it no longer. They turned to face the false door. It was one of the largest Alex had ever seen, a six-foot-high slab of stone with a rectangular indentation at its center painted a faded red ocher and bordered by raised reliefs of columns. Hieroglyphic writing was carved deep into the ancient stone. It was a symbolic gateway to the afterlife, but in about two steps, it was about to get very real.

Alex pulled the scarab out from under his shirt.

"Be careful, Alex," said his mom. Alex heard something different in her voice, not a torn raspiness but a quiver of deep concern that sounded almost as painful. "You too, Ren . . . And even you, Luke. If you are in danger, come back."

Todtman listened with a just-sucked-lemon look on his face that seemed to say: *Come back? They haven't even left yet!* His actual words were only slightly more diplomatic:

"Yes, be careful, of course — but do not waste time! The world of the living and the world of the dead are very close now. We have seen it ourselves: mummies by the thousands, spirits in the streets. The boundaries are falling, and The Order is getting stronger. Look for signs of The Order when you cross over. Even in the afterlife, they will guard their prize closely. Use your amulets to guide you, if you can. We must find the Lost Spells and repair the damage they're done to our world."

Alex looked away. Todtman could say "we" until he was blue in his froggy face, but he wasn't going. He was staying back: Mission Control to their moon shot, and reinforce-

ments if necessary. Still, Alex knew he was right. The worlds were closer now. His mom had used the Spells to open a gateway between them, to bring him back. Now The Order was using the Spells to tear down the walls — to use the power of the world of the dead to rule the world of the living. The old legend was coming true. The Final Kingdom was almost here.

Almost.

They still had one last, desperate chance.

Alex took a deep breath and one more look at his mom. He opened and closed his mouth, like a guppy, but he couldn't even begin to think of what to say. Instead, he just nodded. Reluctantly, she nodded, too. He looked over at Ren and Luke.

"Let's do this," he said with as much bravery as he could muster. It wasn't much.

Luke gave him a sympathetic look. "Nice try, cuz," he said. "But it goes like this . . ." His next words would've fit right in in a football huddle: "LET'S DO THIS!"

Alex had to admit, it sounded better coming from him. He was even a little fired up by it. Without another word, Alex wrapped his hand around his scarab and stepped toward solid stone.

Beside him, Ren said two words, very softly: "For home." Then she stepped forward, too.

Right behind them, Luke said, "It's go time."

The next thing Alex heard was a loud *POP!*

His vision turned red as he passed through the stone, and he closed his eyes instinctively. When he opened them again, he was in a different world. The washed-out electric lighting of the museum was replaced by a warm amber glow. All around him, deeper veins of red and orange and yellow pooled in the air, coming together and hinting at shapes only to pull apart and drain away. Alex looked down at his feet and saw what appeared to be a well-worn dirt path. He looked back over his shoulder and saw a transparent rose-pink rectangle shimmering in the air: the false door, as seen from the other side. Next to it, Ren and Luke stood washed in the yellow-orange light and blinking incredulously.

"Are you okay?" called Alex over the low, steady hum that seemed to surround them.

All three of them clutched their amulets tightly, like lifelines, but Luke gave him a thumbs-up with his free hand, and Ren called back: "I think so. It's not as scary this time."

Alex nodded. The last time they had traveled through the afterlife, it had been a darker and more frightening place. But now, high above, a fiery object was making slow progress across the golden sky. "It's daytime now," he said.

Luke looked up, shielded his eyes, and said, "The sun is all jacked up."

It was true. It was hard to see through its blazing glow, but the object above them wasn't round. If anything, it looked kind of like a boat. Alex was amazed to realize that it *was*

a boat. As many pictures and carvings as he'd seen of it, his next words sounded crazy, even to him: "It's the sun barque of Amun-Re."

"The *sun god*?" stammered Ren.

Alex could see the idea ricocheting around Ren's orderly mind. He seriously hoped she wouldn't lose it. Instead, she closed her eyes briefly, took a deep breath, and opened them. "Okay, whatever," she said. "Let's just get going."

Alex inhaled the fragrant air, clamped down a little tighter on his scarab, and closed his eyes.

It was the biggest test of his life, and it had only one question.

*Could he feel it?*

The scarab could detect the undead and the death magic that created them. It had a strong connection to the Spells, and so did Alex. In Minyahur, the small desert village where his mom had hidden out, studying the Spells, the scarab had nearly burned his hand off when the Spells were close by. And he'd passed out the first time he'd seen them up close. Using the amulet to detect death magic here seemed like a good way to get his hand burned off — this was the *world* of the dead!

But as his eyes closed and his senses stretched out, all he felt — heard, really — was the same buzzing hum getting louder. That's what it was, he realized: the strong, steady signal of the afterlife all around. It was the energy of this strange place, and he didn't need his amulet to hear it.

He relaxed a little more and breathed.

As he relaxed, his senses opened further, and then he *did* sense something. It wasn't a shape or an image as much as a feeling, an almost magnetic pull. The amulet began to heat up in his hand.

He shuffled his feet slightly, turned his shoulders, and then raised his hand.

"The Spells are in that direction," he said. "Somewhere over there."

"Are you sure?" said Ren.

Alex nodded. "I feel a really strong signal. It's almost . . . pulling me there."

He opened his eyes and looked down the length of his arm as if it were the barrel of a gun. He stared into the distance. The air was thick and smelled of earth and water. It still swirled with warm colors and phantom shapes, but the shifting patterns decorated the view more than they obscured it. He could see fields extending outward in every direction, tall stalks of wheat and barley swaying in the wind, washed in golden light. Off in the distance, there were figures moving among the rows of shifting grain, and Alex recognized the timeless, repetitive motions of farmers working the land.

And directly in front of his outstretched arm, past acres of golden fields, was the glittering blue-green band of a river.

The Nile.

As otherworldly as it all seemed, it still made sense to him. The ancient Egyptians believed the dead crossed the Nile on the first leg of their journey into the afterlife. Back at the

museum, they'd prepared for the possibility that they might have to do it themselves.

"So, let me get this straight," said Luke, staring in the direction Alex had pointed. "We're in the land of death, or whatever; there are dudes in these fields, *dead* dudes; something is trying to pull you across a river . . . and you want to *go*?" He lifted his chin toward the riverbank. "You can't even see what's on the other side."

Alex lifted his gaze. The land beyond the winding waterway was obscured by a heavy, fog-like haze. The kingdom of the dead was holding its secrets close.

"We have to," said Alex, trying to sound calmer and more confident than he felt. "I think that's where the Spells are."

Luke considered it for a moment and then shrugged. "You're gonna get us killed," he said. "But at least we're in the right place for it."

"Yeah, let's go," Ren said, eyeing the fieldworkers swaying in the distance. "The faster we find them, the better."

The three friends set off cautiously down the path, the dirt under their feet as black as charcoal. Alex ventured one last look over his shoulder at the fiery vessel inching across the morning sky. He felt its heat on the back of his neck, and when he looked down, he saw his shadow stretching out before him.

They would travel to the west, where the sun died each day.

## To the Nile

They stayed on the path as it cut through a field of waist-high barley. With one hand still wrapped around his scarab, Alex reached out with the other and brushed the top of the nearest stalks. All around them, the light continued to shift and swirl, shapes and colors ornamenting the heavy air. He saw rosy red light pooling in the air ten feet in front of him, forming a perfect circle, like the pupil of an eye. It drained away a moment later, leaving nothing but the vague sensation of being watched.

As his ears adjusted to the steady hum all around, he heard other sounds rise up. Some were faint: airy exhalations that might have been the wind, but sounded more like an old man breathing his last gasp; distant roars that might have been thunder, had the golden sky not been cloudless. Others were louder: A chorus of wailing voices rose up off to their left. Alex whipped his head around, but all he saw was shifting grain.

"Did you guys hear that?" he said, but the voices had already stopped.

"I heard it," said Ren.

Both of them turned to Luke, who shrugged. "I thought it was you two."

Alex turned back toward the fields. Whether or not his ears were playing tricks on him, his eyes were telling a very clear story. The figures working the fields were closer now, the nearest no more than twenty yards away. Their broad backs were slightly stooped and their strong shoulders swung from side to side. Alex couldn't see the blades of the scythes they were carrying, but he knew they were harvesting the grain. Golden stalks disappeared with each swing.

*Shesh shesh shesh* went the blades.

"Are they dangerous?" asked Ren, walking a little closer.

Alex shook his head. "I don't think so," he said. The figures hadn't so much as glanced in their direction.

"So those guys are, like, one hundred percent dead, right?" hissed Luke. "And that's why they look like that?"

They were close enough to see them clearly now. Some had skin the color of stone, but most were shades of blue. They wore simple clothes but regal headdresses that seemed oddly out of place in the sun-washed fields.

"They're shabti," said Alex.

"Yeah," agreed Luke. "They're definitely shabby."

"Shab*ti*," corrected Ren. Then she turned toward Alex and added: "But, uh, you better tell us — I mean Luke — what those are again."

Alex managed half a smile. He knew that Ren liked to know what was going on, and that a little information might help keep her calm in this strange world. Still, he pretended he was explaining it for Luke's benefit.

"The ancient Egyptians believed that the afterlife was just, like, an extension of everyday life. There was no sickness or death, I mean, obviously. But you still had to work, to grow crops and stuff. So they put these little statues in their tombs. They're called shabti, or answerers. Each day, when the dead were called to work, they could send out one of their shabti to answer for them."

Alex told the story as they passed by the first of the silent laborers. *Shesh shesh shesh.* He could see the long, sharp, curved blades of their scythes now, but still the enchanted laborers ignored them. Alex concentrated on keeping his voice calm and steady and willed his feet not to break into a panicked run.

Soon, they passed by the shabti. Now the fields on either side of them were cut low, piles of barley awaiting collection on the ground and little bits of it floating lightly in the golden air.

*Chooo!*

Ren sneezed and Alex jumped. She didn't make fun of him, like she normally would have, though. He knew she was way more freaked out by all this than he was. "Your mom taught you really well," she said instead. "I mean, about the shabti and stuff."

"Thanks," he said. With the fields cut low, they could see the river ahead clearly.

"Why are you thanking me?" said Ren. "I was complimenting your mom."

Alex snorted out half a laugh, and that seemed so crazy that he snorted out a full one. Who would've thought it: laughing in the afterlife.

"I was just kidding," said Ren, too freaked out to laugh but clearly wanting to join in the good mood. "You did a good job learning."

"The thing is," said Alex, "I didn't realize I was learning. It's just that every story she told, I was right there, listening. Every exhibit she worked on, I was right there watching. And . . . I . . ."

His voice trailed off. He was lost in both memory and realization. He had learned so much as a sick kid trailing after his mom in the museum, and now he was using it on his own. He'd chased after her when she disappeared, and then moped when he thought she'd abandoned him. And now he was here leading this mission. Not abandoned, but independent. She'd given him what he needed to navigate this strange world. At least, he hoped so . . .

"Anyway," said Ren, snapping him out of it, "I'm glad you know so much about it."

"Me too," he said. "That reminds me. See all this black dirt we're walking on? That's where the Nile flooded and then pulled back. That's how Egyptians lived for thousands

of years, farming the floodplains of the Nile. Before the big dams were built and the Nile stopped flooding."

"Uh, no offense, dude," said Luke. "I mean, I know you two are having like a nerd moment or whatever — but who cares about dirt?"

Alex didn't deny being a little nerdy around the edges, but he still didn't like to hear it from his cool jock cousin. "I was about to mention the crocodiles," he said. "And the snakes. Those came with the floodwaters, too. Lots of 'em."

Luke and Ren looked all around, their eyes suddenly a little wider.

Alex kept his eyes forward, staring at the massive expanse of the Nile, a legendary river flowing through two worlds at once.

# The Kingdom of the Dead

Ren eyed the edge of the river warily. She'd seen enough nature documentaries to know that that's where crocodiles ambushed their prey. Up close, the current was coffee-colored and thick with sediment, the kind of water that made it very hard to spot crocodiles, and impossible to spot snakes.

"Oh wow!" said Alex.

Ren reluctantly lifted her eyes from the river's murky surface and gasped in astonishment.

The far shore, which had been hidden in haze as they walked, now revealed itself. More fields filled the floodplain on the other side, but beyond them, a vast kingdom stretched to the horizon. White stone temples, majestic houses, and even a few colossal pyramids glowed and shimmered in the golden light. It was a scene from out of a history book, a museum painting come to life.

And moving along the broad avenues, just visible from where she stood, people walked, alone or in small groups. As Ren watched, not blinking and barely remembering to

breathe, she even saw a glittering, horse-drawn chariot, looking like a tiny toy in the distance. It kicked up a plume of dust and sand behind it before turning a corner and disappearing.

*The kingdom of the dead.*

She nearly fainted.

"Let's get that boat," said Alex.

"Uhhh," said Luke, and Ren thought that summed it up pretty well.

She looked at Alex, incredulous. "How are you not freaked out by all this?" She pointed across the water. "By all of *them*?"

"I *am* freaked out," said Alex, and a slight tremble in his voice confirmed it. "But dead doesn't necessarily mean evil. These are the good ones, I think. And, anyway, we have work to do."

"The *good* ones," said Luke. "What, like . . . Casper the Friendly Ghost?"

Instead of answering, Alex shrugged his backpack off and lowered it to the ground. He unzipped it and carefully pulled out the small wooden carving of a boat. It was a little more than a foot long and a little less than three thousand years old. They'd taken it from a storeroom in the museum. Its edges worn down and its paint worn off, it was one of thousands of items that didn't quite merit display space.

But the little boat was about to earn its keep now.

"I don't see how we're supposed to get across this huge river in a toy," said Luke. "What is that, a boat for ants?"

"They put these in the tombs so the spirits could cross the Nile," said Alex. He walked over to the river's edge. Ren

followed a step behind and watched as he knelt down and placed the little boat on the gently rippling surface.

Immediately, the boat's frame pushed up and out, quickly reaching the height of Ren's shoulders. As she and Alex both jumped back to avoid getting knocked over by the bow, Ren thought of the packet of little sponge dinosaurs her dad had given her once, the ones that expanded when you dropped them in water.

By the time the little boat stopped growing, it was a real boat big enough for three. It was made not of wood but of bundled reeds that rose up to a high point on each end. All Ren managed to say was "Whoa."

And then it occurred to her that she was supposed to get in this thing now — and to travel to the other side. Where so many of the dead were. Suddenly, the possibility seemed all too real. "I don't know . . ." she said.

"We have to, Ren," said Alex, stepping forward and gingerly touching the reedy side of the craft. "I am getting such a strong signal from over there."

Ren looked at him. There was something wrong with what he had just said, a hole in the logic, but she couldn't place it. Her brain was too full of wonder and fear.

A moment later, it got worse.

"That is not your vessel," she heard. "The one it was made for has already crossed over." The voice was strong and steady. And it did *not* belong to Alex or Luke. "Where did you get this boat?"

Ren wheeled around to see who the voice belonged to.

Who, or *what*.

He was tall and muscular and dressed in ancient garb. A white-and-yellow shendyt kilt was wrapped around his waist, and a wide, ornate collar necklace hung from his neck. Thickly woven straps crisscrossed his broad chest, meeting at a massive, perfectly round ruby. He held a long, thin staff in one hand. But who could possibly care about any of that when his head — the head talking to them right now — was that of a jet-black jackal?

As she stared in disbelief, he turned to meet her eyes. Her knees felt like jelly, and her punch-drunk brain had its finger on the light switch.

*Talking dog*, she thought vaguely. *Good talking dog man. Don't bite.*

*Anubis.*

The guardian of the underworld.

Not just an ancient Egyptian god but, as Alex's mom would say, one of the big ones.

"I asked you a question," said the deity, the daggerlike tips of two huge white canine teeth appearing as he spoke. "Where did you get this boat? And answer carefully. The afterlife is a perilous place for tomb raiders."

Alex gulped in just enough air to squeak out: "In a museum."

Anubis's jackal ears swung toward the small sound. He looked at Alex, considering. Alex's heart hammered hard in his chest.

Out of the corner of his eye, he saw Ren swaying on her feet. He wanted to run over and help her, but he didn't dare move. He had the distinctly unpleasant feeling that he was being judged. Luke was standing beside her, staring at the ancient god in wide-eyed, slack-jawed wonder. *Please don't say anything stupid*, thought Alex.

"I will accept your answer," said Anubis, and Alex relaxed just a little. Even Ren seemed to stop wobbling. Luke's mouth closed and opened again silently, like a goldfish's. "Your museums empty our tombs just as surely as the thieves do, but at least they take good care of what they find."

Anubis paused and then added cryptically, "And then, too, you have been vouched for." His jackal head looked off to a spot farther up the bank. "It is funny, in a way."

Alex had no idea what any of that meant. *Vouched for? Funny? Did gods like jokes?* He had zero chance of mustering a polite laugh at the moment, so he stuck to what he knew. "Thank you," he said, bowing slightly. "We're sorry about the boat, but we need to cross . . ."

"You may not," said Anubis, suddenly striding forward.

The three friends scrambled to get out of his way. Alex turned to see the deity raise his staff and tap the bow of the boat. As the boat shrank and shriveled, Alex dropped his

head in defeat. A moment later, he saw the little wooden carving once again bobbing like a bath toy on the river. All three of them watched silently as the current caught it and it began to float away.

"We needed that," said Alex to his own feet.

"Why is that?" said Anubis.

Alex looked up slightly, still not daring to make direct eye contact with the deity. "Because we are looking for something," he ventured. "Something important."

"All hope would seem to be lost, then," said Anubis.

And there was something about the way he said it: almost playful. *Is he teasing me*, wondered Alex, *or mocking me?* "The people — well, the things — we're after are *evil*," he protested. "Our world is in *danger*."

Anubis sized him up with glowing green eyes, and Alex was afraid he had gone too far. *Would the next thing he felt be those dagger-like teeth? That battle staff?*

And then . . . Anubis smiled. He smiled in the way dogs do sometimes. It would have been cute, if he weren't a seven-foot-tall death god. "I know they're evil," he said. "That's why I did not let them cross, either."

A hundred questions flooded Alex's mind, but Anubis was already walking away. "I take no part in this conflict, other than to protect my realm," said the ancient guardian of the afterlife. "What you seek and the ones you fear are here on the borderlands. But hurry, for this land is no place for the living, especially at night."

As the god headed up the bank, Alex turned to look at the others. "That really just happened, right?" he said. "You heard all that?"

"Oh, that happened all right," said Luke. "That Snoopy-looking dude was hella real."

"That was Anubis, wasn't it?" said Ren. "I've seen his, like, statues."

Alex nodded and turned back for one more look.

But Anubis was gone.

As soon as Ren registered that fact, she let Alex have it. "I can't believe you were going to magic-boat us over to the *city of the dead* for no reason! The Death Walkers aren't even over there!"

Alex looked at his amulet. "But I got such a strong signal," he protested, his voice breaking slightly.

"Yeah," said Ren, "because that thing detects *spirits*, too." She pointed to the endless city on the far shore. "And, I mean, *hello*, the *kingdom* of the dead?"

"Oh yeah," said Alex.

He looked down at his feet, embarrassed. He saw his shadow stretching out behind him. *Behind him* . . . He looked up. The fiery vessel had crossed over the river and begun its descent.

"Um, we should really get going," he said, reaching down to pick up his pack.

"Yeah," said Luke. "Let's get out of here before the rest of the zoo shows up."

As they walked quickly back up the bank, Alex picked over what Anubis had said: *Did not let them cross . . .* Something big occurred to him.

"The gods are more powerful than the Death Walkers," he said, and as soon as he heard the words out loud, he knew they were true. Back in the Egyptian desert, Sekhmet had obliterated a Death Walker their amulets had been powerless against. Anubis had stared down The Order's stone warriors and turned them back.

"Yeah," said Ren. "Obviously. They're gods. It's kind of in the definition."

Alex knew there was some greater significance to that fact, something he wasn't quite getting. Amazingly, Luke was the one to put his finger on it.

"It would be cool if the gods could put the beatdown on The Order," he said. "Instead of leaving it up to three middle schoolers from Manhattan." Then he quickly added: "Not that we're not awesome."

Alex stared at his cousin. It was a statement so obvious that it had taken Luke to say it. "That *would* be cool," said Alex. "So cool."

As they neared the top of the bank, Ren came up next to him. "You know," she said, "if the gods did that we wouldn't need to use the Spells."

He nodded. His best friend was just as worried about what might happen to him if they used the Spells as he was. She wanted him to live, too — even if she did yell at him sometimes.

"Of course," she added, "that's a pretty big *if.*"

He knew she was right about that, too. Relying on the divine intervention of ancient, animal-headed deities wasn't much of a plan — it was like planning to win the lottery as a career goal. It was a nice thought, but the time for daydreaming was over. Now they needed to figure out how to do it for themselves. Alex scanned the ground near the top of the bank. Anubis had said that what they were looking for was on this side of the bank. *But where?*

He scanned the bank in both directions, and then looked down at his feet. There in the dark dirt of the timeless Nile he saw a scattering of small footprints. He huffed out a little laugh. "I think I figured out who vouched for us back there," he said, pointing down.

The others gathered around. "Are those . . . cat prints?" said Luke.

"Anubis was right," said Alex. "It is kind of funny. Imagine being saved from a dog-headed god . . . by a little cat."

"Pai!" exclaimed Ren, dropping to her knees and tracing the tracks with her fingers.

"It must've been her," said Alex.

They looked all around, but there was no sign of Ren's undead BFF, and the tracks vanished into the harder dirt higher up the bank.

Ren stood up and brushed her hands on her jeans. "Okay, Pai did her part," she said. "I guess it's time I did mine."

She took a deep breath and reached for her ibis.

## A Dangerous New Direction

Ren tried to calm her thoughts. The last time she'd used the ibis, it had shown her a fearful scene from home. Now she was worried about what it might show her, and what it might not. She took hold of the ancient amulet, closed her eyes, and made her question as clear and focused as possible. It was a question the ibis had never answered before, but maybe now it would. Now that they were so close . . .

"Where are the Lost Spells?" she said out loud.

Instantly, a series of images flashed through her mind.

The first: the little wooden boat bobbing along the current near the shore.

The second: a frightening and familiar figure standing near the riverbank. His face and neck were swollen with stings, his body was wrapped in crimson robes, and there was a huge scorpion stinger where his left hand should have been. It was the first Death Walker they'd faced, the Stung Man. In the river behind him, bobbing lazily along, was the little boat.

Finally, she saw a long line of men. They were dressed in ancient garb, but as the first man in line stepped into a glowing portal in the air, his features changed. He aged three thousand years in one step and his outfit was replaced by the ragged wrappings of a mummy as he disappeared through the false door.

Ren's eyes fluttered open.

"What did you see?" said Alex. "Anything?"

She described each image carefully. "It seems like it wants us to follow the boat along the river."

"We need to go north," Alex said.

"That's right," she said. She remembered now: Unlike most U.S. rivers, the Nile flows north, out of Africa and up to the Mediterranean Sea. So that's the way it would carry the little boat. "But why do you think it showed me the Stung Man?" she said.

Back in New York, at the start of all this, they'd used the ancient Egyptian Book of the Dead and Alex's amulet to send him back to the afterlife. But that wouldn't work this time: They were already in the afterlife!

"I don't know," said Alex. "He could be guarding the Spells. We'll have to try to avoid him or at least hold him off until we can find them."

*Hold him off?* thought Ren. *He has a scorpion stinger the size of a desktop printer — and usually about a thousand actual scorpions with him, too.* But she had another concern that was even bigger. "What about the men — I mean mummies?"

she asked. "Do you think those are the ones heading to New York?"

Alex nodded grimly. "Yeah," he said. "Pretty sure."

It made sense to Alex that the mummies would look like the people they'd once been while they were still in the afterlife. Then they'd be mummies again when they stepped back into the world of the living. And he knew The Order's first target was NYC, a high-profile demonstration of their abilities, meant to strike fear into the rest of the world.

But he had a bigger concern, too. Ren had asked the ibis where the Spells were. He'd heard her with his own ears. But he also knew that her attention was divided by her homesickness and concern about her parents. And the ibis knew it, too. The last time she'd tried to ask it about their mission, it had shown her home instead.

*Was this time different?* he wondered as they headed north along the riverbank. *Or were they chasing the wrong thing?*

"So that portal, or false door or whatever," she said, "it leads to New York?"

"Man," said Luke. "I would love to get back to NYC."

"Guys!" Alex snapped. "We need to concentrate on what we're doing here, okay?"

"I know," said Luke. "I'm just, like, seriously missing my PlayStation."

They walked on wordlessly for a while, keeping their eyes and ears open and doing their best to move quietly, though the ground had grown so muddy that their footsteps made small squelches. The three of them were spread out in a line, with Ren farthest up the bank, Alex in the middle, and Luke closer to the river. Together, their six feet were making a chorus of burpy sounds in the soggy soil. Alex turned to the others to tell them to step softly, but as he did, he saw a man in black robes slip silently out from behind a palm tree and step in front of Ren. "Watch out!" he blurted.

But she'd already stopped cold.

She saw the knife, too.

Alex and Luke both grabbed for their amulets, but the man held the knife just under Ren's chin. "There is no need for that," he said. "I just came to see who passes along my bank."

Alex didn't dare unleash a burst of wind with the knife so close to Ren, but the amulet did allow him to understand the man's ancient tongue. "*Your* bank?" he said, trying to keep the fear and concern from his voice.

"I maintain it," said the man.

Luke moved a few squelches closer to Alex and whispered, "I could get him."

Alex shook his head slowly and whispered back, "Not yet. Can't risk it." If Luke hit this guy at top speed, the impact could drive the knife right into Ren.

The man paid no attention to the hushed conversation and continued to talk about maintaining the bank. "If it weren't for me, it would be a swamp. There is a spring — and many snakes. But I keep it nice. Nice for you to pass."

"Uh, thanks?" said Ren, who had quietly taken hold of her amulet, too. She said it through her teeth to avoid opening her mouth too wide and cutting herself on the blade.

"You are welcome!" said the man grandly, lowering his knife just a touch. Then he seemed to remember something sad and shook his head ruefully. "But such work is not easy. I am afraid I must ask —"

"For a small contribution?" volunteered Alex eagerly, suddenly understanding. "Just a reasonable toll, perhaps?"

The man smiled broadly. "I am glad you understand me! Clearly you are a very intelligent boy."

*And you're a bandit and a thief,* thought Alex, but what he said was: "Hold on."

Once again, Alex swung the pack from his back. He stuck his hand in and began rifling through the bottom. Soon he felt the old, cold gold clinking under his hand.

"No tricks," said the man.

Alex pulled his hand out of the pack and held up three ancient coins — another gift from the overstocked museum. "Of course not," he said. "Just a small, um, appreciation."

Thousands of years had dulled the luster of the coins, but the man eyed them greedily as Alex walked them over to him, spread out on his outstretched palm. The man lunged for

them with his free hand, but Alex pulled back and pocketed one of the coins. "We will give you this one when we cross 'your bank' safely on the way back."

The bandit smiled and grabbed the two remaining coins with the quickness of a cobra striking. Alex felt the man's ragged nails scratch across his palm. Then the bandit lowered his knife and began to back away, bowing slightly. "You truly are a smart boy," he said. "And these are fine coins. So I will give you one last bit of information. Beware, strange children, for the borderlands are unsettled. There is discord between the world of the living and the world of the dead."

"Uh, no offense," said Ren, no longer needing to talk through her teeth. "But we kind of know that already."

"Smarter than I thought, then," said the thief, pocketing the coins and sheathing his knife. "But did you know that Ammit herself prowls these lands now, upset by the imbalance?"

"Ammit?" said Alex. "The devourer of souls?" Alex had seen Ammit's strange image many times, carved into the walls of tombs and painted on the scrolls of the Book of the Dead. A demigod with the head of a crocodile, the body of a lion, and the hindquarters of a hippo, she had one grim job: to devour the hearts — and souls — of those who failed the weighing of the heart ceremony.

"Yes," said the man, looking both ways nervously as he stepped back alongside the thick old tree. "The pull of the far shore is strong, but I have stayed on this side for long

ages to avoid her fearsome jaws. Now she has come to the borderlands!"

"Uh, okay," said Ren, clearly ready to be done with this man. "We'll keep our eyes open."

"Your ears," he said. "You will know the devourer by her cry."

And then, without another word, he stepped toward the tree and disappeared completely. Not behind it but, somehow, inside.

"Good thing Todtman thought of giving us those old coins," said Ren, glaring at the old tree. "That guy could've killed me."

"Oh, I don't know," said Alex, giddy with relief to see his best friend still alive. He knocked on the tree trunk as they walked past. "His bark is worse than his bite."

Ren groaned at the pun, and Alex slung the pack back over his shoulder. It was lighter now, without the boat and coins. He felt a few old scrolls, protective spells from the Book of the Dead, rolling around inside.

Luke led the way, high-tech sneakers on timeless soil, as they angled back down the bank and followed the river around a wide corner. New knowledge jumbled together in Alex's head like puzzle pieces in a box:

*Ammit herself prowls the borderlands . . .*

*The gods are stronger . . .*

## Against the Grain

"There it is!" said Luke, pointing toward the river.

The little wooden boat was lying on its side on the river-bank. Alex looked back over his shoulder as they walked toward it. He couldn't say exactly how far it had come — or they had come — since they'd first set this thing in the water. All he knew was that the golden light was starting to fade, and the colors swirling in the air were getting darker and more ominous, bloodreds replacing rosy pinks, blues edging toward black. The growls and groans and huffs and wails that had sounded far-off before seemed louder now, closer. Alex didn't like any of it, and the darkening world wasn't his only concern. "We need to be careful." he said as Ren bent down to pick up the boat. "If the boat's here, the Stung Man could be, too."

Kneeling in the sand with her hand a few inches from the boat, Ren paused and looked back toward him. "Maybe we got here first," she said. "Maybe I was wrong."

As she spoke, Alex saw a large black scorpion scamper up

from the little pocket of shade under the boat's hull. "Ren!" he gasped.

"What?" she said, her fingers just inches from the scorpion's flexed tail, the curved stinger twisting into position for a strike.

"Scorpion!" shouted Luke.

Ren jumped up and back as the angry arachnid struck out at empty air.

"Where did that come from?" said Ren. "Do you think it's one of *his*?"

The first Death Walker had faced a grisly demise from scorpion stings thousands of years earlier, and back in New York, the venomous insects had been a surefire calling card of the Stung Man. But here, in between palm trees and the Nile, the little creepy-crawler seemed to fit right in. "Maybe not?" Alex said hopefully.

"Uh, what about those ones?" she said, her voice suddenly shaky.

Alex turned and saw why. The bank was suddenly dotted with scorpions. Some were large and black and others were small and pale, but all of them were packing potent venom and heading down the bank, their exoskeletons clicking and clacking softly.

"This place is really starting to bug me," muttered Luke.

Alex grabbed his amulet, planning to clear a path through the arachnid army with a gust of desert wind. Instead, he got a warning. A sharp pulse, like a radar signal bouncing off a

**122**

mountain, rang in his mind. Alex spun around. And there he was.

"I was hoping we'd meet again," said the Stung Man. He stood just up the bank, no more than twelve feet away.

"Oh no," breathed Ren, grabbing for her own amulet.

The Stung Man advanced toward them with long, confident strides, and the scorpions scurrying all around him.

"What happened to his face?" whispered Luke. Alex realized it was his cousin's first encounter with this Walker and the swollen, discolored flesh of his eternally unhealing wounds. But there was no time for explanation — only action.

Ren raised her hand and delivered a blinding white flash that caught the Stung Man by surprise. He closed his eyes too late and grunted in annoyance.

Meanwhile, Alex delivered a whipping, whistling lance of wind that scattered dirt and scorpions as it cut up from the bank to the line of palm trees. "Go!" he shouted, and the friends took off running toward the tree line. There was nothing to be gained from fighting the Stung Man out in the open, before they'd ever located the Spells, and the only plan that made sense was escape.

As they raced up the bank, Alex pictured the massive stinger that took the place of the Stung Man's left hand. He could almost feel it shooting forth and piercing his back with its cruel, curved point. He ran faster as Luke whooshed past him in a cheetah-powered blur. Half a step behind him, Ren's feet slapped dirt. "Come on, come on!" he called over his shoulder.

Luke was at the crest of the bank. Moving at hyper-speed, he had already molded the dark soil of the floodplain into a dozen perfectly round dirt balls. Now he delivered the first one down the slope in a high-kicking baseball pitch.

A dull *THOKK!* of exploding dirt gave way to an indignant shout from the Walker.

Alex didn't need to turn around to know that Luke's first pitch was a strike. Instead, he eyed the fields just beyond his cousin. The grain was higher here, as if unharvested for some time — perfect for hiding three kids!

"Into the field!" he called.

Luke whipped one more major league dirtball down the slope as Alex and Ren reached the top of the bank and sprinted straight past him. Luke turned and followed, immediately overtaking the others. Their own frantic footsteps mixed with the beat of the Stung Man's sandals slapping the dirt behind them. As the sound of the Walker's pursuit grew closer — hoarse shouts and muttered curses mixing with heavy footfalls — Alex tensed up, preparing for the terrible pain of the massive stinger piercing his back.

And then he felt it.

The rough slap of tall sprouts of barley hitting his face as they burst into the field. "Keep going!" he said as the Stung Man roared his disapproval behind them.

Alex crashed through the tall ripe stalks, his vision just a whirl of green and gold and tan. His heart pounded and he gasped for breath, feeling like he was sucking in nearly as much grain and dust as air.

For a few chaotic moments he lost track of the others and panicked. *Had Ren fallen? Had Luke been brought down by the stinger?* But then he heard Ren. "This is going to be murder on my allergies!" she huffed from right behind him. The crash of stalks laid low in front of him told Alex his cousin was still at full speed.

But if he could hear his friends, so could the Stung Man. "Slow down!" he gasped. "We have to be quiet if we want to lose him."

The crashing subsided. "Okay," Ren said softly from beside him.

"Good plan," said Luke from a few yards ahead.

Alex took the lead as they snaked their way through the field single file. The grain grew taller the deeper they went, and soon even Luke could stand up straight with no fear of being seen.

"Okay," whispered Alex. "Let's stop for a second."

They stood still, catching their breath and listening carefully. The only sound Alex could hear was the wind gently rustling the grain. He took hold of his amulet and searched, but the intense radar signal was gone. All he felt was the same general buzzing hum as before. "I think we lost him," he said. "I'm not getting any signal from the amulet."

"None?" said Ren. "Not the Lost Spells, either?"

Alex shook his head. "I think they must be hidden again," he said. They knew it was a possibility. When The Order had captured the Spells from his mom's desert hideout, they'd

**125**

also captured the ancient cloaking spells she'd wrapped them in.

"We'll never find them now," said Ren angrily, punctuating the thought with a small sneeze. *Choo!*

"Not cool," said Luke.

*Had they really come all this way — into another world! — only to come up short?* Alex refused to believe it. "Wait," he said as the three knelt down next to each other in the sea of swaying grain. "We did see the first thing the ibis showed you. And then we ran into the Stung Man."

"Okay, so what does that mean?" asked Luke.

"We banished him here. But Todtman said that if The Order got the Spells, the Walkers we'd banished would be able to come back," Alex explained. "So if the Stung Man's still hanging around here, then maybe it means he's helping to guard the Spells."

"Okay, maybe," said Ren. "But they're not going to hide the most powerful spells in the world in some field. Remember what else Todtman said, right before we left? 'Even in the afterlife they will guard their prize closely.' They wouldn't just leave them out in the open."

Alex considered it. "Right . . . so we're looking for some kind of building, and we know it's on this side of the river and that we're probably pretty close."

"Not many buildings around here," said Luke, plucking a stalk of barley from the ground. "It's not exactly midtown."

*Midtown . . . Skyscrapers . . .* It gave Alex an idea. He looked up at the sky, cut into sections above him by the waving grain. "We need to get up high and look."

Ren looked back the way they'd come. "Maybe if we climbed one of those trees by the river?"

"We can't risk going back," said Alex. "The Stung Man could still be there."

Luke eyed the top of the grain. "I might be able to, like, high-jump it," he mused. "For, like, a second."

Alex pictured his cousin jack-in-the-boxing up over the fields, getting a quick glimpse at most. Then he had a better idea. Better . . . and worse. He dropped his head. "Oh, this bites," he said. He'd seen kids do this at the pool at the YMCA. He'd always been too sick and weak to join in, and the lifeguards always blew their whistles to stop it, anyway. He looked up at his undersized friend. He was so much stronger and healthier since his mom had used the Spells to save him — but he still couldn't believe what he was about to say.

"What?" said Ren.

Alex sighed. "Do you know what a chicken fight is?"

## Guard Crocs

Alex boosted Ren up on his shoulders. Luke was the obvious choice for the job — taller and stronger — but the big jock had balked. "This is seriously all you," he'd said, putting his hands up and backing up a step.

Alex did his best, but it was more of a launch than a lift. As soon as Ren was more or less in position, Alex lurched up and forward. Ren wobbled and rose, and rose and wobbled. Luke reconsidered slightly, helping to steady her. But five seconds later, it all came crashing down. Ren toppled from Alex's shoulders, taking him with her. And when Luke tried to catch them, he wound up on the ground, too. The three fell in a heap among some crushed stalks of barley.

"Did you see anything?" asked Alex from the bottom of the pile.

"I saw some roofs!" crowed Ren.

Alex pumped his fist: *Yes.* "Let's go," he said. And as the first skittering, chittering sounds of scorpions advancing through the tall grasses reached their ears, Ren and Luke didn't argue.

Alex and Luke followed Ren's lead. They kept low and tried to disturb the tall stalks as little as possible, easily outpacing their tiny, tail-heavy pursuers. Soon, they came to the edge of the field. They stopped just short, peering through the last few rows of barley.

Ren's sense of direction had been unerring: A complex lay before them. Three square stone buildings were arranged in a triangular formation. And at its point stood Ta-mesah. As an Order operative, he'd nearly finished off Alex and Ren in London. Now, as a hulking, ten-foot-tall Death Walker with the head of a huge crocodile, he stood sentry in front of the largest building.

In front of the other two buildings, two enormous crocodiles basked in the late-day sun. "They've got to be twenty feet long," said Luke.

Alex peered through the thin veil of barley as it swayed in a light breeze. The air was dark gold now, and it swirled and glimmered with shifting shapes, but as he watched, he saw three glowing rectangles hold firm.

He pointed them out to the others. "Portals," he said. "More false doors, like the one we came in through."

"This is like the Grand Central Terminal of the afterlife," Ren whispered.

Suddenly, Ta-mesah's gaze shifted and he scanned the edge of the field. Alex's breath caught. *Had he heard them?* he wondered. *How was that even possible? Crocodiles barely have ears!*

But then Alex's own ears picked up a rustling to their left. The friends sank a little farther back into the stalks

and watched as the Stung Man emerged from the field and approached Ta-mesah. The two conversed briefly. The new Death Walker was so much larger than the old one — thanks to his mammoth stone statue — that the exchange looked like a father and son talk.

*Father.*

The thought hit Alex hard. *His own father had caused all this: a father he had never known, a father he never would . . .* He shook his head hard to clear it and then turned to the others. "I'm pretty sure I can guess what they're talking about," he said.

"So much for the element of surprise," said Ren.

Alex took hold of his amulet and felt his pulse race with ancient energy. He leaned in and tried to pick up at least some of what they were saying. It was no use. At this distance, their words were just a low mumble. A moment later, the Stung Man walked past Ta-mesah and into the tall open archway of the central stone building.

"That's got to be the one with the Spells," whispered Ren. "It's bigger, and guarded by Death Walkers. The other two are just guarded by reptiles."

Luke eyed them. "Those are some Jurassic Park–looking reptiles."

"Yeah, but crocodiles are dumb as mud. They've got brains the size of walnuts. And most of that is for hunting."

"That's the part that worries me!" hissed Luke.

Alex eyed the formidable stone structure. It was the size of a small house but built like an old bank. It had one

visible entrance, which was currently blocked by a ten-foot-tall undead ambush predator. And at least one more Death Walker was already inside.

"What do we do?" said Ren.

"I don't know," answered Alex, eyeing the long shadows stretching out behind the buildings. "But whatever it is, we have to do it fast."

"Maybe if one of us, like, lures him away," Luke offered. "And the others sneak inside . . ."

"And straight into a giant scorpion stinger?" countered Ren.

"Okay," he said. "What's your big idea?"

Ren's mouth opened, but nothing came out.

Suddenly, a huge sound filled the air. It was as loud as thunder and sounded like a combination between a roar and a low, rumbling growl.

"What the what?" blurted Luke.

Ta-mesah flinched visibly and then froze. A few moments later, he slowly lifted his long snout to sniff the air. Alex realized that what had been a crocodile mask in life had now become the Death Walker's head. Even more amazing: This ten-foot-tall, croc-headed undead powerhouse was very clearly *scared*.

On either side of their master, the two massive crocodiles called back in response. Their low, huffing growls sounded like layers peeled off from the original sound. Suddenly, Alex understood where that thunderous roar had come from — and why even Ta-mesah was afraid. He remembered the old thief's words: *You will know the devourer by her cry . . .*

He turned to others, wide-eyed. "It's Ammit."

Ren had just removed her hands from her ears and nodded. She knew the legend, too. It was fear of Ammit's jaws at the weighing of the heart ceremony that caused the Death Walkers to flee the afterlife in the first place. And as the roar split the sky again, Alex recognized it as the angry product of a croc's mouth and a lion's lungs.

Ta-mesah recognized it, too. Alex watched him slink back toward the building and disappear inside the open mouth of its doorway. *The gods are stronger* . . . The crocs called back once again and then fell silent. Alex sized up the sinister sentries. They were big, but their legs looked short and stubby. "This is our chance to get inside," he said.

After arguing earlier, Ren and Luke were suddenly on the same page. "Are you nuts?" they said simultaneously.

"Now they're both in there!" said Ren.

"Maybe they're hiding?" ventured Alex.

"Maybe they're *waiting*!" she countered.

"It's our only chance," he said. "Once he comes back out, we'll be stuck here till dark — and then it will be just as dangerous outside."

Luke looked around. "Those spooky voices are definitely getting louder," he admitted. "It's like a ghost concert out here — and I don't like the sound of that roar, either."

Ren still looked unconvinced, though, and Alex played the only card he had left. He pointed to the nearest portal, hanging in the air. "Somewhere nearby, there's another of

these that an army of the dead is marching through to New York."

Ren's expression shifted quickly from skeptical to resolute. She looked back toward the buildings. "Okay," she said, "but what about the crocodiles?"

Alex sized them up one last time. The animals were at least sixty feet from the doorway. Here at the edge of the field, the friends were half as far away — and with legs twice as long. "Don't worry about them," he said.

"Yeah, they look even slower than you two," said Luke. "And that's saying something."

Ren glared at the menacing crocs. "We've come a long way for this," she said. "What's thirty more feet?"

As the crocs settled back onto their bellies to bask in the last rays of sun, Alex realized how true that was. They really had come a long way. He had gone from a life on the sidelines to one in the thick of the action. From a kid too fragile for gym class to one preparing for a life-or-death sprint straight toward danger. Kneeling next to him, the cousin who had betrayed them in the desert was now an Amulet Keeper himself.

And Ren? As Alex gathered his legs underneath him and crouched down low, he took one last look over at his best friend. She'd struggled to come to terms with a world of magic and mummies, secret signs and changing rules. From London to Luxor, she'd struggled mightily with her ibis. But here in this strange otherworld, she had harnessed its

power to lead them right where they needed to go. And she was preparing to sprint straight toward the unknown.

Ren turned and caught him looking. "What?" she said.

"Nothing," said Alex.

"Whatever," said Ren. "Now, what's your plan for the Walkers?"

"We'll catch them by surprise or sneak around them," he said. "We'll use our amulets, if we have to. We've done this before."

Ren gave him a deeply skeptical look. "Not with two . . ."

"Okay, fine," said Alex. "I just came up with a new plan. It comes in three parts."

He crouched down deeper and relayed the first part: "On your mark . . ."

He touched his hands to the ground in front of him.

"Get set . . ." He raised up into a sprinter's stance. Beside him, Luke did the same. The two boys clearly had the same plan. Which was . . .

"Go!" blurted Alex as he and Luke took off running.

"Wait, what? That's it?" called Ren, but she took off right behind them.

In a blink — much faster than Alex had imagined possible — the two huge crocs took off running, too.

It was dinnertime.

## Light in the Darkness

Ren's legs pumped furiously as the huge carnivores converged on the friends from either side, rushing toward them in a brisk, improbable gallop.

"How are they so fast?" Alex yelped.

"I saw them gallop like this in a nature documentary once," called Ren. "I assumed it was on fast-forward!"

As the crocs closed in, Ren saw Luke reach up toward his amulet and disappear in a blur. *Fast-forward indeed*, she thought. He reappeared a moment later, under the stone archway at the building's entrance.

Now it was just her and Alex left on the menu. She had two choices: rush straight forward toward two waiting Death Walkers or stop and be eaten. *He called this a plan?* She was so angry at Alex that she almost wished he'd trip. She turned that anger to energy, edging past him despite his longer legs. The open doorway was just up ahead now, ten feet away. Luke waved them forward from inside: *Come on! Come on!* The crocs were coming from either side, maybe twenty feet away. She did the math.

They would make it. She eased up ever so slightly — as Alex went sprinting past Luke into the dark open mouth of the building.

Behind them, the massive crocs collided with a sound like two thick T-bone steaks being slapped together. Ren rushed inside, and Luke reached out to slow her down. "Thanks," she said. She scanned the dark entryway: no immediate sign of the Walkers. She felt a brief flash of relief, but it vanished as she turned back toward the entrance and realized their croc troubles weren't over yet. Either of the creatures could fit inside the archway, filling the entry with snapping jaws and blocking off all escape.

The two beefy beasts untangled themselves from their collision. Then slowly and in perfect unison, they turned their big beady eyes toward the entrance — and the tender little morsels inside.

"They're going to come in here, aren't they?" said Luke. "And then we're pretty much done for."

"Yep."

The larger of the two behemoths took a step toward the entrance, a string of saliva hanging from its slightly open mouth. Luke whispered, "I can't believe I'm doing this."

"Wait," said Ren. "Don't go out there. We'll figure something out in here, hide in the dark or something."

"Nah," said Luke. "You two do your thing. I'll hold off these things. I'm not the smartest guy — but you said it yourself: Crocodiles are dumb as mud."

He touched his amulet and disappeared back into the daylight. A split second later, he appeared in front of the monstrous crocs. "Here, lizard, lizard, lizard!" he called.

The closest one lunged. Ren held her breath — but Luke was already gone.

She exhaled and turned back into the darkness. She hoped he'd be able to distract the cold-blooded killers for long enough — and she hoped he wouldn't get eaten in the process. All of which meant one thing: She trusted him again. She even kind of liked him. Risking your life repeatedly for someone tends to have that effect.

It was the other one she was still mad at.

"Alex?" she hissed, heading down the dark tunnel of the entryway, her wide-open eyes desperately searching the darkness for friend and foe alike.

There was no response for a few steps, and then she heard his voice: "I'm here."

She flinched with fear and then swatted out blindly at him.

"Where's Luke?" he said.

"Saving our bacon," she answered, slapping what felt like his shoulder. "Great plan, by the way: *On your mark, get set, go!*"

"It worked, didn't it?" he said.

As glib as his words were, his voice told her that he was scared. His voice and common sense: Anything could be in here with them. *Would the next voice in her ear rise from the lifeless lungs of a Death Walker?* She lowered her hand, sucked

in a deep breath, and waited for her eyes to adjust to the darkness.

Slowly, the fading light filtering in from the open entryway revealed a high-ceilinged hallway. It ended five feet from them in a massive stone door. "That thing looks like it weighs a ton," Ren whispered. "Like, literally, a ton."

"At least we know where the Spells are," said Alex.

"Yeah, and the Death Walkers," said Ren. This was bad. No light or sound escaped from inside, so there was no way to know what awaited them, and she was sure the big stone slab would grind loudly against the floor if they opened it. She wondered if they even could. She glanced over at Alex's shadowy silhouette. *Maybe he can push it open with his amulet*, she thought. *But what then?*

She looked down at her own amulet, glowing softly in the murk. She still hadn't been able to move heavy objects with it the way Alex and Todtman could. The ibis was a symbol of Thoth. He was the ancient Egyptian god of wisdom, writing, and moonlight, and apparently he didn't do manual labor. Still, the ibis had its own unique abilities.

Standing there in the dark, she got a bright idea.

Alex could hear his heart beating as he crouched down on one side of the door. Ren was barely visible on the other side, and he dearly hoped she knew what she was doing.

Finally, the moment they'd been waiting for — and dreading — arrived.

Stone ground loudly against stone, drowning out even Alex's racing heart, as the door began to open inward. Flickering firelight leaked out into the hall, only to be eclipsed by a massive figure.

Ta-mesah's reputation preceded him — and so did his snout. Before he'd even pushed his toothy visage all the way into the hall, a second figure appeared directly behind him. In the wash of firelight Alex would see the glossy venom bulb at his side.

*Now, Ren*, he thought.

He closed his eyes tightly as she sprang to her feet.

*FWOOOP!*

Even through his eyelids, the blinding white flash lit Alex's vision.

Ta-mesah grunted in pain and surprise, and the Stung Man once again covered his eyes too late, nearly stinging his own face in the process.

Unnoticed, Alex slipped quietly past them, through the door, and inside the chamber.

The room was half lit by a small stone pool with yellow-orange flames dancing on its surface. Alex desperately searched the deep shadows.

Speed was key now. The rapid-fire slap of Ren's footsteps had already disappeared down the hallway. Taking a page from Luke's playbook, she was trying to lure at least one of

the dazzled Death Walkers into pursuit. But there was no guarantee they would take the bait.

Alex's thoughts were interrupted by movement. A shadowy blur buzzed past his ear. Turning to get a better look at it, he saw a second shape fill his vision: dark purple in the faint firelight and the size of a Thanksgiving turkey. He ducked and it flew inches over his head, tearing out half a dozen strands of hair as it went.

Alex gasped from the pain, but the sound was drowned out by an angry buzzing that grew louder with each passing second, as if he'd just stepped on a hornets' nest.

*Hornets*, he thought. *Oh no.* An image flashed through his mind: a ragged figure, teeming and torn, on a rooftop in Cairo.

Suddenly, the deafening buzz fell silent. A hollow, desolate voice that rose up in its place, and a nightmare stepped clear of the shadows, revealing itself in the flickering glow.

Ren bolted out of the dark entryway as if shot from a gun. There was no need to adjust to the daylight. Dusk had come to the land of the dead. She looked around desperately for any sign of approaching croc jaws. Instead, she saw Luke literally grabbing one of the toothy beasts by the tail. It seemed like the definition of a bad idea, but Luke caught sight of her and shouted an explanation. "They were giving up on

trying to catch me," he shouted. "Just trying to keep their attention!"

"Look out!" Ren shouted in response.

The croc swung its big head around but couldn't reach him. The second croc gave it another go, lunging at him from nearby. But before it could even sniff Nikes, Luke vanished in a blur. In his sudden absence, the crocs turned toward Ren and eyed her greedily. Ren swallowed hard. She didn't know if she looked more appetizing, but she was sure she looked slower. They sprinted toward her.

Behind her, she could hear heavy footfalls echoing through the entry hall. Two sets. Both Death Walkers were in pursuit — and close. She was in between a croc and a hard place. *Would she be torn apart? Stung to death? Something worse?*

She took off running, putting everything she had into one quick burst of speed.

Her legs strained, her head pounded, her lungs burned — and her plan worked.

The two crocodiles shot like rockets toward the spot where she'd been standing, just outside the entrance to the building. The closest one lunged for her, just missing her left leg as she scooted past it and into the clear. Even with walnut-sized brains, the crocs knew better than to collide again. But it hadn't occurred to them not to block the exit. The second croc lunged at Ren, too, partially climbing over the other one's back to do it. Together they formed a wide wall of twisting reptilian flesh just outside the entryway.

The Walkers hit the brakes, stopping just short of the living roadblock. Ta-mesah released a hoarse, huffing growl. He grabbed the big beasts by the backs of their necks and tossed them aside with mindboggling strength.

Before the crocs even landed, Ren hit the wall of barley like an arrow, disappearing inside.

"Nice move," she heard. The voice came from right beside her, and she jumped nearly as high as the tall grain. But it was only Luke. She shushed him and grasped her amulet tight so that she could understand the Walkers' words.

"Forget her," rumbled Ta-mesah, scanning the wall of grain and slowing to a walk. "She is just trying to lure us away from the boy."

Still trying, Ren reached out with her free hand and rustled the stalks all around her. The Walkers ignored the desperate gesture.

"True," said the Stung Man. "And he is dead by now. Let us go see if there's anything left of him."

Ren's blood ran cold. *The crocs, the Stung Man, Ta-mesah — they were all right here — but he was confident Alex was dead. Had she let her best friend run straight into a trap? Was there something else lying in wait inside? Something even worse?*

## Facing the Founder

Alex wasn't dead. Not yet, anyway.

The bizarre figure before him was toying with him, as a cat would a mouse. "I founded The Order long ago, when civilization itself was still young and Egypt was new."

The founder paused, his rasping voice winding down like a buzz saw. Alex stared at him, horrified and transfixed. A churning swirl of purple and black enveloped him like a thick, liquid suit. Now and then an insect's eye or a translucent wing appeared in the mix, only to be sucked back into the maelstrom. Large, wasp-like bodies bubbled up and disappeared. Sometimes a gap appeared and Alex caught a glimpse of the founder's desiccated body beneath. Alex understood now that this was the very first Death Walker.

"I see you have met my friends," said the founder. He plunged one bony, clawlike hand into his own swirling chest and plucked one of the ghostly wasps. Free from the teeming mix, it grew from the size of a sparrow to the size of an eagle and snapped at the air with jagged needle-sharp teeth.

Without even looking at it, the founder plunged it back in. "They started as spirits — human souls. They were drawn to me, because my spirit was stronger. But over the centuries, I have taken over those spirits. We have become a sort of hive. Now they hunger for other souls to consume." He paused. "As you will see in a moment."

Alex knew that the founder would soon devour him, body and soul. He knew he should fight, but the idea seemed absurd. *What could I possibly do to this ancient creature?* Right now it was one being, more or less. Blasting it with wind or launching some object at it would just scatter the hive — which would pick him clean in seconds.

Alex's heart raced with fear and sank with despair at the same time. Because the real pity of it was that he had come so close to his goal. So very close.

On a raised stone platform directly beside the founder lay the Lost Spells of the ancient Egyptian Book of the Dead. They were covered over with the thin linen of the concealment spells, but he knew they were there. They had given him a second life, and he could feel them in his blood.

"Yes, the Spells," said the founder, following his eyes. "For so long we searched for them: a power far greater than our own, a power beyond imagination. And now they are ours. Perhaps I should thank you, but you have caused us trouble as well. So instead, you will die."

Alex searched his mind desperately for some escape. He was too far into the room to sprint for the door. There was

nothing substantial to hide behind. Even if fighting was futile, he would have to try.

Alex heard heavy footsteps at the door behind him. He didn't dare turn around, but he knew that the other Walkers had returned.

The founder smiled. Vain in the way powerful men have always been, he'd simply been waiting for an audience. He raised one hand, and the hive began to grow there, like a grotesque, inflating fist. Wings sprouted, buzzing loudly; eyes appeared.

But Alex clung tightly to something the Death Walker had just said: *A power far greater than our own.*

The founder was more powerful than him. Ta-mesah was more powerful than him. Even the Stung Man, whom he'd defeated before, was beyond harm here. But none of them were the most powerful thing in this room.

As the leader lowered his churning arm toward him, Alex used the power of the scarab for the smallest of tasks.

He flipped aside the light, age-yellowed linen of the concealment spells.

A wave of power spread through the room like a ripple on smooth water. It was barely visible — just a brief wink and bend to the firelight — but the effect was profound.

The founder held his vengeful spirits as he turned to look at the powerful ancient text. The other two Death Walkers, who'd been hovering near the door to avoid being caught in the carnage, took a step back.

Alex was barely aware of any of it. His head swam and his knees nearly buckled. All he could do was stare at the Spells that had brought him back. As he did, the ancient scroll's ink-black text began to glow a soft gold.

*This is your chance*, he told himself. *Your last chance.*

For a moment, no one moved. Even the swarming spirits fell nearly still. And then, his legs wobbly and his vision lit by stars and phantom symbols, Alex teetered forward.

The founder took a step to block him, but Alex willed his dazzled eyes to focus and his breathless lungs to speak. "Get back!" he managed. "I have activated the Spells!"

"You can't wield this power," said the founder. He punctuated his words with a dismissive snort. But he didn't take another step.

Alex wobbled forward like a baby deer on ice. "Of course I can," he said, his voice little more than a pained gasp.

"He's used the Book of the Dead before," said the Stung Man. "He banished me here before the doors were fully opened."

The founder looked at the Stung Man carefully. "The Book is one thing," he said. "The Lost Spells are another." He turned back to Alex and repeated himself: "You can't wield this power!"

Alex stumbled past him, passing mere feet from the deadly swarm. "Why not?" he mumbled. With the Spells so close, he felt like he was speaking underwater, but he poured

everything he had left into his next words. "My mother used them . . . *And my father.*"

The founder glared at him. "Enough. I will destroy you."

The words formed clearly in Alex's troubled mind: *The gods are stronger . . .*

"No!" he shouted. "With a word, I can summon the Devourer! Her ancient name glows at the top of this page. Don't you see it?"

It was a bluff. A total bluff. The top line could have said Cheez Whiz for all he knew. He could barely see the walls with all the stars swirling in his eyes, much less read a scroll. With one last lurch, he stumbled toward the stone platform. Just inches from the Spells, his blood ran hot and his head went blank. He flung his free hand up gracelessly, but it worked. The concealment spells flapped upward like a wing and then fell across the face of the scroll.

Alex's head cleared slightly, and he scooped the ancient texts up against his chest: the thin, gauzy concealment spells and the heavy old scroll they guarded. It felt like hugging an electric eel, but he held on tight.

"One word!" he blurted, doubling down on his bluff.

Then he turned unsteadily and lurched out of the room.

With hate in their eyes, his stunned enemies let him pass.

Out in the hallway, he pulled the linen veil tight over the old scroll and took off running.

## The Sensation of Flight

As soon as Alex began to run, the Walkers realized he'd been bluffing and came after him. Alex bolted out the short hallway at full speed and rushed between the crocs, now lying motionless on their backs. He heard Ta-mesah's heavy footsteps slap the stone floor of the hallway and then soften as they hit dirt. *He was right behind him!*

"Over here!" Ren called from somewhere in the field.

Alex angled toward the sound and grimaced as Luke added: "Don't look back, cuz!"

He did his best to protect the ancient Spells with his arms as he ducked his head and rammed into the barley. Luke and Ren were waiting a few rows in.

"I have them!" Alex gasped. "We need to get back to the portal where we came in!"

"Okay," said Ren, already turning to run. "We can head to the riverbank and follow it back!"

The three friends crashed and stomped through the tall, fragile stalks.

With his friends beside him, their long-sought prize in his arms, and the concealing crops all around, a wave of hope washed over him. The Spells had saved his life twice now — and he'd just gotten a glimpse of their power. Three unstoppable Walkers had been held hostage by the mere threat of it.

But it wasn't just the Spells they feared: It was Ammit. The gods really were stronger. Anubis had turned the Walkers back at the river. He was the guardian of the afterlife, and his word was law here. But Ammit was the enforcer of that law, and her jaws brought oblivion.

As Alex ran, the stalks stinging his face, a wild thought occurred to him: *Maybe they could win.*

*And if they did . . .* This whole time, he'd been almost as afraid of finding the Spells as of not finding them. They could save his world, but they could also end his life. He'd been willing to risk it before.

But now? Knowing that this plot began long before him, that his mom had never abandoned him, and that the Spells in his arms scared his enemies stiff . . . He still wanted to win, but feeling the wild elation of escape, the sensation of flight as he ran alongside his friends, he knew something else. He wanted to live, too. *But how?*

A sound much louder than three grain-stomping kids rose up behind them. Alex looked back over his shoulder and saw the barley bend forward in a massive wave. As it did, Alex felt a swift slap strike his whole body at once. "Guh!" he blurted, stumbling onto one knee.

Ren was knocked to the ground beside him. Only Luke managed to keep his balance. All around them, acres of slender stalks were pushed to the ground as they were overrun by the invisible wave. Regaining his balance and turning once again, Alex saw the source. The hulking frame of Ta-mesah stood in the twilit distance. His arms were extended and his palms thrust outward.

He had used his formidable powers to flatten the grain.

The three Amulet Keepers were suddenly out in the open. Movement caught Alex's eye and he raised his gaze to the gray sky, which was turning a deep, bruise-like purple behind them, clouding over with a swarm of fast-flying shapes.

Ren scrambled to her feet, eyes darting back at the rows of flattened grain and up at the swarm of hungry spirits. "The portal's too far away," she said. "We'll never make it!"

"We have to try," called Luke, reaching down to help Ren up. He alone had the speed to escape, but he wouldn't do it without them.

They turned and ran across the flattened field.

Ta-mesah had flattened the grain all the way to the edge of the field, and Ren squinted into the dim distance as she ran.

And there it was: an army on the march.

An uninterrupted line of men appeared out of a glowing gateway in the air at one end, only to march steadily forward

and disappear into the air at the other. Ren had seen this before, when her amulet had shown it to her. She knew they were stepping out of one false door and into another, traveling from Egypt to New York by a macabre shortcut through the afterlife.

An odd feeling washed over her overheated system. As the infernal buzzing grew louder and closer and as the Death Walkers closed in, she stared at the spot where the undead soldiers were disappearing. *New York*, she thought. *At least I'll die close to home.*

The fading gray twilight was filled with darkening swirls and whorls and streaks. Wails and growls and disembodied gasps filled her ears. Soon this would be the menacing nighttime world she'd seen on her first trip to the afterlife — if she lived that long. She turned her attention to the uneven ground in front of her. As she did she saw a faint but familiar glow hanging in the gray air just up ahead. Her muscles burning and her legs pumping, she looked a little closer.

*"PUH!"* she gasped as she felt a hard, sharp push from behind.

She stumbled forward, falling through the spectral light and into darkness.

## Back Where It All Started

Sure, Alex felt bad about pushing his best friend through the glimmering portal. And maybe he felt a little weird about grabbing his cousin by the hand and tugging him through. But he felt worse about tripping over Ren once he leapt through himself, and worse still when Luke fell through on top of him.

"Duh-off!" he blurted as his foot caught Ren's leg, and he blurted something worse when Luke sandwiched him onto the hard floor. He did his best to land on his shoulder and protect the ancient Spells from the impact.

As Luke rolled free, Alex shot a look back to make sure nothing was coming through the portal after them. *Had they lost them in the dim light and distance?* he wondered desperately. *And if so, for how long?*

He turned to examine their new surroundings. They could be anywhere there was a false door, including some old tomb deep beneath the ground. As he looked around, he realized that they *were* in a tomb. But the mix of natural and electric light told him that this tomb was in a museum.

"Why does it look so —" Ren began.

"Familiar," said Alex. He was sure now: the immaculately restored old stone, the little silver information plaques, the lights burning softly overhead . . . He turned back to the others, unable to keep the smile from his face. "We're at the Met," he said. "We're home!"

They were in the big, reconstructed tomb at the entrance to the Egyptian wing, the one that always had a line snaking through it in the summer. Alex peered out of the tomb mouth and saw the back of the north-side ticket booths. Beyond that, huge banners hung down from the ceiling of the Great Hall. Sunlight streamed in the museum's high windows. It had been twilight in Egypt, but it was still midday in New York.

"Finally," said Ren, her voice breaking with emotion.

The three climbed to their feet, grunting and groaning as their bumps and bruises required. Alex carefully refolded the concealment spells. His head swam, and a hot, static energy tingled through his fingers as he touched the scroll beneath them, but he felt better again as soon as he pulled the linen veil tight. He removed his old backpack and stuffed the bundle deep inside, putting the old scrolls already in there on top to pin the protective linen in place.

"I'll take that," said Ren. "I know they make you kind of swoony."

Alex didn't argue — they did make him swoony. He handed over the pack, and she put it on.

Alex looked out into Room 100 of The Metropolitan

Museum of Art, a place as familiar to him as the lobby of his own apartment building. The lights were low, and the room was empty. The museum was closed tight in the middle of the day. Alex edged out of the tomb mouth.

"See anything?" asked Ren, a few steps behind him.

"Hear anything?" added Luke, a few steps behind her.

"Nothing," he said, turning back to them. They were quite a sight. Ren's nose was running from her allergies, and tears from her watering eyes had carved tracks through the thick layer of dirt and grain dust on her cheeks. Luke looked like the "Before" picture in a laundry detergent ad.

"How did you know this portal led back to New York?" asked Ren.

"I didn't," Alex admitted, lowering his voice as they eased silently out of the room and toward the ticket booths. "But I figured that's where all those mummies were headed, and this one was close by. Plus, you know, we were about to get torn into a million pieces by those wasp things."

Ren nodded, satisfied with his deductive reasoning.

"Good call," added Luke.

They edged past the empty ticket booths and looked out into the grand marble expanse of the museum's entrance hall. The huge old building felt solid and familiar, but far from safe. Just up ahead, near the center of the hall, flashing red light washed in through the tall glass doors and painted the walls and floors. The friends rushed toward it.

"It looks like a war zone," said Ren once they reached the big glass doors.

Alex could only nod. Wooden barricades and stacked sandbags lined the streets in front of the museum. The flashing lights came from two NYPD cruisers parked on Fifth Avenue, bookending two large, blocky armored personnel carriers with thick knobby tires. Alex craned his neck to look up East 82nd Street. He saw a cloud of thick gray-and-black smoke billowing up in the distance. Somewhere nearby, a fire was raging.

Silhouetted figures shifted inside the police cruisers, but there was no traffic and the normally packed sidewalks were deserted. A city of millions was on lockdown. The only sound was the rumble of the army vehicles' idling engines purring through the safety glass. *Police, military, open fires, and empty streets* . . . He could hardly believe this was the same bustling city where he'd grown up.

"My parents," moaned Ren. "I hope they're okay."

"I'm with you on that," said Luke solemnly. And Alex thought of his well-meaning aunt and uncle, and all that Luke had suffered to keep them safe.

"Yeah," Alex said, "but before we find our families —"

"I know, bro," said Luke. "What's the plan?"

"Call Cairo," Alex said, the red lights washing over his dirt-smeared face. "I can't use these Spells — they knock me for a loop — but my mom can. And then she can, you know, save the world."

"Yeah, that part sounds important," agreed Luke.

The friends took one more look out at the war zone where they'd grown up and then headed toward the main office.

"So how did you escape from all those Death Walkers back there, anyway?" Ren asked Alex.

Alex managed half a smile. "I told them Ammit was on the way."

"They are really scared of that dude, huh?" said Luke.

"She's a lady," said Alex. "Sort of. But yeah: really scared."

They walked quietly for a while and then Ren leaned in toward Alex and said a few hesitant words: "I was thinking . . ."

Alex smiled at her. "That doesn't surprise me."

She got to the point. "The Walkers are afraid of the gods. And the gods definitely don't seem to like the Walkers. Did you hear the way Anubis talked about them? He *knew* they were evil . . ."

"They don't exactly keep that a secret," said Alex.

"Don't you get it?" she said. "What if the gods could do something more than scare them? What if they could do *what they're scared of*? They're afraid of that ceremony, the weighing of the heart. They're afraid of being *judged*. What if there was someway to, I don't know, put them on trial?"

"That would be *awesome*," said Alex. It was as if his best friend had read his mind — and then taken his thoughts a step further. The two had known each other nearly their entire lives, and their thoughts often ran along the same lines, like two trains on parallel tracks, with Ren's maybe half a length ahead. But all tracks still led to the same ques-

tion that had stopped Alex before. "But how do we get the gods to do it?" he said.

"Yeah," Ren answered. "That's the thing."

A few minutes later, they were in Alex's mom's office. Alex had the emergency cell phone she kept in her bottom drawer pressed to his ear. His finger shook as he held it steady next to a line midway down the *H*s in his mom's address book: "Dr. Hesaan, Cairo."

Now they had to hope that one flickering bar of service — Alex imagined one last stubbornly functional cell tower somewhere in the Bronx — would be enough to connect two crisis-crippled cities six thousand miles apart.

The phone rang: once, twice, three — "Who is this?"

The connection was weak, but the voice was familiar. Alex exhaled mightily and put the phone on speaker for the others. "Hey, Dr. Hesaan," he said. "It's Alex. Can I talk to my mom, or Todtman?"

"So they have telephones in the afterlife now," said Hesaan. "Strange days . . . But they are both here. Just a second."

It was Todtman who came on the line. He listened carefully to what Alex had to tell him. "New York?" he said.

"Yeah," breathed Alex, hardly believing it himself. "Right back where it all started."

Todtman was silent, thinking.

"Where it started and where it will end," he said at last. "You must stay where you are. We will come to you."

Alex could only imagine how long that would take. "What if they find us first? They're going to figure out where we went sooner or later."

"Then let us hope it is later. We are on the way. Stay out of sight, and keep the Spells safe."

Ren grabbed the phone from Alex's hands and got right to her point. "I can't stay here," she said. "I have to go home and check on my parents. It's not far."

"I am sorry, Ren, but you must stay there. We will need you for this. We will need everyone. You have been away from home a long time, but the risk is too great. Peshwar and her army control most of the city by now."

"But —" she protested.

"Please, Ren, stay safe," pleaded Todtman. "This will all be over soon . . . One way or the other."

The line went dead.

But outside the office, a stronger buzz was already growing.

## Company

Alex rushed toward the door and closed it as quickly and quietly as he could. He listened closely as the noise grew louder and angrier. "It's coming from the hall," he whispered.

"It's one of those bugs, isn't it?" said Luke.

Alex tried to think of something — anything — else it could be. But he couldn't. He nodded slowly, his eyes on the frosted glass panes alongside the door.

The buzzing grew louder, closer.

A shadowy shape flashed past out in the hallway, and Alex gasped. He looked over at Ren, asking the question with his wide-open eyes: *Did it see us?*

The buzzing grew softer and then, very suddenly, louder. Alex turned back toward the door — where a dark shape was hovering on the other side of the frosted glass. The spirit wasp flew back a few inches and then rammed its body into the pane. *WHUMP!*

Alex's hand fumbled beneath his shirt for his amulet.

*WHUMP! WHUMP!*

It tried two more times to break the glass, but then seemed to reconsider. For a long moment, it just stared in at them with dark, malevolent eyes. Then it turned and disappeared back down the hallway.

"Oh no," said Ren.

"What?" said Alex. "Isn't it a good thing it went away?"

Ren shook her head. "It's a scout," she said. "It found us."

"Oh, snap!" said Luke. "It's going back to snitch."

The three friends took off after it, but by the time they reached the hallway, they'd lost the speeding spirit.

"We have to stop it before it goes back through the portal!" said Alex urgently.

With his amulet, Luke was more than fast enough to catch the bug as it bugged out — but he didn't know his way around the museum. Instead, he ran alongside the others as they navigated the twisty interior, taking every shortcut they knew. They finally caught sight of the thing in the Great Hall. "There!" called Alex.

"Give me something to throw over it!" called Luke. But they had nothing. Luke tried to strip off his Under Armour top while at a full run and wiped out on the slick tile, sliding across the polished floor with his shirt over his head.

It darted through the ticket booths, utterly ignoring the "suggested donation" sign.

A few moments later, Alex and Ren sprinted into Room 100 just in time to see the infernal bug enter the big tomb.

Ren tried to blast it with her ibis, but the bug was already inside the stone entryway.

"No!" cried Alex as the thing flew full speed into the false door. The buzzing disappeared instantly.

*Whoomp!* Luke appeared by their side, holding his shirt in one hand and his amulet in the other. "Where'd it go?"

Alex lifted his chin toward the ancient portal.

The only sound in the quiet room was the three friends, breathing hard.

"I think we're going to have company," huffed Alex.

A man's voice boomed through the room: "Oh, but you already do."

## The Day Turns Red

"Gah! Todtman!" huffed Ren as Alex clutched his chest. "Don't scare us like that!"

"*Tut mir leid,*" said the German, leaning on his walking stick. "I am sorry. But I am more sorry that we could not stop that pest. I had just turned the corner when I saw it flash by."

As if to demonstrate the process, Dr. Bauer rounded the corner. Alex rushed over to hug her. "Careful, hun!" she said, and he pulled up short and did his best to hug her healthy side. She reached down and ruffled his hair. Then he did a double take. "Wait, where did you two come from?"

Todtman flashed his quick, sly smile and said, "There are many false doors in this museum."

"But you only have one amulet," said Ren.

"I'm an Amulet Keeper, too, though," said Dr. Bauer. "And I held on *very* tight."

Todtman waved away the pleasantries and scanned the three kids quickly. "Where are the Spells? Are they safe?"

Ren swung the backpack off. Todtman clucked once in disapproval. "They are thousands of years old, irreplaceable. They are not . . . a math workbook."

"Actually, they're surprisingly durable," said Dr. Bauer, taking the backpack from Ren. "Strong magic makes for strong scrolls."

Alex watched his mom gracefully shift the backpack from one hand to the other.

"You're moving a lot better," he said.

She turned and smiled. "I am full of Hesaan's arthritis medication."

"Is that safe?" said Ren, and it occurred to Alex just what a good doctor she would make.

"None of this is safe," said Alex's mom, unzipping the pack and peering inside. "But it does numb the pain."

Alex watched her pluck out the extra scrolls and lower them to the floor. There was only one scroll that mattered now, in the pack and in the world. "Mom," said Alex, hesitating, unsure of what exactly he was asking. "Can the Lost Spells do . . . other things?"

"Yeah," added Ren. "Can they, like, talk to the gods?"

Dr. Bauer looked from one to the other. She knew when they were up to something. "All Egyptian spells invoke the old gods in some way," she said. "But it's not a conversation. It's more like calling out a name and hoping for an echo. And the Lost Spells are quite specialized. They deal with the afterlife, its gateways and guardians."

"Guardians?" said Alex and Ren together.

"Enough questions," said Todtman. "We must use the Spells immediately. The Death Walkers and their army will be here in moments, too many and too powerful to oppose. We must repair the rift *now*."

He turned toward Dr. Bauer, put his hand on her arm, and looked her in the eyes. "Maggie," he said. "Can you use the Spells here, now? We have little time."

She took one more look inside the pack, then glanced into the dark entryway of the tomb. "In there," she said. "We should be close to a portal for this, within sight. It will have more effect that way. And if we close one, we close them all."

They filed back inside the old tomb. Before they made it halfway down the entryway, a huge crashing noise thundered out of the inner sanctum, followed by the brittle screech of cracking stone. All around them, the big stone structure began to rumble and shake. Something was coming through the portal. Something *big*.

"Let's get out of here!" called Alex.

"There's another portal in the Temple of Dendur," said Alex's mom. "We can use that!"

They hustled out of the shaking structure toward the familiar temple. It was housed in the largest room in the museum, even bigger than the Great Hall. It had always been Alex's favorite place at the Met. He'd spent days gazing out of the room's soaring glass wall into Central Park, peering into its midnight black reflecting pool, or looking

up at the ancient temple itself, brought over from Egypt and reconstructed block by block here.

A heavy stone block crashed to the floor behind the friends as they headed deeper into the Egyptian wing. They wound their way through the maze of half-lit rooms, past grand granite statues and cases of glittering jewelry of gold, carnelian, turquoise, and lapis lazuli. A carving of the cow-headed goddess Hathor gazed out at them with big, sad eyes as they rushed by. A quick glance was enough for Alex to recognize each exhibit. He'd spent his childhood here, and many of the items were as familiar to him as the decorations in his own bedroom. *Would it all end here as well?*

He shook his head hard to clear it, but the thought would not be cleared.

They reached the temple quickly, but it was not the safe haven they'd hoped for. Daylight streamed through the panes of the soaring three-story glass wall, and just outside a battalion of mummies swayed in sun.

"There are like a brillion of them!" said Luke.

It looked more like a few hundred to Alex, a small fraction of the overall army, but it was still more than enough to tear the Keepers limb from limb. "What are they waiting for?" said Ren.

The answer came in a brilliant flash of crimson light outside the windows. As the day turned red, Alex swung around and saw the leader of the undead strike-force. The lioness-headed Peshwar stood at the front of her troops,

supersized in death just as Ta-mesah had been. In her long, clawlike hand was a crackling crimson energy dagger.

"Take cover!" shouted Todtman.

As the Death Walker whipped her hand up and forward, the friends ducked behind the row of statues just inside the double doors. An explosion shook the room as the energy dagger blew a huge hole in the massive glass wall.

The mummies began clambering clumsily inside, pausing only to allow their leader to step gracefully through the jagged opening.

"We have to get out of here," called Todtman. But as he turned toward the door, Alex saw him stop cold. Todtman began to slowly back up as Ta-mesah dipped his fearsome head through the doorway. A moment later, the Stung Man appeared, and a fierce buzzing grew in the room behind him

"Over here," called Dr. Bauer. "This way."

Not daring to take their eyes off the approaching enemies, the group followed her voice toward the southeast corner of the hangar-like room.

"You cling to your lives like you cling to those Spells," rumbled Ta-mesah, leveling his lifeless gaze at the huddled friends. "And soon, you will have neither."

But Dr. Bauer knew the great museum well, and she'd chosen this corner for a reason. A small side door there connected back to the western edge of the Egyptian wing.

Alex knew it, too. And he knew they didn't need to conquer their enemies. All they needed to do was protect his

mom long enough for her to use the Spells. He tightened his left hand around the scarab. "Go!" he shouted as hurricane force wind shot out from his right hand.

He formed his fingers into a tight spear, concentrating the wind, and aimed it right for Ta-mesah's face. The force had little effect on the massive Walker — but at least Alex couldn't hear what the big creep was saying anymore.

A handful of mummies, their formerly bone-dry corpses half-soaked from wading through the reflecting pool, attempted to scramble around Ta-mesah's hulking frame. Alex dialed back the mystic wind and let them. Then he redirected the blast low, mowing the mummies down like bowling pins.

With the powerful wind no longer blasting his face, Ta-mesah charged forward, but his thick legs got tangled with the squirming mummies on the floor in front of him. Trying to kick free, he snapped one of mummies nearly in half and went down in a heap on top of the others.

The Amulet Keepers took advantage of the opening and darted through the side door, into darkness.

## Sacrifices

The rooms on the western side of the wing had no windows, and were lit only by a few Exit signs. Alex blinked into the ruddy murk in time to see the others filing quickly into the next room. As he rushed to catch up, Alex could hear the shuffling stampede of bony feet behind him.

As the group cleared the next room, Alex yanked the glass door closed behind them. *That ought to hold them . . .* he thought. *For about three seconds.* Empty eye sockets were already gaping at him as he locked the door with his amulet. Leathery hands were already pounding on the glass as he turned to run.

They just needed a few quiet minutes within sight of a portal for his mom to use the Spells. So close to their goal, he got a wild, cornered feeling, knowing that the Spells could kill him. His mom knew that, too. She'd had the Spells for weeks and been unwilling to take that chance. His feelings a jumble, he both hoped and feared she'd risk it now.

He looked up at his mom, one hand clutching the Spells, the other grasping her injured side. He wanted to run along-

side her — she'd sacrificed so much for him — but he stayed a few steps behind instead. He wanted even more to protect her.

Behind them, the glass door exploded under some massive, unseen force. The friends ducked their shoulders and entered Room 100 from the opposite side of where they'd left it. Pursued by a wave of mummies and Death Walkers, they could do nothing but rush straight past the last of the portals. Alex exhaled when he saw no sign of the founder as they passed the ruined temple — but he simply hadn't been looking hard enough. From one shadowy corner, a hovering member of the hive began to beat its wings furiously. The buzz rose to a high-pitched whine.

"Zap it, Ren!" called Alex.

*FWOOP!*

White light washed the corner clean of shadow and seemed to stun the wasp spirit. It dipped in the air, the outer layer of its body turning to purple vapor. The urgent whine fell back to a buzz, but it was too late. Another wasp turned the corner to join it, and then a dozen more.

Ren let out one more burst of mystic light as covering fire as the friends rushed out of the room. As the thundering stampede of mummies began to merge with the angry hum of swarming spirits, Alex closed and locked the big glass double doors behind them.

They rushed back through the ticket booths, but in front of them lay the wide-open expanse of the Great Hall.

"We'll never make it across," said Todtman. "They'll tear us apart before we get halfway."

"Behind there," said Dr. Bauer, pointing to the long counter along the wall where the museum sold memberships and event tickets.

Ren turned and, running backward, released two more blinding flashes at the bodies and souls massing behind the heavy safety-glass doors. If their pursuers saw them slip behind the counter, it was all over.

A moment later, they were all crouched behind the tall, dark counters.

"We need a plan," said Ren in an insistent, hissy whisper. "We can't just keep running and hiding."

"If we stop running and hiding, we're dead," said Luke.

The pounding on the big glass doors was turning to a brittle crackling as Todtman crept up alongside Alex and his mom. "You two stay here," he said.

"What?" said Alex as his mom said, "No!"

He ignored them both. "The nearest portal is right behind you. We will lead them away. Stay quiet and perfectly still until we are gone. Then move fast — and do not fail!"

"But it's me they're looking for," said Dr. Bauer. "Me and the Spells."

"I know," said Todtman. He closed his hand around his amulet. His eyes closed and his face reddened with effort. Two shimmering shapes appeared beside him: a boy and a woman, rough approximations of Alex and his mom.

"Whoa," gasped Alex. He reached out to touch his phantasmal twin, but his hand passed through.

**170**

"It is only in your mind," said Todtman.

*Prr-KRISH!* The big double doors exploded outward. The crimson light washing the walls left no doubt as to the cause. As bits of safety glass rained down on the tile, the others sprang into action.

"Good luck," whispered Ren, before slipping out from behind the counter and into harm's way.

Alex was too stunned to respond and only managed to gasp "Ren" at the spot where she had been. It took everything he had, and his mom's reassuring hand on his shoulder, to stay still as the others risked their lives leading The Order forces across the Great Hall and into the vast museum beyond.

"Over here!" Alex heard Luke call as he used his speed to lure the lurching mummies and their deathly leaders as far away as possible. "No, over *here*!" he called as he zoomed farther down the hall.

The strobe-light flash of Ren's amulet washed the walls, followed by a crimson response from Peshwar. There was a loud explosion, but Alex exhaled as he saw a second flash, this one farther away. He knew that most of The Order's forces would chase Todtman and his phantoms. He could only hope the old man could stay out of their deadly range.

Just feet away, on the other side of the counter, mummies lurched and spirits buzzed. The big Death Walkers followed in turn, like tanks taking the field after the infantry. But after a few loud and terrifying minutes, the Great Hall fell silent. The others had succeeded in luring the enemies

farther into the museum, up its marble stairs and into its masterpiece-filled galleries.

Ren, Todtman, and Luke . . . They were all risking their lives for this. Alex felt overwhelmed by their bravery, but more than that, he felt an obligation to do his part.

"Let's go," he said, helping his mom to her feet.

They had one more shot — bought at great cost — and they could not waste it.

His mom nodded and rose. Their feet crunched through the shattered glass as they approached the first tomb, the stone cracked from where the Walkers had come through. It was dark and quiet inside Room 100. Except for . . . an ominous and all-too-familiar buzzing.

The founder was still inside the fractured tomb. The oldest Walker had released some of his hive to the chase, but the man himself had found his new nest.

Slowly, very slowly, Alex and his mom backed away from the entrance.

"Where now?" whispered Alex.

"Dendur," answered his mom.

Eyes wide-open for any more stragglers, they hurried back toward the Temple of Dendur.

Ta-mesah took one more swipe at Alex's image only to see his massive hand pass harmlessly through it. He released a ruffled huff that flared his croc nostrils.

**172**

"They are illusions," hissed Peshwar. "Tell us where the real ones are, old man."

Todtman stood in the shadowy back corner of the room, breathing hard, blood trickling from his nose and split lower lip. All around him, Greek statues bore silent witness to a brave man's last stand.

Cut off from the exit by two massive Death Walkers, he could run no more. "They are right here," said Todtman, gesturing to the two phantom figures next to him. "Don't you see them?"

"I see your crude trick," rumbled Ta-mesah, eyeing the shimmering shells. "The simple work of a street magician."

The flickering images vanished, and the smallest of smiles creased Todtman's froggy features. "Not such a crude trick," he said as a red glow lit up the room, turning the pale marble statues a garish pink.

The energy dagger grew long and wicked in Peshwar's hand. Todtman was certain his next words would be his last. "After all," he said, "it has kept you both here, so far from where you need to be, for so very long."

Peshwar snarled as she whipped the deadly dagger straight toward him. Todtman tried to leap to the side, but his crippled leg betrayed him one last time. The crackling crimson dagger sank deep into his chest, and a heart that had begun beating some six decades earlier in a small village in Bavaria convulsed and fell still.

His body crumpled to the cold tile floor.

## The Lost Spells

Alex and his mom were inside the shallow alcove of the Temple of Dendur. The Lost Spells were spread out across the floor, and the letters of the ancient text glowed softly as she chanted the first few lines in a rhythmic, almost trance-like voice. The power of the Spells had saved him once, but now it was taking a heavy toll. His vision was speckled with stars and phantom symbols, and his head was woozy. He sat gracelessly, legs straight out, shoulders against the side of the temple for support.

Suddenly, his mom stopped chanting and looked up. The glow began to fade, and Alex's head began to clear ever so slightly. "I can't do it," she said.

Alex struggled to understand her through the slowly lifting fog in his mind. "You need the scarab," he said, reaching for the chain around his neck with clumsy fingers.

"No," she said. "It's not that. The scarab lets you read the language, understand the spells — that's how it lets you use the Book of the Dead. But I already read this

language and understand these spells. It's . . . you. Alex, you're my son."

As overwhelmed as his mind was, he knew exactly what she meant. But he also remembered the sacrifice the others were making to buy them this time. "I know, but —"

She cut him off. "If I close these doorways, if I undo the damage that I did . . ."

She didn't have to finish. Alex knew the rest all too well: She could snuff him out like a birthday candle. How could he convince his own mother to risk his life? "But if you don't . . ." he began. He didn't need to finish that sentence, either. They both knew how it ended: in a death-shadowed world ruled by madmen.

He met her eyes through the nebula of tiny stars that lit his vision.

"I am proud of you," she said, "and I love you, and . . . I will try."

He saw a single tear roll down her cheek, and then he saw a huge figure looming up behind her.

"Oh no," he gasped, but it was already too late. The leader reached down and plucked the woman who had once been his wife from the floor by her shoulder.

She screamed and kicked back at him with her boots. It was useless. "Alex," she called. "The amulet."

*Yes,* he thought. He'd seen her use it before and knew she was a more experienced and powerful Amulet Keeper than he was. But as he reached up for the chain once again,

the leader spared a quick glance for his son. He flicked his free hand in Alex's direction, and an invisible wave of force slammed Alex back into the temple wall. Alex's head bounced off stone with the sound of a coconut considering cracking. A jolt of pain shot through him, and he fought to stay conscious. As his eyes fluttered half closed, he saw his mom tossed across the tile platform in front of the temple. She landed on her injured side and slid like a broken toy.

"No!" he called weakly.

He struggled to stand, but battered from the blow and woozy from the Spells, he was like a boxer who couldn't peel himself from the canvas. His legs twitched and jerked but refused to gather underneath him. One numb hand pawed his chest, managing only to push the scarab around, not grasp it.

His mom's body was still now, and as he stared at it, hoping for any sign of movement, the room began to fill up behind her. He caught snatches of it through his peripheral vision. The hulking figures of Ta-mesah and Peshwar, the ornate robes of the Stung Man, the sea of ragged wrapping as the mummies followed, the growing buzzing in the air. He didn't know if they'd been called back by their leader or if their chase was simply over.

Finally, he saw his mom's hand twitch open and closed. Her legs straightened out and she flopped over onto her back. Alex could let himself breathe again.

Meanwhile, The Order's forces had massed beneath the temple's raised platform, staring up at their leader. Alex saw

something move out of the corner of his eye and turned to see Ren and Luke rush into the room last, following the forces they'd been trying to lead away, still trying to get their attention. They stopped cold inside the entrance, just short of the undead army in front of them.

Alex saw the look of shock on Ren's face as she spotted his mom's crumpled body. Then he saw her face collapse as she spied him slumped inside the alcove.

"It is over, Amulet Keepers," called the leader, his booming voice echoing through the massive space.

Ren's small voice rose up in response: "Then give us our friends and we'll leave."

A layer of mummies moved in between his friends and the door they'd come through, sealing off any escape. "You will get nothing," said the leader, "and you will go nowhere."

Alex tried again to stand but succeeded only in flopping back to the floor — and attracting Peshwar's attention. "The boy is alive, and near the Spells," she hissed from her place near the edge of the platform. "Kill him now."

The leader looked back. "He can't even rise to his feet in the presence of the Spells," he said. "Much less give voice to the chants. He is no danger to us."

"Your weakness for the boy puts us in danger," said Peshwar.

The leader stared down at her. "Are you challenging me?"

She bowed her head, pointing the empty sockets of the lioness skull at the floor, but still she spoke. "Kill them all," she said. "It's easy. Like this."

She tossed something toward the platform. As it clattered to a stop at the leader's feet, Alex recognized Todtman's walking staff.

The realization that Todtman was dead hit him like a punch to the heart. But under Peshwar's cruel gaze, he felt that sorrow turn to something else. Anger and loyalty and loss mixed in his battered body — and it gave him strength. His fingers found his amulet and finally closed around its familiar form. The ancient energy flowed through him. He looked over at the Lost Spells. He pulled himself closer.

His father was right: He couldn't stand in their presence or chant their words. But as he edged closer to the old scroll, he thought he just might be able to read them. The Spells were specialized, his mom had said. They dealt with the afterlife, with its gateways and guardians.

As Alex's vision filled with fresh pinpricks of light and his head lolled limply on his neck, he looked for the name of one guardian in particular.

"Behind you!" called Peshwar.

"The boy!" growled Ta-mesah.

Alex knew the leader was turning toward him, knew he had only seconds left, but he dared not look up — and there it was! The name he was looking for.

With all his remaining strength and all the breath left in his lungs, he called that name. Just one word, but he filled it with all the anger and sadness and helplessness he felt. His enemies had broken the rules, not just the laws of this world,

but the laws of life and death. And they had done so cruelly and for the basest of all reasons: power. As full of stars as his vision was, it was hard to tell, but he thought the word might even have glowed a little, flickered on the page, as he said it.

A moment later, a fresh wave of force from the leader sent Alex flying backward across the tile. He slammed hard into the back of the alcove. He managed to protect his head this time, but he felt something crack in his chest.

*Just like my mom*, he thought as he once again teetered on the edge of consciousness. He peered out of the alcove and saw his father staring in. The Spells were between them, ten feet away. It might as well have been ten miles.

The room was quiet, save for the buzz of the spirits, and still, save for the gentle swaying of the mummies.

"He has failed," Peshwar hissed into the calm.

The reply came almost immediately, but it wasn't from the leader or any of the other Walkers. It wasn't from any of the Keepers, either. It wasn't in words at all, in fact. Peshwar got her answer in the form of a great and terrible roar. The cry shook the room.

Part lion.

Part crocodile.

Part thunder.

Alex leaned his battered frame back against the temple wall and smiled.

His call had been answered.

# The Devourer

Alex never saw the great beast enter the room. Turning his head toward the source of the terrible roar, she was simply there. She was the size of a truck and as terrifying as she was improbable. Her huge crocodile head dwarfed that of Ta-mesah and gave the Walker no more than a glance as she swept her vision across the room.

Alex's head swam and fresh pain stabbed him deep inside. He was terrified for his mom, who was still lying helplessly on the platform. He had called Ammit in desperation, but had no way of knowing what this otherworldly presence might do.

Ammit was the ultimate enforcer of good and evil in ancient Egypt, the one who devoured the souls of the unworthy, destroying them forever. But now the rules had been cheated, the boundaries between the worlds torn open, and this much was clear: Ammit was mad.

She released another roar, so fearsome and so close, that Alex could do nothing but cover his ears. Then, with slow, deliberate steps, she began to move toward the platform. Her

enormous front paws, those of a massive lion, pushed forward with the fluid ease of a jungle cat, while her huge back feet, those of a hippo, plodded forward to join them.

As she moved, she brushed by rows of swaying mummies. At the slightest touch, they disintegrated into clouds of dust and scraps of linen. Two more steps and she had reached the platform. With surprising grace, she pulled herself up.

Suddenly, there were only two people left in her path. Once again, the leader reached down and plucked Alex's mom up by the shoulder. This time she could offer no resistance, but from his perch inside the temple, Alex saw her eyes flutter open. She stared at the strange creature and breathed her name in awe: "Ammit . . ."

The beast came a few steps closer and seemed to examine her.

A jolt of fear shot through Alex's system. His mom was in danger: direct, immediate danger.

Surrounded by The Order forces, the creature's paralyzing presence had seemed a reprieve. But now he understood how stupid he'd been. This was the devourer, and she was here for a reason.

Alex gasped a word of his own: "Mom . . ."

But it was the other half of the family tree that responded. The leader thrust Alex's mom forward toward Ammit. She pried uselessly at his powerful fingers. Alex managed to get his legs underneath him. He desperately wanted to rush over and help her. But what could he do? Even with his amulet,

he'd be little more than another pair of hands prying use-lessly at a death grip.

"Yes," called the leader. "Take her. She is the one you want. She opened the portals. *She* started all of this. We merely responded to these changes, traveled between the worlds as a floating leaf would follow a river."

Alex glared at him. But the words still stung. She *had* opened the portals, but she'd done it for him. She didn't know what would happen, but she had risked everything.

He looked at his mom, twisting in the grip of a madman.

He looked down at Todtman's staff.

He looked across the room at Ren, who had risked so much for friendship. He saw Luke still standing next to her, with the speed to escape but the loyalty to stay.

"No!" Alex called out from his sheltered stone alcove. "It's because of me. The portals were opened to let me back. Don't take her." He rose slowly to his feet. "Take me."

"No, Alex, don't," called Ren.

But the words were already out.

Ammit turned her head, and one cold crocodilian eye fell on Alex. He saw the vertical slit in the center narrow as it focused on him. She turned her body toward him now, golden lion fur rippling. Alex put his hand out to steady himself as he walked past the spot where the Spells lay and toward the avenging demigod. He felt the pain in his side and tasted the blood in his mouth, but he kept walking.

"Yes, take the boy," purred the leader. "He's the cause."

**182**

Ammit paused. Her head swung back and faced the leader. Her strong, huffing breaths rippled his robes as they looked at each other. Alex's mom hung an arm's length away, and Alex was nearly out of the temple now.

Ammit looked over at him one more time, and then back at his mom.

Then, with a speed Alex would not have imagined possible, Ammit's head swung back. Her jaws flashed open, extending all the way down to the floor and revealing rows of huge white teeth.

Alex heard a huge gulp of air as the devourer pulled her prey toward her.

Alex's heart stopped and his eyes closed as the enormous jaws snapped shut.

Quiet.

Alex slowly opened his eyes. His mom was still there. The leader's arm began to fall limply from her shoulder.

Just his arm.

The rest of him was gone.

He had been devoured in one swift bite, by a creature who had seen so many hearts weighed and so many souls judged that she was quite capable of doing it herself.

"Yes!" shouted Ren.

"In your face!" added Luke.

Alex's heart started again. He breathed.

The leader's arm hit the floor with a soft thud. No longer the size of a small tree trunk, it was just a human arm again, tightly wrapped in strips of linen.

Alex's mom wobbled on her feet, and Alex wanted to rush over to help her. But he could still barely stand himself.

Ammit swung around and took a few plodding steps toward the edge of the platform. She opened her mouth again, not to devour but to roar. Ammit's cry shook the room. When it was done, she stood firm at the front of the platform, in between Alex and his mom and The Order's forces. The meaning seemed clear: protection.

Alex's mom walked unsteadily back toward the temple — and the Spells inside.

"Are you okay?" Alex said, stumbling out to help her.

"No," she said. "But I know what I need to do. I looked into Ammit's eyes, and I saw something there. I think I understand her."

As Alex's mom knelt down over the Spells, the ancient text began to glow once more. She took her time now, confident in the protection afforded her.

*Would the Death Walkers dare attack Ammit to try to stop this?* Alex wondered. His answer came in a crackling of crimson energy and the rising buzz of a purple swarm, but that was the last he saw. As the ancient words rose on the air, his head swam and his knees buckled. He knelt on the cool tile as his vision filled with light and color. Behind him, he knew, his mom was reciting the rest of her chosen spell.

A minute later, Alex's head cleared. *I'm still here!* He understood now: His mom wasn't the only one under Ammit's protection. Somewhere in front of him, he heard the creature give one last satisfied huff. The swirling colors faded from

his vision as he stood, but he still didn't believe his eyes. All around, the mummies lay like dominoes on the floor, their bodies curling in on themselves stiffly.

It was a sight both gruesome and glorious, because there were new mummies among them, as well. Alex wheeled around and found each one in turn. Ta-mesah and Peshwar were merely mummies in masks, their bodies no larger than they'd been during their hateful lives. The Stung Man was a mummy, too, albeit a much older one, as timeworn and leathery as any of the others. And oldest of all, the founder, who was now little more than a skeleton wrapped in ragged yellow cloth in the far corner of the room.

Alex looked back toward Ammit, but she was gone. She had vanished just as mysteriously as she had appeared, although with far fewer witnesses.

"I don't under —" he began, but suddenly arms wrapped around him from behind. His mom. They hugged each other softly, both injured now. A moment later, two more arms wrapped around them. Ren had no intention of missing out on the victory party.

Alex turned his head to take a breath. Through vision clouded not by mystic stars but by the first hint of tears, he saw Luke standing a few steps farther back. Not much of a hugger, Luke gave his cousin a big thumbs-up. "Bauer power," he said.

The others hugged for a while, though.

"Todtman," Ren said, and Alex could feel her shoulders heave with a small sob.

"I know," said Alex's mom. "He was a good man."

But that wasn't good enough for Ren. "He was a *great* Egyptologist," she said.

And that did it for Alex — a sob shot through him, too, as happy tears and sad tears rolled down his cheeks. The tears mixed there softly, joining together and continuing on, like the waters of the mighty blue Nile.

Finally, the group hug pulled apart.

"What happened to them all?" asked Ren, sniffling and gesturing around the room. "To the Death Walkers, I mean."

Dr. Bauer looked around the room, counting the fallen. "We sent them to the ceremony," she said.

"The weighing of the heart?" said Alex.

His mom nodded. "Yes, they can't avoid it any longer."

Ren shook her head. "That is one test they are *not* ready for."

"That's okay," said Alex. "I'm pretty sure Ammit has already decided on their grades."

Even amid the sorrow and loss, the friends managed to exchange a few soft laughs. Even Luke, who pretended he knew what they were talking about.

# Epilogue: The Business of Living

Cairo had always been a somewhat chaotic place — ask anyone who's ever rented a car there — and so it was back to something like normal when the friends arrived for Todtman's funeral. His final wish was to have his ashes scattered in the waters of the Nile as it rolled north to the sea. It was done from the deck of a large, slow-moving boat, among a few rows of stoic Germans and what seemed to be about half the world's museum curators. Alex and Ren leaned over the side to watch the ashes scatter and fall.

*"Auf wiedersehen,"* whispered Ren, who had decided to learn German in Todtman's honor.

Alex already spoke some, but he stayed silent and just watched. This time, his tears really did mix with the waters of the Nile.

And what was there to do after that but get back to the business of living? Alex's mom and Ren's dad were busier than ever, trying to get the Met's battered Egyptian wing up and running again. There was, for obvious reasons, a surging

public interest in ancient Egypt. At night, Dr. Bauer studied the Spells, making sure everything was as it should be.

The wider world did its part: picking up the pieces, reburying the dead. Eventually, things returned to something like normal. Even for the families at the center of the maelstrom, who found themselves at a dinner party at the Durans' place a month later.

Alex's mom and Ren's mom and dad talked about the things parents talk about, Luke helped himself to seconds, and Alex and Ren chattered on about the school where they were once again classmates.

Alex felt something brush against his ankle and flinched. His nerves were, to be honest, still a little on edge.

"Oh, don't worry about her," said Ren, reaching down and scooping up a sleek black cat.

"You got a cat?" said Alex.

Ren's dad looked over, finished chewing, and said, "Or she got us. Just showed up on the doorstep. Pretty weird considering we're on the fourteenth floor. Anyway, she wouldn't leave until Ren got home."

"And then we couldn't get her to let the cat go," added Ren's mom.

Alex looked at the cat's golden eyes and coat of elegant jet-black fur as it purred softly in Ren's arms. There was something so familiar about it all. "What's her name?" he said, leaning in to pet the newest addition to the Duran family.

Ren leaned in, too. "Don't you know?" she whispered.

Alex looked from her to the cat and back again. "No way," he said. "Pai?"

The cat looked up at him, centuries of wisdom in her golden eyes. "Mmuh-Rack!"

Alex shook his head. He'd always heard that cats had nine lives. He had no doubt this former mummy would enjoy her second one.

He looked around the table at his family and friends. He was pretty sure he would, too.